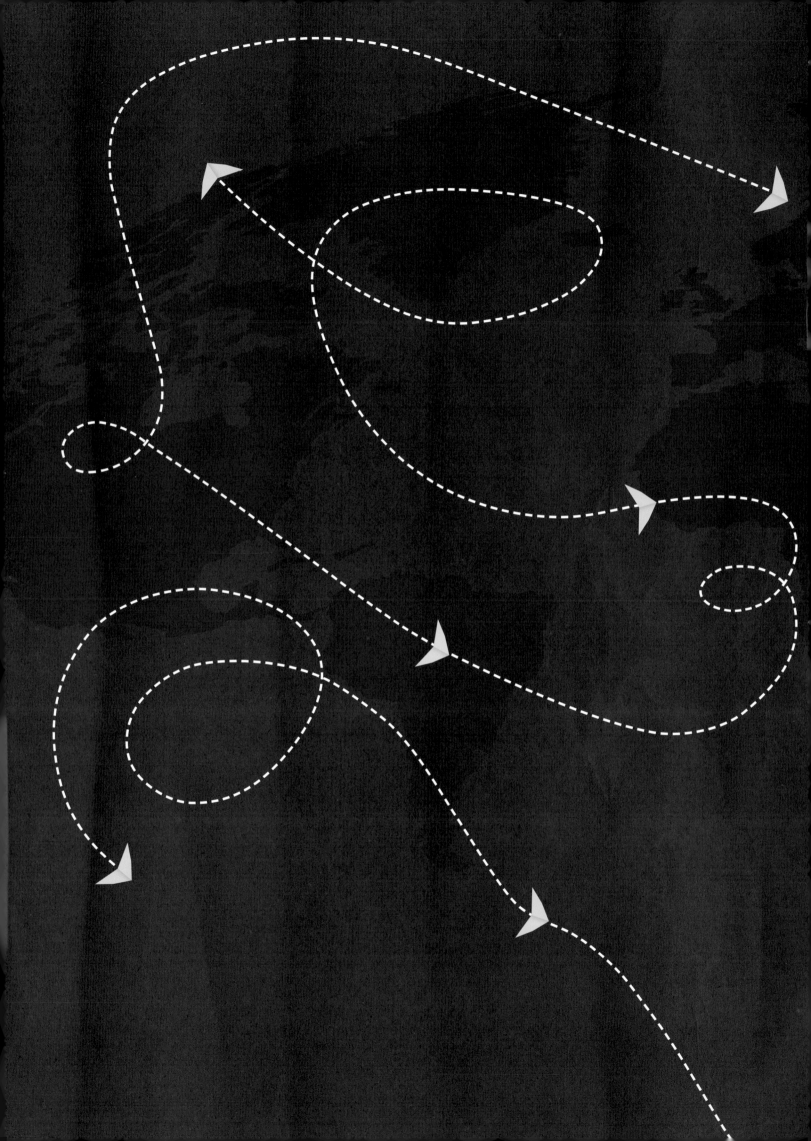

weird but true!

WORLD
2025

Let's get this party started!

Incredible facts, awesome photos, and weird wonders— for this year and beyond!

NATIONAL GEOGRAPHIC
WASHINGTON, D.C.

CONTENTS

This is dino-mite!

Introduction 8
Weird in the World 10

CHAPTER 1
WEIRD THIS YEAR 12

Save the Date 2025 14
Weird Ways to Have Fun 16
Surprising Stats About the Number 25 18
Weirdest Races in the World Runners-Up 20
Weirdest Races in the World And the Winner Is 22
Weirdest Animals Runners-Up 24
Weirdest Animals And the Winner Is 26
Weirdest Photos Runners-Up 28
Weirdest Photos And the Winner Is 30
By the Numbers What's in a Year? 32
Weird News From Around the World 34

CHAPTER 2
INCREDIBLE NORTH AMERICA 36

Weird in the World 38
Peculiar Places 40
What's Weird About This? Hierve el Agua 42
By the Numbers Monarch Migration 43
Bonkers Buildings 44
Vibrant Volcanoes 46
Creature Feature 48
Weird Wonders Caddo Lake 50
Madcap Museums 52
Star-Studded Facts About Hollywood! 54
By the Numbers Chichén Itzá 56
Personality Quiz 58
Freaky Fossils 60
Weird Vacations 62
Weird Wonders Sailing Stones 64
Human-Made Masterpieces 66
Rocky Wonders 68
Quiz Whiz 70

CHAPTER 3
SPECTACULAR SOUTH AMERICA 72

Weird in the World 74
Peculiar Places 76
Eye-Catching Oddities 78
Weird Wonders Salt Mines of Maras 80
Weird Vacation Destinations 82
By the Numbers El Ateneo Grand Splendid 84
What's Weird About This? "Coloso" 85
Dry as a Bone 86
Ridiculous Rides! 88
Bizarre Bugs! 90
Personality Quiz 92
Groovy Galápagos 94
Weird Wonders Marble Caves 96
Perplexing Plants 98
Strange Structures 100
Kooky Colors! 102
Mind-Blowing Facts About South American Birds 104
Quiz Whiz 106

CHAPTER 5
AWESOME AFRICA 144

Weird in the World 146
Bizarre Vehicles 148
Curious Creatures 150
Record Breakers 152
By the Numbers Ouarzazate Solar Power Station 154
Creative Critters 156
Cool Constructions! 158
Weird Wonders Jaw-Dropping Sand Dunes 160
Remarkable Rocks 162
Personality Quiz 164
Weird Wonders Wildebeest Migration 166
By the Numbers The Nile 167
Fascinating Facts About King Tut! 168
Weird Wonders The Forest of Knives 170
Full Circle! 172
Weird Water 174
Ancient Mysteries 176
Quiz Whiz 178

I spy with my BIG eyes...

CHAPTER 4
UNIQUE EUROPE 108

Weird in the World 110
Naturally Bizarre 112
Weird Shapes 114
Surreal Sports 116
Extreme Art 118
Room With a View! 120
What's Weird About This? Hotel Ship 121
Eye-Catching Oddities! 122
Fascinating Facts About Weird Yearly Events 124
Animal Antics 126
Personality Quiz 128
Strange Stations 130
By the Numbers Acropolis 131
Weird Wonders Flower Fields 132
Cold as Ice 134
Into Thin Air 136
Unexpected Theme Parks 138
Bizarre Buildings 140
Quiz Whiz 142

CONTENTS

CHAPTER 7
OUTSTANDING AUSTRALIA & OCEANIA 216

Weird in the World 218
Island Oddities 220
Surprising Facts About the Great Barrier Reef 222
Weird Wonders Crab Invasion 224
Go Big or Go Home 226
Weird Days Out 228
By the Numbers Kangaroo 229
Personality Quiz 230
Taking Flight 232
Distinctive Dwellings 234
Animal Antics 236
Weird Wonders Bungle Bungles 238
Aussie Oddities 240
Quiz Whiz 242

CHAPTER 6
ASTOUNDING ASIA 180

Weird in the World 182
Animal Magic 184
Color Pop! 186
Fantastic Facts About the Great Wall of China 188
Cool Critters 190
By the Numbers Gardens by the Bay 192
A Bridge Too Far 194
Weird Wonders Plank Road in the Sky 196
Stargazing 198
Personality Quiz 200
Breathtaking Builds! 202
By the Numbers The Taj Mahal 204
What's Weird About This? Artist Liu Bolin 205
Making a Splash 206
Festival Fun 208
Extreme Eateries 210
Madcap Museums 212
Quiz Whiz 214

CHAPTER 9
SENSATIONAL
SEA & SPACE 264

Weird in the World 266
Underwater Weirdness 268
Down to the Depths 270
What's Weird About This? Nemo's Garden 271
Tidal Transport 272
Weird Wonders Great Blue Hole 274
Who Put That There? 276
Bizarre Behavior 278
By the Numbers International Space Station 280
Jokes in Space 282
What's Weird About This? Blood Moon 283
Space Robots 284
Far, Far Away! 286
Unlikely Items in Space 288
Astronomically Amazing Info About Planets 290
Quiz Whiz 292

Index 294
Photo Credits 302

CHAPTER 8
AMAZING ANTARCTICA 244

Weird in the World 246
Weird Wonders Under the Ice 248
Cool Facts About the People in Antarctica 250
Unusual Underwater Creatures 252
Perfect Penguins 254
By the Numbers The Coolest Continent 255
Ice and Fire 256
Ocean Oddities! 258
Icy Travel 260
What's Weird About This? The Endurance 261
Quiz Whiz 262

Is it getting a little chilly in here?

INTRODUCTION

WEIRDNESS IS ALL AROUND US ...

and we're here to celebrate the wackiest of the bunch!
From random to outrageous and offbeat to seriously strange, this book is jam-packed with all the things that help keep our planet interesting. Because let's be honest, normal would be pretty dull, right? Get ready for the ride of your life as you check out the most unusual animals, landmarks, museums, and more in each continent.

You want weird? You've come to the right place!

FINDING YOUR WAY AROUND

Before you set off on this epic journey, find out what's **Weird This Year** in Chapter 1. For 2025, we've got the **weirdest races, animals, photos,** and **news** from around the world. Then travel around the globe one continent at a time. Be astonished by **Weird Wonders,** hang out with **Weirdly Cute** creatures, learn incredible stats in **By the Numbers,** and find out **What's Weird About This?** Test yourself with quizzes as you go, and reveal what your answers say about **your personality.** There's way more weirdness in store. Just turn the page to reveal all. **Ready, set ... go!**

WEIRD in the WORLD

A giant ball, whirling through SPACE, covered in WATER and a few patches of LAND (or continents, as we call them). What a PECULIAR place to live!

Sweden has MORE ISLANDS than any other country in the world—267,570 of them.

Only two countries use THE COLOR PURPLE on their national flags—Dominica and Nicaragua.

I like to swim in sea-cret.

Scientists have spotted fewer than 50 GOBLIN SHARKS in the ocean.

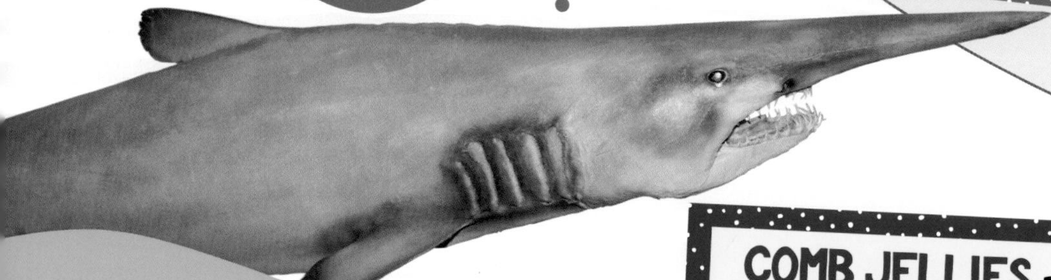

ARCTIC

NORTH AMERICA

United States

ATLANTIC OCEAN

Dominica

Nicaragua

Liberia

SOUTH AMERICA

PACIFIC OCEAN

SOUTHERN

COMB JELLIES are Earth's OLDEST KNOWN ANIMAL GROUP—they've been around for more than 600 MILLION YEARS!

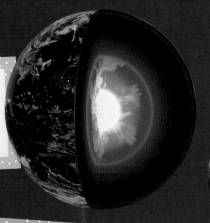

Earth's IRON CORE is as large as MARS and can reach temperatures as HOT as the surface of the SUN.

OCEAN

Sweden

EUROPE

ASIA

Mount Everest

Myanmar (Burma)

PACIFIC OCEAN

AFRICA

INDIAN OCEAN

OCEANIA

AUSTRALIA

North Island

OCEAN

ANTARCTICA

EVEREST, the world's HIGHEST MOUNTAIN, is getting TALLER by .16 INCH (4 mm) every year.

The world's LONGEST PLACE-NAME is Taumata-whakatangihanga-koauauotamateaturi-pukakapikimaunga-horonukupokai-whenuakitanatahu. This TONGUE-TWISTING hill is on New Zealand's North Island.

Just THREE COUNTRIES in the world use only IMPERIAL MEASUREMENTS (like inches and feet)— Liberia, Myanmar, and the United States.

WEIRD THIS YEAR

Saddle up, you're in for one wacky ride!

If you're on the lookout for the WEIRDEST, strangest, and most bizarre things in the world, you've come to the right place!

13

SAVE THE DATE 2025

With something strange to celebrate every month, 2025 is going to be one wacky year. Whether you're nuts about numbats or deeply into dinosaurs, there's a date for you ...

JANUARY 4

PERIHELION DAY
Feel slightly warmer today? That may be because Earth is at its closest to the sun on its slightly oval orbit. This year it falls on the fourth, but every 58 years or so, Perihelion Day creeps forward a day.

FEBRUARY 11

EXTRATERRESTRIAL CULTURE DAY
Roswell, New Mexico, U.S.A., is famous as a rumored UFO crash site. Although there's no proof of the crash, you can still join in this human celebration of alien visitors and perhaps invite one over for some snacks.

MARCH 7

NATIONAL SOCK MONKEY DAY
The sock monkey, a simple stuffed toy sewn from socks, is said to have been invented in the 1930s. It's now a stitched-up superstar with its own special day. Celebrate this crafty classic by making your own primate pal.

APRIL 27

MORSE CODE DAY
Morse code was invented in the early 19th century to send messages over long distances using electricity. It works by transmitting and receiving a series of short and long electric signals, or dots and dashes, that represent letters of the alphabet. (For example, the emergency signal SOS would be: . . . _ _ _ . . .) Check out the code, and dash off your own top secret message.

MAY 6

NO HOMEWORK DAY
Let's hope that teachers know what day it is! For those who celebrate, today is a rare chance for students to rest their brain cells. Whether for hanging out or for hobbies, everyone needs a break from studying sometimes.

JUNE 1

DINOSAUR DAY
Dinosaurs ruled the world from around 230 million to 66 million years ago. While we still have the descendants of avian dinosaurs—or birds—with us, today is a good moment to celebrate the extinct *T. rex* and its contemporaries by checking out fossils at a museum or watching a dinosaur movie.

JULY 1

NATIONAL CREATIVE ICE CREAM FLAVORS DAY

Iced desserts have been around for hundreds of years—and so have creative flavors. Ancient Greeks ate honey or fruit-flavored ice, and ancient Arabs were partial to spiced pomegranate sorbet. If those flavors don't do it for you, how about pizza, lobster, or jalapeño? Forget vanilla and chocolate chip! Test your taste buds today with something unusual.

AUGUST 6

NATIONAL WIGGLE YOUR TOES DAY

Stuffed into socks, squeezed into sneakers, our toes are often neglected. Today's the day to salute your dynamic digits. Free your feet and give your toes a good wiggle. Feels good, doesn't it? (Now, what's that smell?)

SEPTEMBER 7

NATIONAL PET ROCK DAY

It doesn't have to be fed, it's totally house-trained, and it doesn't even need exercise! The pet rock is the absolute easiest pet to care for. If you don't have a pet rock to share this day with, just go outside, pick up a random stone, and glue some googly eyes on it. It's not hard!

OCTOBER 9

NATIONAL MOLDY CHEESE DAY

Mold can develop on food that's been left for far too long, but in cheesemaking, it's a good thing. For blue cheese, an edible penicillium mold is used to ripen it and add flavor. Don't be put off by the stink—go for Gorgonzola or sample some Stilton today.

NOVEMBER 1

WORLD NUMBAT DAY

What's a numbat?! The numbat is a small, stripy marsupial found in isolated areas of Australia. With fewer than 1,000 numbats left in the wild, World Numbat Day raises awareness about this endangered species.

DECEMBER 8

PRETEND TO BE A TIME TRAVELER DAY

If you're not already a time traveler, today's the day you can play one. To take part, choose a year from the past or future you've arrived from, then pretend to be shocked by the culture and gadgets of the day. Definitely dress the part, too!

Has anyone seen my flying car?

WEIRD WAYS TO HAVE FUN

Video games? Soccer? TV? Been there, done that! Check out these entertaining activities for the offbeat thrill seeker ...

Swimming With Crocodiles

Hanging out with crocodiles underwater isn't everyone's idea of fun, but at Australia's Crocosaurus Cove, people line up to join the giant reptiles. Saltwater crocodiles, or "salties," can grow up to 20 feet (6.2 m) in length and weigh 2,370 pounds (1,075 kg). Lurking in water by riverbanks, they have no problem launching an attack on water buffalo, kangaroos, wild pigs, or humans, if they stray too close. With a 3.3-ton (3-t) bite force, crocs will seize their prey and then drag it into the water to drown it. If this doesn't scare you off, you can get into the "Cage of Death" at Crocosaurus Cove. You'll be lowered into the crocodile enclosure, kept safe by an acrylic tank, to enjoy watching a major predator in action—while both of you take snaps!

THE COVE ALSO HAS A SPECIAL "FISHING FOR CROCS" PLATFORM WHERE YOU CAN DANGLE TREATS FOR YOUNG SALTIES TO HUNT.

Trampolining in Caves

You've probably been on a trampoline before. But have you ever bounced in a cave? If you're worried about bonking your head, don't be. Zip World in Llechwedd Slate Caverns, Wales, has got it all worked out. They've given an abandoned mine a complete makeover, turning the old tunnels into a playground for jumpers of all sizes. "Bounce Below" is one part of the setup. Built in a cave twice the size of Notre-Dame Cathedral, it's a series of six suspended trampoline nets connected by chutes. The highest is 180 feet (55 m) off the ground. Zip World also features zip lines you can hook up to for a half-mile (1-km) slide that runs 1,400 feet (427 m) above an open-air quarry. You're going to need a head for heights—and depths!

Go-Karting on Japanese Roads

It's like one of your favorite video games, but now you can do it for real! In some Japanese cities—Tokyo, Osaka, and Okinawa—you can take a go-kart tour around town. Ahead of the tour, you get a short lesson on how to drive your kart, then you get to pick a costume, such as a cartoon animal or superhero. It's a ton of fun, but go-karters have to be careful on the road. Karts are only about half as tall as cars, so they're hard for drivers to see. That's why the karts go out as a team ... and wear highly visible outfits. (No racing allowed!)

SURPRISING STATS

weird but true!

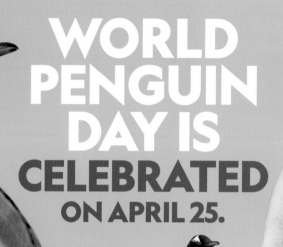

WORLD PENGUIN DAY IS CELEBRATED ON APRIL 25.

25 is what you get when you **ADD** together the **FIRST** five **ODD NUMBERS.**

$$1 + 3 + 5 + 7 + 9 = 25$$

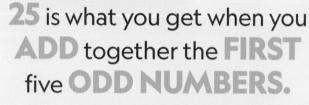

ALL THESE RELATIVES SHARE ABOUT 25% **OF THEIR DNA:** half-siblings, grandparent with grandchild, and aunt or uncle with niece or nephew.

To be elected to the **UNITED STATES HOUSE OF REPRESENTATIVES,** you need to be at least **25 YEARS OLD.**

IN 2019, AUSTRALIA'S **NIC WHITE** SCORED THE **FASTEST EVER POINTS** IN A PREMIERSHIP RUGBY UNION FINAL, JUST **25 SECONDS** INTO THE MATCH.

25 SKYDIVERS JUMPED FROM A BALLOON—BREAKING A WORLD RECORD.

American **DANNY WAY** achieved **THE HIGHEST AIR** on a **SKATEBOARD** when he launched himself **25 FEET (7.7 M)** into the air from a **QUARTER-PIPE RAMP.**

No horsing around!

"Pony" is slang for **£25** in the **U.K.**

The ancient Indian board game Pachisi, which inspired **Parcheesi,** gets its name from the Hindi word for the top score, 25.

19

WEIRDEST RACES IN THE WORLD RUNNERS-UP...

Being weird can leave you breathless! This year, we've rounded up the world's most outlandish races. They will take you across deserts, through UFO country, and even into the clouds! *Whew!*

Human Versus Horse

On a racetrack, a human running against a horse would be no contest. But what about over a rugged course of hills and streams? The Man v. Horse challenge has been taking place in the rolling landscape of Llanwrtyd Wells, Wales, since 1980. The 22-mile (35-km) route was designed to make it an even match for human athletes racing against horses with riders. Still, it took 25 years before a human got the better of a horse, when Huw Lobb crossed the finish line in two hours five minutes, beating the fastest horse by two minutes.

Fast Food

This is some serious service. Waiters and waitresses compete to deliver orders in a flash in the annual Waiters and Waitresses Race. The competition takes place in several different cities each year and involves hundreds of service staff hurrying over a course, balancing a tray of bottles and glasses on one hand. The competition dates back about a hundred years to a Bastille Day event called the Course de Garçons de Café in Paris, France. The fastest waiter to complete the modern-day course, without spilling anything off their tray, can take home a prize of about $1,000. Not a bad tip!

Space Race

Little green men, lace up your running shoes! Area 51 in Nevada, U.S.A., is a top secret U.S. Air Force facility notorious for local reports of unidentified flying objects. Some people believe the wreck of an alien spaceship is being kept under wraps there! Highway 375, which passes this high desert site, has been given the fitting title "Extraterrestrial Highway." And this is exactly where competitors run in the annual Extraterrestrial Full Moon Midnight Marathon. For this night-time race, which is up to 32 miles (51 km) long, runners have to wear a reflective vest and carry a flashlight. Some participants dress up as aliens. And, of course, runners should keep their eyes peeled for unusual lights in the sky!

Race With a View

The only way is up for competitors in the Empire State Building Run-Up. During this race, 150 athletes attempt the 1,050-foot (320-m) ascent of the iconic New York City skyscraper. They have to make their way up 1,576 stairs—86 flights in all—from the ground floor to the observatory on the top floor. It's a journey that would take just one minute in the elevator. The men's record is held by Australia's Paul Crake, who managed it in a heart-pounding 9 minutes 33 seconds in 2003. The women's record of 11 minutes 23 seconds was claimed by Austria's Andrea Mayr in 2006. You have to be dedicated to make it all the way to the finish, but what a view!

Are we there yet?

WEIRDEST RACES IN THE WORLD

And the Winner Is ...

WINNER

Marathon des Sables

For some, running a 26-mile (42-km) marathon is just not tough enough. So they run an ultra-marathon, which is several times farther than a regular one. Still too easy? Then how about you race through the Sahara, over sand dunes, rocks, and salt plains, in temperatures up to 122°F (50°C)? This is the Marathon des Sables (Sand Marathon), a test of human endurance over six days and 156 miles (250 km) across inhospitable terrain. Every marathon entrant must carry their own backpack containing food and sleeping gear, too. More than 22,000 competitors have run the course since the charity event launched in 1986, with the youngest coming in at age 16 and the oldest at 83.

IN 2019, A STRAY DOG NAMED **CACTUS** RAN THE MARATHON DES SABLES AND WAS GIVEN THE RACE NUMBER "000."

Does anybody have a pup-sicle?

The competition is really heating up!

OVER THE YEARS, COMPETITORS HAVE FACED **SANDSTORMS** AND EVEN **FLOODING!**

WEIRDEST ANIMALS
RUNNERS-UP ...

From very tiny primates to super-old fish, these creatures are awesomely odd. It's a truly loopy lineup ...

Tarsier

Meet the tarsier, the second tiniest primate in the world. At just 6.5 inches (16 cm) tall, plus tail, it could fit in your hand. The tarsier lives in the jungles of Southeast Asia, clinging to trees with its long fingers and toes. From the treetops, it can jump incredible distances, leaping up to 70 times its body length between branches. The tarsier can't move its eyes left or right, but it can swivel its head in a nearly complete circle to look around. In addition to giant peepers, tarsiers also have amazing senses of hearing and smell, which they use to hunt insects and lizards.

THE TARSIER'S EYES ARE AS BIG AS ITS BRAIN.

Let's have a staring contest!

Greenland Shark

You'd need a ton of candles to decorate a Greenland shark's birthday cake. As the world's longest-living vertebrate, this giant of the icy seas can live for a whopping 400 years. This means there's probably a shark swimming around that's older than the Liberty Bell, or even the Taj Mahal. The Greenland shark can grow up to 23 feet (7 m) long and weigh up to 1.5 tons (1.4 t), but it takes its time growing up: The shark doesn't reach reproductive age until it's about 150 years old. Despite being the largest fish found in the Arctic Ocean, this old-timer wasn't caught live on camera until 1995.

Treehopper

There are many types of treehoppers—about 3,200 species—and one thing they all have in common is being totally weird. Some of these little insects are masters of disguise, easily camouflaging themselves as thorns, leaves, wasps, or even bird or caterpillar droppings. Others steal the show with bizarre shapes growing from the middle sections of their bodies. The Brazilian treehopper is one of the strangest. It wears a "helmet" of hairy orbs that may mimic a parasitic fungus. Another species found in Ecuador called *Cyphonia clavata* has a helmet that resembles an angry ant. These strange growths—which are actually modified wings—make the treehoppers look thoroughly unappetizing to predators.

Blue-Footed Booby

No, this bird has not accidentally waddled through a puddle of paint—it really has blue feet. For booby males, the brighter the blue the better. During mating season, they show off their colorful feet by marching past a potential mate and presenting her with a stick or a stone. What charmers! Boobies live off the west coast of Central and South America, and on the Galápagos Islands. They spend most of the day flying in a group, looking for anchovies and sardines in the water. When they spot a snack, they can dive at up to 60 miles an hour (97 km/h) to pluck the salty fish from the sea. The name "booby" comes from the Spanish word *bobo*, meaning "foolish." Though they might look clumsy on the shore, these talented fliers and fishers have nothing to feel blue about.

WEIRDEST ANIMALS

And the Winner Is ...

WINNER

Pom-Pom Crab

Give a big cheer for the pom-pom crab!
With a fancy patterned shell and claws clamped tightly around colorful anemones, this tiny tropical crab looks like an underwater cheerleader. The stinging anemones are not for decoration, though. The crab uses them to keep predators at bay. The crab grows to just one inch (2.5 cm) across and could fit on a coin—a tempting morsel for a passing fish. Its pincers are pint-size, too, more like tweezers than fighting claws. The pom-pom crab would be easy prey on its own, so waving anemones is a smart defense. They'll sting any fish that comes too close! Along with borrowing the creatures as boxing gloves, the clever crab also snacks on food collected by the anemones. *Claw*-some!

PUSHY POM-POM CRABS WILL STEAL ANEMONES FROM OTHER CRABS.

Three cheers for sea anemones!

ANEMONES CAN REGROW AFTER BEING SPLIT IN TWO SO THE CRAB ALWAYS HAS TWO POM-POMS.

WEIRDEST PHOTOS
RUNNERS-UP...

OK, OK—I'll moo-ve!

You have to see it to believe it! Check out these quirky photos of shocking sights and strange perspectives.

Cow-bird

Is it a cow? Is it a bird? Actually, it's both. This tricky shot shows a nilgai—a kind of antelope—being attacked from behind by a feisty sarus crane. That's what happens when you wander too close to a crane's nest. At about five feet (150 cm), the sarus crane is nearly as tall as a nilgai. It's eight-foot (2.4-m) wingspan is longer than a nilgai, too! The sarus only lays one or two eggs at a time, so it's very protective of its brood, even when a curious cow comes over.

THE SARUS CRANE IS THE TALLEST FLYING BIRD IN THE WORLD.

Inside an Instrument

With its warped wooden walls, spooky stains, and unusual lighting, this eerie scene seems like it could be a room in a haunted house, but you'd find it difficult to pay a visit. This photo of the inside of a 200-year-old cello was taken by the Romanian artist Adrian Borda. Borda lives in Reghin, a city famous for making violins; he borrowed instruments from a repair shop for his interior photographs. Despite his interest in musical instruments, Borda can't play a note.

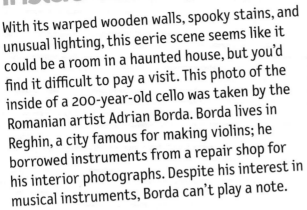

Rad Dad

This fish certainly has its mouth full, but it's not lunch. Look closely and you'll see that every bead-like object in the fish's jaws has eyes. They're babies! The jawfish lives in warm tropical waters and hides in a burrow on the seafloor. When the female lays her eggs, the male gulps them into his mouth for protection from predators. To keep them clean, he occasionally spits them out and sucks them back in again. Then, after about a week, the eggs hatch, and the baby jawfish are free to swim away. Dad can finally seek out a real meal. *Gulp!*

Icy Lighthouse

Every year the Port of Cleveland is battered by gale-force winds. This causes frosty waves to crash against the West Pierhead Lighthouse, transforming it into a chilled-out sculpture. Like a fairy-tale castle, this lighthouse on the edge of Lake Erie becomes encased in giant icicles, but incredibly, its beacon continues to operate. Is the poor lighthouse keeper trapped inside, living on snow cones and slushies? Don't worry. The lighthouse has been automated since 1965, so it still operates—just without a keeper.

WEIRDEST PHOTOS
And the Winner Is ...

WINNER

Doodle House

You might get in trouble for drawing on walls, but artist Sam Cox's doodling has turned his home into a star attraction.

Cox—or Mr. Doodle, as he likes to be known—has drawn cartoons and patterns on every wall, floor, window, ceiling, piece of furniture, and appliance inside and outside of his six-bedroom home in Kent, England. Mr. Doodle can be hard to spot indoors, as he likes to wear clothes decorated with his drawings, too. **Don't try this at home!**

TO COVER THE WHOLE HOUSE, MR. DOODLE USED **238 GALLONS (900 L) OF WHITE PAINT, 401 CANS OF BLACK SPRAY PAINT, 286 BOTTLES OF DRAWING PAINT, AND 2,296 PEN TIPS.**

BY the NUMBERS

That's weird!

WHAT'S IN A YEAR?

So, what did you do this year? We've got a hunch. Check out these jaw-dropping stats about what an average person does each year. You might be surprised!

THE AVERAGE ADULT **WALKS** ALMOST **1,180 MILES** (1,900 KM) **IN A YEAR,** ALMOST **HALF THE WIDTH** OF THE CONTINENTAL **UNITED STATES.**

ON AVERAGE, WE SLEEP FOR **2,920 HOURS EVERY YEAR.** THAT'S THE SAME AS **SNOOZING** FROM **JANUARY** UNTIL **MAY.**

ON AVERAGE, **A HUMAN DRINKS 2,000** TO **3,000 GLASSES OF WATER IN A YEAR.**

YOU DREAM FOR AROUND **TWO HOURS** EVERY NIGHT, SO YOU'VE PROBABLY CLOCKED **730 HOURS** OF **DREAM TIME** IN THE **PAST YEAR**—THAT'S AROUND **A WHOLE MONTH.**

ON AVERAGE, PEOPLE SPEND OVER **4 HOURS A DAY** ON THEIR **PHONES.** THAT'S ABOUT **2 MONTHS A YEAR!**

I can't believe my luck!

IN A YEAR, THE AVERAGE PERSON WILL **FLUSH A TOILET 2,500 TIMES,** USING ABOUT **4,000 GALLONS (15,000 L) OF WATER.**

IN A TYPICAL YEAR, THE AVERAGE **AMERICAN CONSUMES 40 POUNDS (18 KG)** OF **CHEESE.**

WEIRD NEWS
FROM AROUND THE WORLD

What wacky happenings have been grabbing the headlines? Here's the latest from the world of weird.

SNOOPY TAKES FLIGHT

CALIFORNIA, U.S.A.

Snoopy has finally launched his doghouse skyward. Charlie Brown's world-famous beagle was able to take to the skies thanks to a drone placed inside his kennel by Otto Dieffenbach of Flyguy Promotions. Dieffenbach has given flying lessons with his quadcopters to classic characters including superheroes, droids, and even Santa. He calls his airborne marvels IFOs, or "Identifiable Flying Objects."

UPSIDE-DOWN ART

DÜSSELDORF, GERMANY

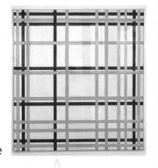

An abstract artwork by famous Dutch painter Piet Mondrian has been displayed upside down for 75 years. German gallery curator Susanne Meyer-Büser noticed the mix-up with the work "New York City I." Experts think turning the painting the right way around might damage it, however, so it must stay the way it is. Exhibition visitors will have to do handstands to appreciate it as the artist intended.

ANCIENT NIT COMB HIDES HISTORIC FIRST

LACHISH RUINS, ISRAEL

The earliest known sentence written using an alphabet has been found carved into a 4,000-year-old comb made of ivory and used for brushing lice eggs out of hair. The text is written in the ancient language of the Canaanites, who lived in the Middle East around 4,000 years ago and who are thought to be the first people to use an alphabet. The translated message says, "May this tusk root out the lice of the hair and the beard."

SOUTH KOREANS GET YOUNGER

SOUTH KOREA

Another year, one *less* candle on the cake?! When the South Korean government passed a law that officially adopted the international age system, people who had used the customary Korean method of counting had a year or two trimmed off their ages! Traditionally, South Koreans have considered babies to be one year old at birth, adding a year each January 1. The legal change meant that people who were about to reach a milestone birthday like 10 had to wait a little while longer before reaching double digits!

CREEPY SEA CREATURES UNCOVERED

COCOS ISLANDS, INDIAN OCEAN

This eerie, fanged conger eel lives in the dark depths of the ocean. It's one of several new sea beasties uncovered by scientists from three miles (5 km) down in the Indian Ocean. Others include a fish with tall fins it uses like stilts, a pale pancake-like batfish, a dragonfish with a double-hinged jaw, and several creatures with glowing organs. Nature is full of spooky surprises!

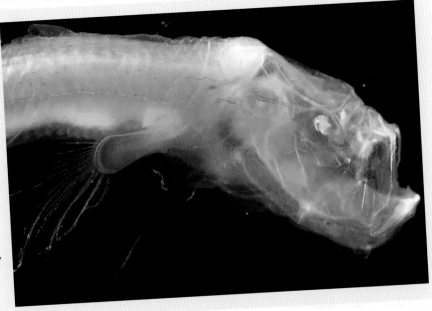

NEUTRON STARS ARE EXPLAINED USING CHOCOLATES

GOETHE UNIVERSITY, FRANKFURT, GERMANY

It's cosmic candy! Scientists studying neutron stars are now comparing these galactic wonders with chocolates. Neutron stars are the tiny but extremely dense result of a supermassive star collapsing, like our sun being squashed to the size of a city. In describing their structure, scientists have turned to the chocolate box, likening "light" neutron stars that have a soft shell over a hard center to a chocolate-coated nut and "heavy" neutron stars that are hard with a soft center to a truffle. Who knew a sweet tooth could help you understand astrophysics?

MAMMALS HUNTED DOWN DINOSAURS

LUJIATUN, CHINA

A recently discovered fossil of two animals that were buried in an instant by a volcano blast around 125 million years ago shows an early mammal dealing a death blow to a dino three times its size! The badger-like mammal had a beaked *Psittacosaurus* (or "parrot lizard") dinosaur in its jaws. Paleontologists have previously speculated that mammals scavenged dead dinosaurs for food, but this is the first evidence that they actually hunted them, too.

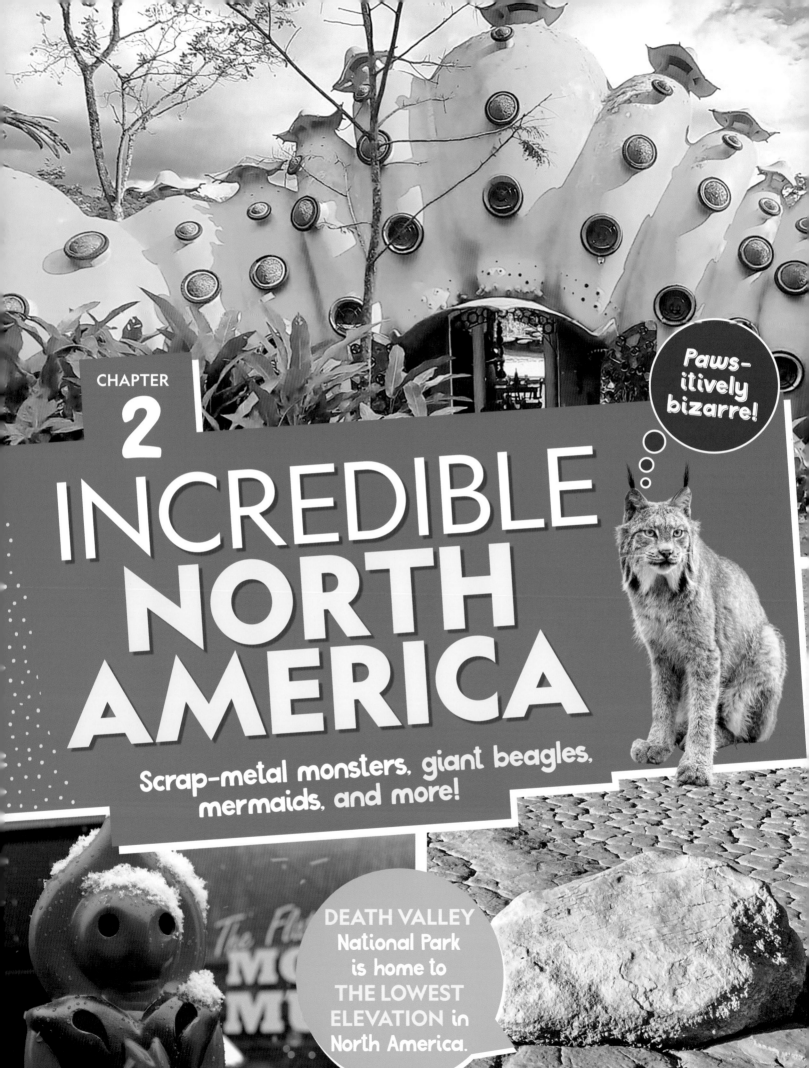

Paws-itively bizarre!

INCREDIBLE NORTH AMERICA

Scrap-metal monsters, giant beagles, mermaids, and more!

DEATH VALLEY National Park is home to **THE LOWEST ELEVATION** in North America.

Butterflies TASTE with their FEET.

MANATEES are more closely related to ELEPHANTS than to other marine mammals like seals or dolphins.

WEIRD in the WORLD

QUIRK or MANUFACTURED MANUFACTURED

Whether it's a natural **QUIRK** or **MANUFACTURED STRANGENESS**, North America is packed with **ODD PLACES, ANIMALS,** and **INVENTIONS.**

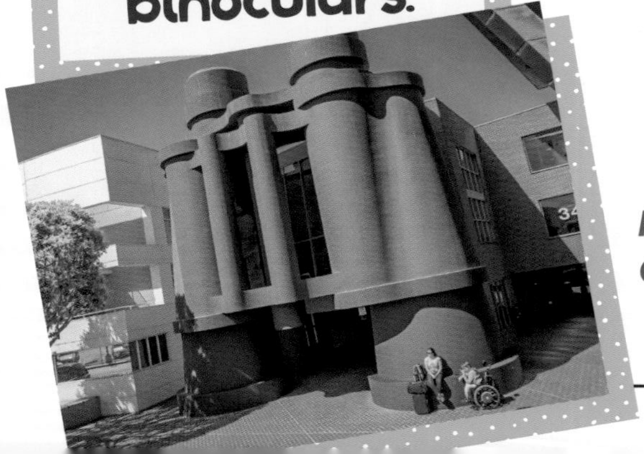

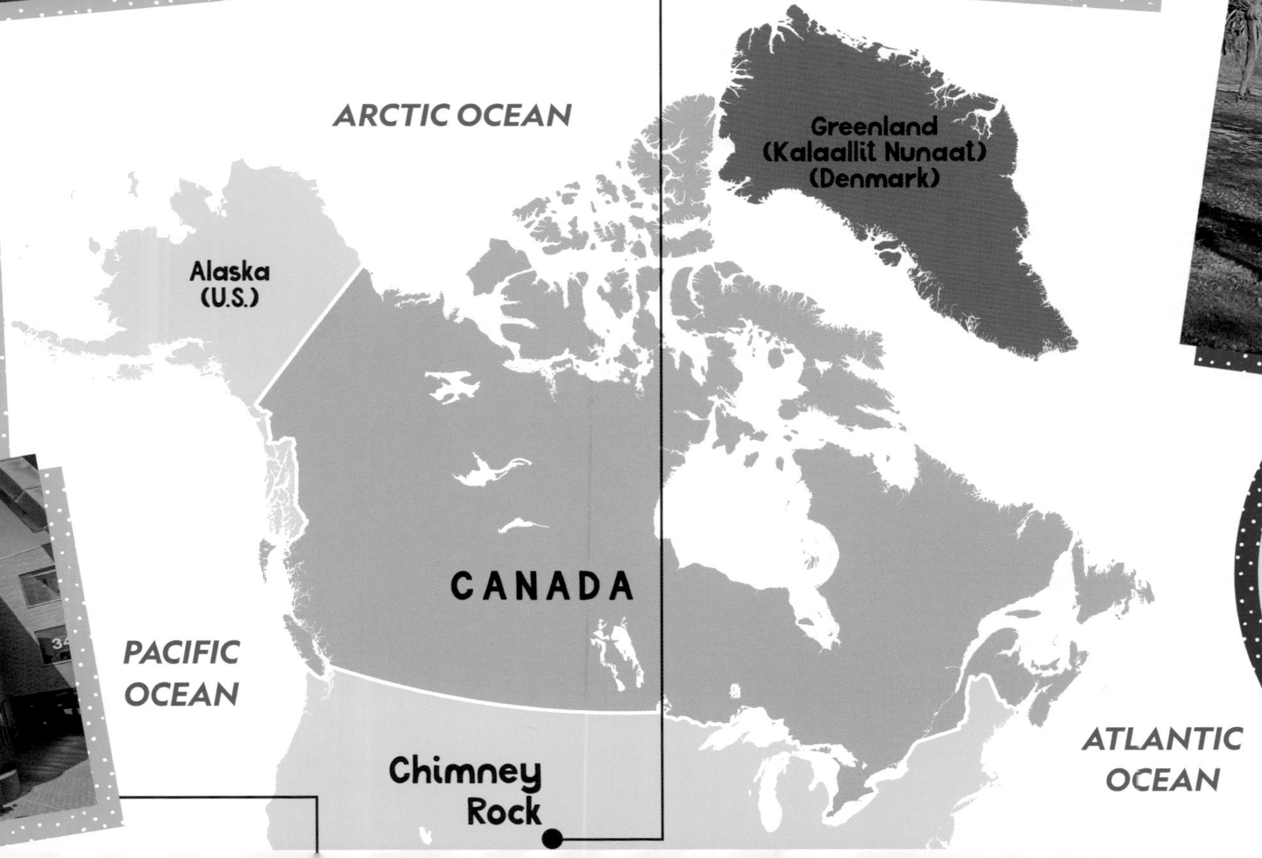

In Erie Dinosaur Park in Kansas, junk car parts have been turned into 17 dinosaur models.

ATLANTIC OCEAN

Greenland (Kalaallit Nunaat) (Denmark)

Rising 325 feet (99 m) over the Nebraskan prairie, Chimney Rock was once used as a marker for the wagon trails of the Old West.

ARCTIC OCEAN

Alaska (U.S.)

CANADA

Chimney Rock

PACIFIC OCEAN

At Google's offices in Venice, California, the entrance to one building is a pair of supersize binoculars.

UNITED STATES

- Venice
- Erie Dinosaur Park
- Houston

MEXICO

Palmitas

Gulf of Mexico

GUATEMALA
BELIZE HONDURAS
EL SALVADOR
NICARAGUA
COSTA RICA
PANAMA

THE BAHAMAS
CUBA
JAMAICA
HAITI
DOMINICAN REPUBLIC
Mopion Island
Caribbean Sea

ASIA
EUROPE
AFRICA
Arctic Ocean
Atlantic Ocean
Pacific Ocean
NORTH AMERICA
SOUTH AMERICA

Arrivals at Houston, Texas's George Bush Intercontinental Airport are welcomed by an astronaut cow! (It's just a sculpture.)

Tiny Mopion Island in the Caribbean is home to only a single straw parasol.

More than 200 houses in the Mexican town of Palmitas are covered with swirly rainbow patterns.

PECULIAR PLACES

Go on—crack a smile!

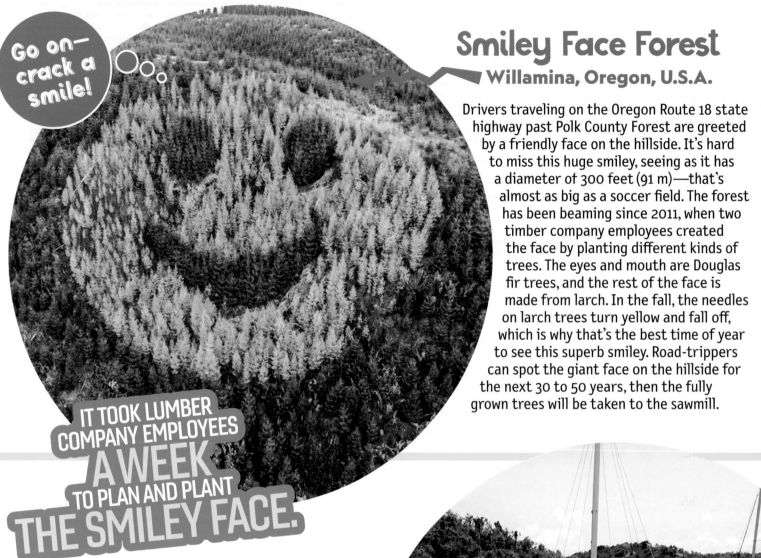

Smiley Face Forest
Willamina, Oregon, U.S.A.

Drivers traveling on the Oregon Route 18 state highway past Polk County Forest are greeted by a friendly face on the hillside. It's hard to miss this huge smiley, seeing as it has a diameter of 300 feet (91 m)—that's almost as big as a soccer field. The forest has been beaming since 2011, when two timber company employees created the face by planting different kinds of trees. The eyes and mouth are Douglas fir trees, and the rest of the face is made from larch. In the fall, the needles on larch trees turn yellow and fall off, which is why that's the best time of year to see this superb smiley. Road-trippers can spot the giant face on the hillside for the next 30 to 50 years, then the fully grown trees will be taken to the sawmill.

IT TOOK LUMBER COMPANY EMPLOYEES A WEEK TO PLAN AND PLANT THE SMILEY FACE.

Pizza Pi
St. Thomas, U.S. Virgin Islands

If you want to attract the waiter's attention at this popular restaurant, do it with a wave! Swimmers at Christmas Cove in St. Thomas can grab a bite during their dip—from a floating pizzeria! Original owners Sasha and Tara Bouis spent two years adding a pizza oven and solar panels to an abandoned boat to create the Pizza Pi. A small armada of boats sails up to collect tempting treats from the restaurant's window, which is open every day. The pizzeria also offers a delivery service using a dinghy to distribute food—fast! Customers can munch on a sausage, ham, and bacon pizza or sink their teeth into the Georgia Peacharia, which is topped with mozzarella and peaches!

OPEN

PIZZA Pi

Auditorio Station

Mexico City, Mexico

This London Underground station is far from home! The Auditorio "El Metro" Station was given its British makeover in 2018 to promote the United Kingdom as a tourist destination. (Note: You definitely can't get to the U.K. from Mexico via an underground train!) Besides the world-famous London "Tube" logo, this working station sports tiled walls, "mind the gap" platform warnings, and posters in English. Organizers of Auditorio's unveiling even invited a Mexican Beatles tribute band to play their hits for passengers.

The Time Travel Mart has claimed to have fresh doughnuts—from 1985.

Echo Park Time Travel Mart

Los Angeles, California, U.S.A.

Do you have a prehistoric appetite? Then the Echo Park Time Travel Mart is the place to go. The time-twisting temptations offered in this way-out retail store include cans of woolly mammoth chunks and fresh dinosaur eggs. Don't worry—these products are not 70,000 to 65 million years past their expiration dates. They're just a line of wacky imagined products offered by a store supporting Los Angeles students. The mart has stock from the past, present, and future, so if you want to smell like a Norse raider, you could try Viking Odorant. Menacing Mongol hordes on your border? Try Barbarian Repellent. There are even products just for robots, with a selection of emotion chips to plug in—including love, happiness, fear, and guilt.

What's **Weird** About This?

If you're expecting to get splashed by these falls, think again.
Just outside Oaxaca, Mexico, is Hierve el Agua, which means "The Water Boils" in Spanish. Over thousands of years, calcium-rich waters from hot mineral springs have poured over the 99-foot (30-m)-tall valley cliffs and formed hardened, stalactite-like shapes. It's more of a rockfall than a waterfall!

BY the NUMBERS

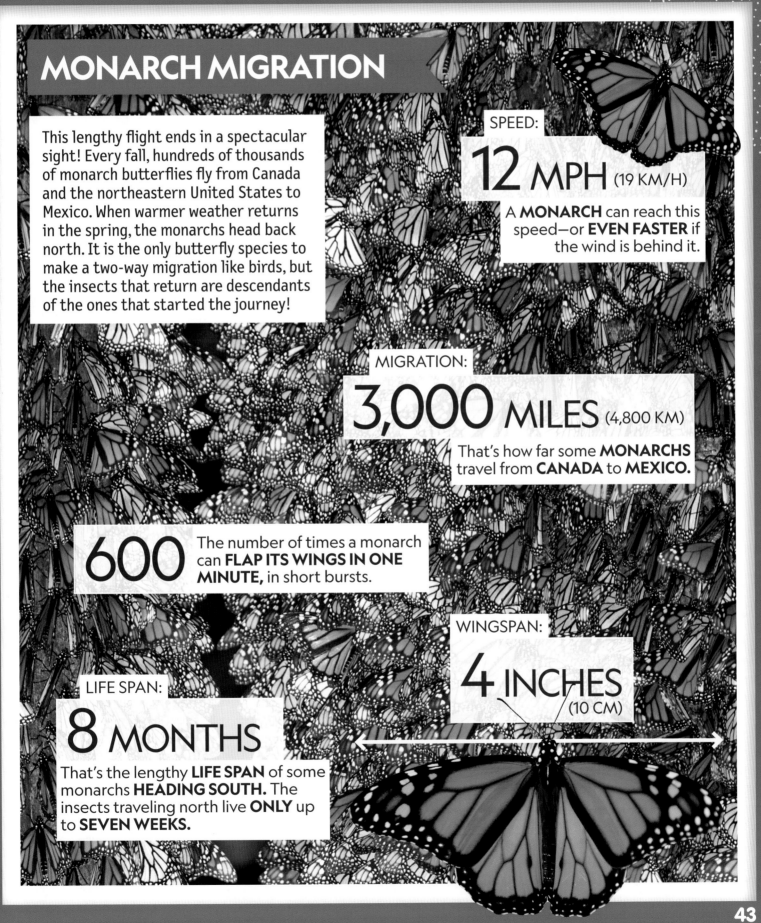

MONARCH MIGRATION

This lengthy flight ends in a spectacular sight! Every fall, hundreds of thousands of monarch butterflies fly from Canada and the northeastern United States to Mexico. When warmer weather returns in the spring, the monarchs head back north. It is the only butterfly species to make a two-way migration like birds, but the insects that return are descendants of the ones that started the journey!

SPEED:

12 MPH (19 KM/H)

A **MONARCH** can reach this speed—or **EVEN FASTER** if the wind is behind it.

MIGRATION:

3,000 MILES (4,800 KM)

That's how far some **MONARCHS** travel from **CANADA** to **MEXICO.**

600

The number of times a monarch can **FLAP ITS WINGS IN ONE MINUTE,** in short bursts.

WINGSPAN:

4 INCHES (10 CM)

LIFE SPAN:

8 MONTHS

That's the lengthy **LIFE SPAN** of some monarchs **HEADING SOUTH.** The insects traveling north live **ONLY** up to **SEVEN WEEKS.**

BONKERS BUILDINGS

Cathedral of Junk
Austin, Texas, U.S.A.

This building is garbage. Literally. Constructed in the suburban backyard of its artist, Vince Hannemann, the so-called Cathedral of Junk is a structure built with all kinds of discarded items, including bed frames, pipes, bicycle wheels, CDs, TVs, guitars, dolls, and even toilets! At its height, the sculpture reached three stories. Though visitors have happily provided scrap materials to add to the cathedral, some neighbors have complained about it being an eyesore. Still, the impressive tower of trash has survived protests, passed engineering safety inspections, and remains a popular place to visit for kids who love to climb. Make sure to ask before adding your own junk to the pile. Hannemann is choosy about what goes into his offbeat masterpiece.

Restaurante La Oruga
Altamira, Costa Rica

There's something creepy-crawly about Costa Rica's Restaurante La Oruga, but it's not bugs on the menu. This diner in La Amistad International Park is shaped like a gigantic green caterpillar wriggling out of the rainforest. *Oruga* is Spanish for "caterpillar," and the restaurant design, by local artist Francisco Quesada, is based on a specific Central American species, *Rothschildia lebeau,* which transforms into a magnificent moth. This weird and wonderful eatery serves up plenty of Costa Rican specialties. And there's an ice-cream parlor shaped like a mushroom outside!

LA AMISTAD IS HOME TO TWO-THIRDS OF ALL SPECIES FOUND IN COSTA RICA.

The World's Only Corn Palace

Mitchell, South Dakota, U.S.A.

Murals are usually made with paint or glass, but one amazing building in South Dakota is adorned with corn instead! Originally constructed in 1892 and rebuilt several times since then, the Corn Palace was designed to celebrate the annual crop-growing season and harvest. Every year, folk artists decorate the walls with an original themed mural. Ancient Egyptian motifs were used in 1911, while space was the theme in 1969—the year of the first moon landing. Recent themes have included "Under the Big Top" and "South Dakota's Home Grown." In the latest murals, university students created designs using 12 shades of naturally colored corn, including brown, red, green, black, and blue!

Welcome to the corniest place on Earth!

Like a **giant** paint-by-numbers kit, the **mural design** is traced onto paper, showing where **each color of corn** should go!

Smith Mansion

Cody, Wyoming, U.S.A.

This precarious pile of planks looks like it could come tumbling down any second, but it has been perched on a hill in Wyoming's Wapiti Valley for 40 years. Engineer Francis Lee Smith spent more than a decade working on his ambitious construction, which was meant to become a family home. Sadly, Smith died in a fall while working on an upper balcony, and the house was left unfinished. Despite its sad past, the project has many fantastic—and strange—features. The five-story house of logs includes numerous balconies and staircases, a tree-stump dining table, and a mini indoor basketball court. On the other hand, it has no discernible bedrooms and no power supply. Because the mansion is private property, visitors can't go inside. But it's still a stunning sight from afar.

VIBRANT VOLCANOES

I feel the need for speed!

Volcano Boarding
Cerro Negro, Nicaragua

On the slopes of this Central American volcano, what goes up must come down ... fast! When Cerro Negro last erupted, in 1999, boulders tumbled down the western side, while black ash spewed into the air, coating the eastern side. This smooth surface inspired a new activity—volcano boarding! Since 2004, visitors have been renting boards before hiking up a path created by the fallen boulders. The strenuous journey takes an hour in 90°F (32°C) heat, close to craters spewing out stinky sulfur. At the summit, riders put on their jumpsuits and goggles before sitting on their boards and setting off on a rapid five-minute descent. Speeds are measured with a radar gun—a heart-stopping 60 miles an hour (96.6 km/h) is the record. Going that fast has its risks, though, which is why sitting down is safer than standing up for amateurs, and even that is best left to adults. Riders who fall can end up with a jumpsuit full of ash and blistered limbs from the heat!

Río Celeste
Tenorio Volcano National Park, Costa Rica

Surrounded by lush Costa Rican forests, this vibrant river seems to appear out of the blue. And that's fitting, because the Río Celeste is very, very blue. Along the incredible neon turquoise waterway, visitors will find a spectacular waterfall and many hot springs. The main attraction, though, is the Río Celeste's amazing color, which is completely natural. This ultra-blue waterway begins where two colorless rivers meet. Buena Vista River contains a large amount of aluminum and silicon. Sour Creek is highly acidic because it flows near a volcano and is rich in sulfur. When these two rivers join together, their minerals interact and create a vivid blue color. Sightseers should avoid the rainy season, though—sediment carried by heavy rain can turn the water a dull brown!

A local legend claims that Río Celeste is so blue because God was painting the sky— and dipped the brush in the river!

Craters of the Moon
Idaho, U.S.A.

It's like taking a trip to outer space, without ever leaving Earth! The unusual terrain of Idaho's Craters of the Moon National Monument and Preserve covers 753,000 acres (305,000 ha)—nearly four times the area of New York City. About 2,000 years ago, magma forced its way up through cracks in the ground. The surface of flowing lava was cooled by the air, creating caves and tunnels made with walls of hardened lava. However, volcanic rock is delicate and breaks easily, so the roofs of lava caves often collapse, revealing passages that were once hidden away! Craters of the Moon is also home to groups of impressive-looking spatter cones. They're formed when the force of an eruption decreases and lava builds up around the vent, forming small, steep-sided structures—a little souvenir of the volcano's immense power.

Yellowstone Supervolcano
Yellowstone National Park, Wyoming, U.S.A.

If a volcano sounds dangerous, then a supervolcano should definitely be avoided, right? Well, not really! The word is used to describe volcanoes that have produced massive eruptions, but that doesn't mean that they erupt frequently. One of the world's most famous supervolcanoes is in Yellowstone National Park. It has had at least three major eruptions in the past. The last was a lengthy 640,000 years ago and may have released more than 240 cubic miles (1,000 cubic km) of material into the sky. Yellowstone's magma reservoir is buried underground, but hot springs on the surface bubble up from the boiling chambers below. With its glorious rainbow colors, the Grand Prismatic Spring is a stunning sight. And it's all thanks to bacteria: As the water spreads out, it cools from the center, creating rings decreasing in temperature. Each ring is home to different types of bacteria. These tiny organisms react in different ways to the sunlight and give the springs their vibrant colors!

CREATURE FEATURE

Wall of Frogs
Santa Barbara, California, U.S.A.

At some point in 1989, a lone plastic frog was left behind on a stone wall in Santa Barbara, California. No one knows why, but it caught on. Ever since then, the frog has built up quite the following. It's now surrounded by hundreds of croaking companions. The hilltop Riviera area of Santa Barbara is generally known for its breathtaking views and Mediterranean-style mansions, but now the Wall of Frogs has joined its list of attractions. Alongside the pileup of frogs and toads on Paterna Road, silly signs announce: "Frog Parking Only. All Others Will Be Toad," and "Will Work for Flies." Visitors are welcome to add to the amphibian assembly, but anyone thinking of helping themselves to a free toy can hop off. There is said to be a curse cast on any would-be frog thieves.

Beautiful Wood-Nymph Moth
Eastern United States

Yuck! There's a blob of bird poop that needs to be cleaned up. Or is there? If you look closely, you may see a pair of furry legs attached to this blob. It's not a bird dropping at all, but the clever disguise of the beautiful wood-nymph, *Eudryas grata*. In flight, the beautiful wood-nymph matches its name with gorgeous white, brown, and gold wings between 0.5 and 1.8 inches (13–46 mm) across. Though it might not be a beauty when it perches on a leaf, this moth's camouflage is a beast of an adaptation. After all, what predator would think to go for a pile of bird poop?

I'm pooped!

Manatee Hot Spot
Florida, U.S.A.

Could you mistake manatees for mermaids? That's what some early sailors thought they were when they spied these big, blubbery creatures at sea. Though they're not as dainty as mermaids, manatees—or sea cows—have their charms. Manatees are gentle, often playful, and graceful swimming mammals. They graze, like cows, on plants found on the seabed. Who wouldn't jump at the chance to swim with these underwater wonders? Crystal River in Florida is the only national wildlife refuge for this protected marine species. Hundreds of manatees gather there in the winter months to enjoy warmer water and feed on eelgrass. Visitors to Crystal River can view the manatees and make friends with these adorable animals—but no hugging, as cuddly as they are.

At up to **14 feet (4 m) long, manatees** are the **ocean's largest** plant-eaters.

Canada Lynx
Canada and Alaska, U.S.A.

The adorable whiskered face of the Canada lynx may look like that of your average house cat. And at 20 inches (50 cm) tall, it's not much bigger than one—but don't expect it to nap on your lap! A loner that lives in remote conifer forests of North America, this wild feline is specially adapted for stalking prey over deep snow. Its huge paws are wide like snowshoes and have fur underneath for traction. Its back legs are longer than its front, so it can gracefully pounce over drifts to snare a snowshoe hare. The Canada lynx also has long, distinctive black ear tufts and a shaggy beard, though scientists really can't say why. With so many unique features, this elusive animal is easy to recognize—if you ever manage to spot one!

WEIRD WONDERS

Caddo Lake is a strange and spooky place that can feel like another world to visitors. This wild bayou surrounds you as you weave between bald cypress trees rising from the swampy waters. Curtains of Spanish moss drape from the trees' low branches, and the air is alive with animal calls. This haunting wetlands covers up to 33,000 acres (13,350 ha) and stretches from Texas into Louisiana. You can kayak past tree trunks and spiky aboveground roots (called cypress knees) while trying to spot the lake's wildlife, which includes 200 bird, 30 amphibian, 60 reptile, and 55 mammal species. Keep your eyes peeled for the swamp's most famous resident, the alligator. The largest reptile in North America, with a bite three times more powerful than a lion's, the American alligator could take a chunk out of your paddle, at the very least!

More than
90 SPECIES OF FISH
call Caddo's shallow waters home, making it Texas's most diverse lake.

CADDO LAKE

Texas and Louisiana, U.S.A.

MADCAP MUSEUMS

Museum of Pizza Culture
Philadelphia, Pennsylvania, U.S.A.

For anyone craving a slice of cheese or pepperoni, there's a place you can go to indulge in all things pizza. Pizza Brain in Philadelphia, Pennsylvania, claims to be the world's first pizza museum, and it's crammed with cheesy memorabilia. With more than 500 objects on display, the museum has earned its own world record for the largest collection of pizza-related items. From plastic toys to movies to recordings singing the praises of pizza, the place is plastered with paraphernalia—even a crusty clock to tell you it's time for takeout. If the tasty displays start making you drool, you can get a freshly baked slice from the on-site pizza ovens.

THE MUSEUM OF PIZZA CULTURE HAS SERVED PIZZA-FLAVORED ICE CREAM.

American Visionary Art Museum

Baltimore, Maryland, U.S.A.

Ever wanted to see your artwork displayed in a museum? The American Visionary Art Museum in Baltimore, Maryland, gives self-taught artists just that opportunity. Founded in 1984 by Rebecca Alban Hoffberger, the museum galleries exhibit paintings and sculptures not by well-known, professional artists but by farmers, homemakers, mechanics, or anyone with an artistic dream. The museum also helps organize one of the wackiest races on Earth, the annual Kinetic Sculpture Race. It involves volunteers in costumes racing their own mobile artistic creations 15 miles (24 km) over road, water, mud, and sand. A typical race could feature motorized monsters, cycling crocodiles, rafting burgers, and dashing dinos—the wilder the designs, the better.

Peculiarium
Portland, Oregon, U.S.A.

Described by its owners as an "art gallery dedicated to learning and terror," even the origin story of the Freakybuttrue Peculiarium is a little strange. Supposedly (who knows if it's true), the adventurer Conrad Talmadge Elwood traveled the world collecting strange and mysterious exhibits! Today, visitors can enjoy a whole host of weird—and not-so-true—wonders, including a dog with three eyes, a haunted dollhouse, Bigfoot, and an alien autopsy scene where you can become the patient! Its collection of creepy life-size mannequins includes Krampus, famous from folktales where he punishes naughty children at Christmas! He was supposed to be a temporary festive exhibit but was so popular with visitors, he's now a permanent resident. Although Krampus is not real, a jokey sign says, "Unattended children will be fed to Krampus!"

Who are you calling peculiar?

Desserts at the **Peculiarium's café** are topped with **edible crickets** and **scorpion pieces!**

Flatwoods Monster Museum
Sutton, West Virginia, U.S.A.

In 1952, a bright object was spotted over the small town of Flatwoods, West Virginia. Six locals went to investigate the farm where it landed and—according to legend—came face-to-face with a 10-foot (3-m)-tall hooded humanoid creature with a bright spade-shaped red head, glowing eyes, and clawlike hands. The visitor hissed at them and sent the group running away in terror. There's no hard evidence to back up the story, but more locals reported encounters with the potential alien later that year. Now the creature, known as the Flatwoods Monster, has been immortalized with its own museum. The museum features reports of the visitor from the skies as well as models of the monster and its landing site. Was it an alien? Was it a meteor? Was it completely made up? You decide!

STAR-STUDDED FACTS ABOUT

weird but true!

THE ORIGINAL

HOLLYWOOD

SIGN, in CALIFORNIA, U.S.A., read **HOLLYWOODLAND.**

The Hollywood Walk of Fame doesn't just honor human celebrities—

BUGS BUNNY, SHREK, AND GODZILLA all have stars.

Foley artists create sound effects for movies. The sounds of hatching **VELOCIRAPTORS** in *Jurassic Park* were really **ICE-CREAM CONES BREAKING.**

AN OVERTURNED **POULTRY TRUCK** IN 1969 MIGHT BE THE REASON A **COLONY OF FERAL CHICKENS** LIVES BY THE HOLLYWOOD FREEWAY.

The lights on top of the **CAPITOL RECORDS TOWER** spell out "Hollywood" in **MORSE CODE.**

HOLLYWOOD!

MAKING *PIRATES OF THE CARIBBEAN: ON STRANGER TIDES* **COST A MASSIVE** **$410 MILLION.**

Hollywood is the **INSPIRATION** for other film industries, including **BOLLYWOOD** in **INDIA** and **HOGAWOOD** in **JAPAN**.

The classic Christmas film ☀ *IT'S A WONDERFUL LIFE* was filmed in the **SUMMER—** ☀ during a **HEAT WAVE**.

Director James Cameron said his **MAIN REASON** for making the film *TITANIC* was to dive to the **WRECK OF THE REAL SHIP**.

An actor's **scream** from a **1951 film** has been used as a **sound effect** in more than **400 FILMS** and TV shows, including *Toy Story* and *Raiders of the Lost Ark.*

AHHHHH!

BY the NUMBERS

CHICHÉN ITZÁ

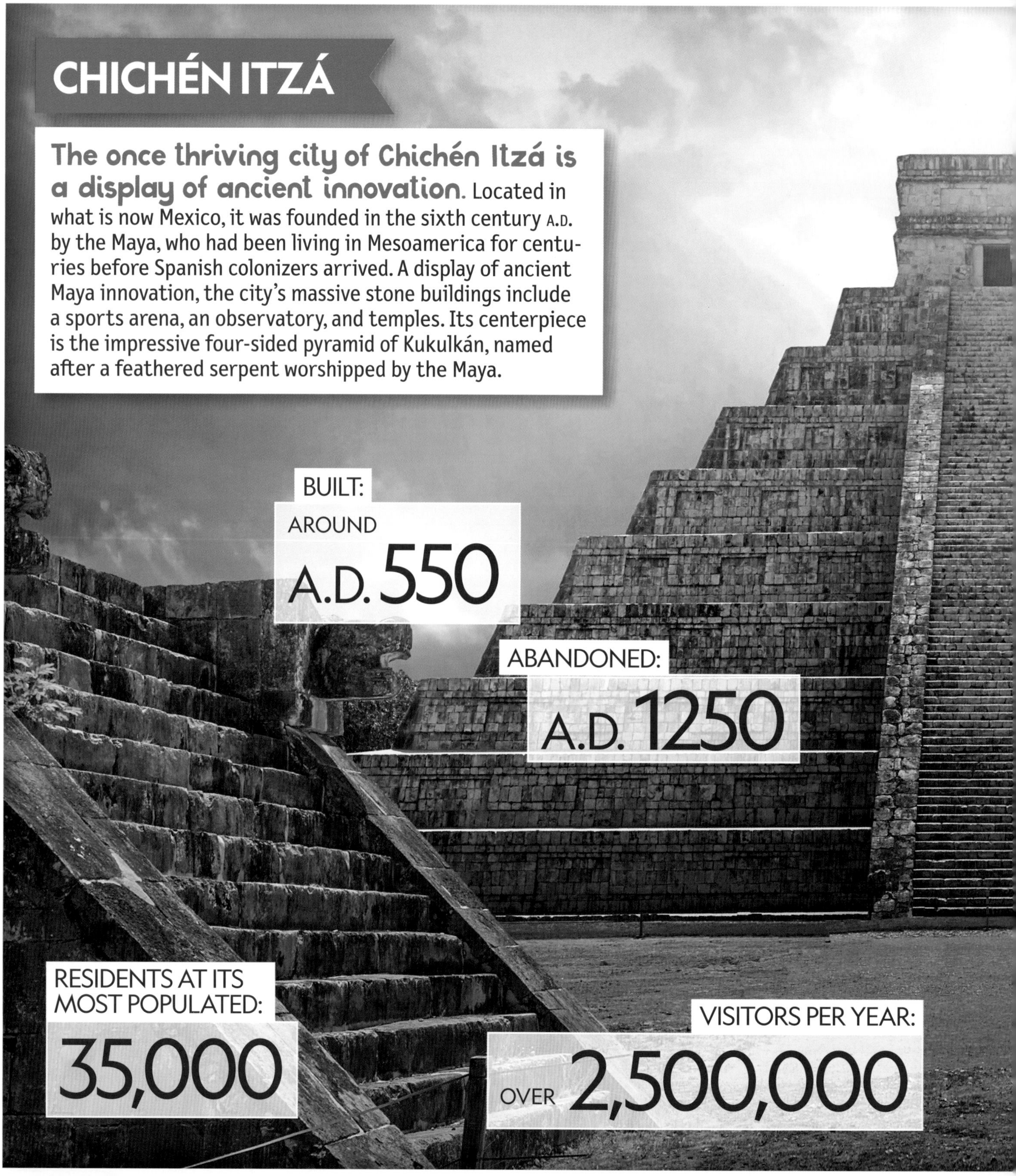

The once thriving city of Chichén Itzá is a display of ancient innovation. Located in what is now Mexico, it was founded in the sixth century A.D. by the Maya, who had been living in Mesoamerica for centuries before Spanish colonizers arrived. A display of ancient Maya innovation, the city's massive stone buildings include a sports arena, an observatory, and temples. Its centerpiece is the impressive four-sided pyramid of Kukulkán, named after a feathered serpent worshipped by the Maya.

BUILT:
AROUND
A.D. 550

ABANDONED:
A.D. 1250

RESIDENTS AT ITS MOST POPULATED:
35,000

VISITORS PER YEAR:
OVER 2,500,000

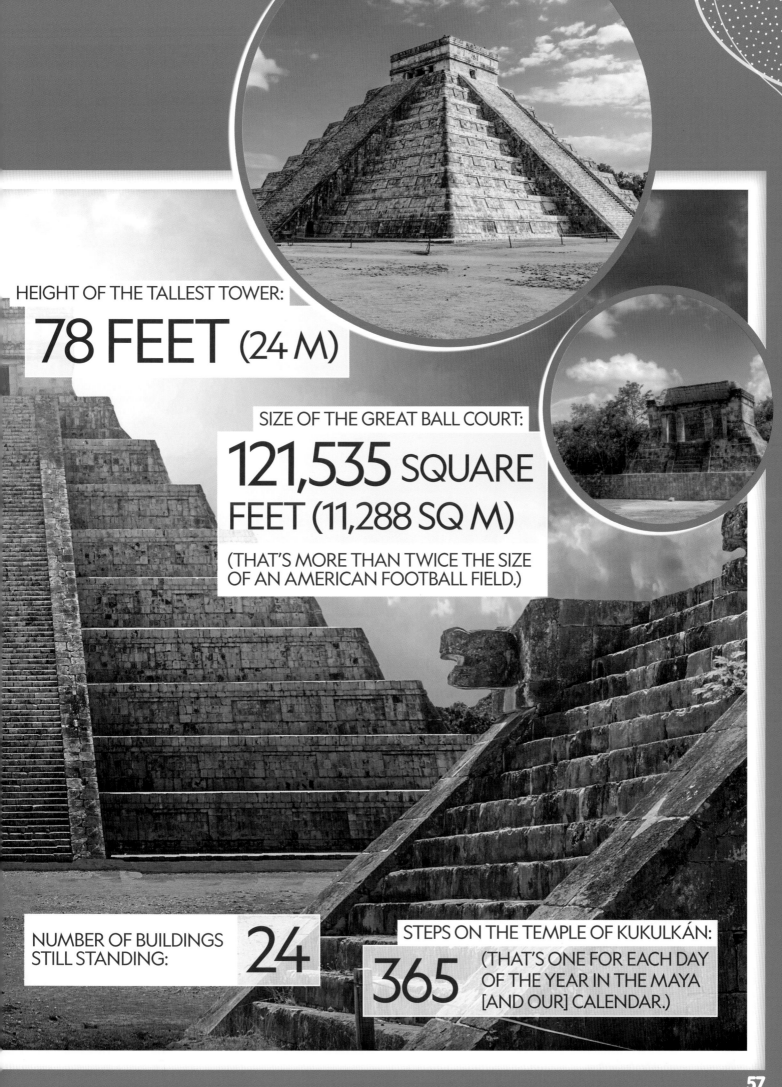

HEIGHT OF THE TALLEST TOWER:

78 FEET (24 M)

SIZE OF THE GREAT BALL COURT:

121,535 SQUARE FEET (11,288 SQ M)

(THAT'S MORE THAN TWICE THE SIZE OF AN AMERICAN FOOTBALL FIELD.)

NUMBER OF BUILDINGS STILL STANDING: **24**

STEPS ON THE TEMPLE OF KUKULKÁN:

365 (THAT'S ONE FOR EACH DAY OF THE YEAR IN THE MAYA [AND OUR] CALENDAR.)

PERSONALITY QUIZ

Imagine North America's quirkiest tourist sites are looking for help over the summer. **Which job are you weirdly suited for?** Take the quiz to find out.

1 Do you like to hang out with friends?
a. Yes! I love company!
b. Mostly old friends
c. Just my close friends. I'm choosy.
d. I like a lot of me time.

2 How artistic are you?
a. I have great taste.
b. I'm very creative.
c. I love to build things. Does that count?
d. I'm not that interested in art.

3 Favorite food?
a. Cheese
b. Doughnuts
c. Leftovers
d. Fish

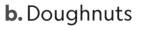

4 Describe your bedroom.
a. It's where I keep all my treasures.
b. It's my cave.
c. Honestly, it's a total mess.
d. Private. Keep out!

5 Best vacation day?
a. Going to a theme park
b. Visiting historic sites
c. Seeing a new city
d. Chilling at the beach

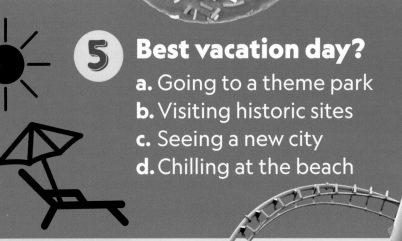

6 **What do you collect?**
a. Toys and games
b. Fossils and rocks
c. Everything!
d. Nothing—I'm a minimalist.

7 **What best describes you?**
a. Enthusiastic
b. Curious
c. Resourceful
d. Relaxed

8 **What do you like to read?**
a. Joke books
b. Sci-fi
c. Comics and magazines
d. Adventure stories

Mostly A's
Your perfect job would be ...
Assistant at Philadelphia's Museum of Pizza Culture. Your sense of humor and love of collecting will perfectly suit this pie-obsessed exhibition. You don't have to be a chef to work here, but you've got to have taste, especially for all things retro and cheese-topped.

Mostly B's
Your perfect job would be ...
Cashier at the Echo Park Time Travel Mart. Your love of things old and new will suit the fun, prehistoric, and futuristic stock at this out-of-time store. The hours are flexible, but make sure you get paid in modern currency.

Mostly C's
Your perfect job would be ...
Curator at the Cathedral of Junk. Here you can recycle to your heart's content and express your artistic side at the same time by adding to the towers of trash. And no worries about tidying up afterward.

Mostly D's
Your perfect job would be ...
Tour guide on the lonely beach of Mopion Island. You could show visitors around this tiny sandbar in just seconds, then spend the rest of your time alone, enjoying the peace, sunny weather, and warm Caribbean waters.

FREAKY FOSSILS

Giant Ants
Wyoming, U.S.A.

Paleontologist Bruce Archibald didn't have to do much digging to make an impressive fossil discovery—it was sitting in a drawer at the Denver Museum of Nature and Science! As soon as he saw it, Archibald realized it was the first full-bodied fossil of the giant ant in North America. At two inches (5 cm) long, this impressive insect was the same size as a modern-day hummingbird! The same giant ants have also been found in Europe. Scientists aren't sure whether they migrated east or west, but either way would have meant crossing the Arctic region. That would normally be too cold for the insects, but during the Eocene epoch, between 56 million and 34 million years ago, there were short periods when the temperature shot up, which is probably when the ants made their long journey over land bridges.

Modern-day *Dorylus* **ants in Africa can grow to be two inches** (5 cm) **long!**

I've got my eyes on you!

Opabinia
British Columbia, Canada

What has a long trunk, a backward-facing mouth, and five eyes? This might sound like a joke, but it's an accurate description of a marine animal that lived 508 million years ago in the Cambrian period! *Opabinia* belonged to the arthropod group, which have hard exoskeletons but no backbone, and was about the size of a mouse. But it's that absurd-looking head that makes this extinct creature so memorable. Its long proboscis ended in a claw that would carry particles of food from the seafloor to its mouth. *Opabinia* probably didn't have any teeth, so it could only have eaten small, soft fragments. You might think this bizarre creature is unique, but in 2022 another pre-historic marine animal, *Utaurora comosa*, was identified as belonging to the same family. It had five eyes, too!

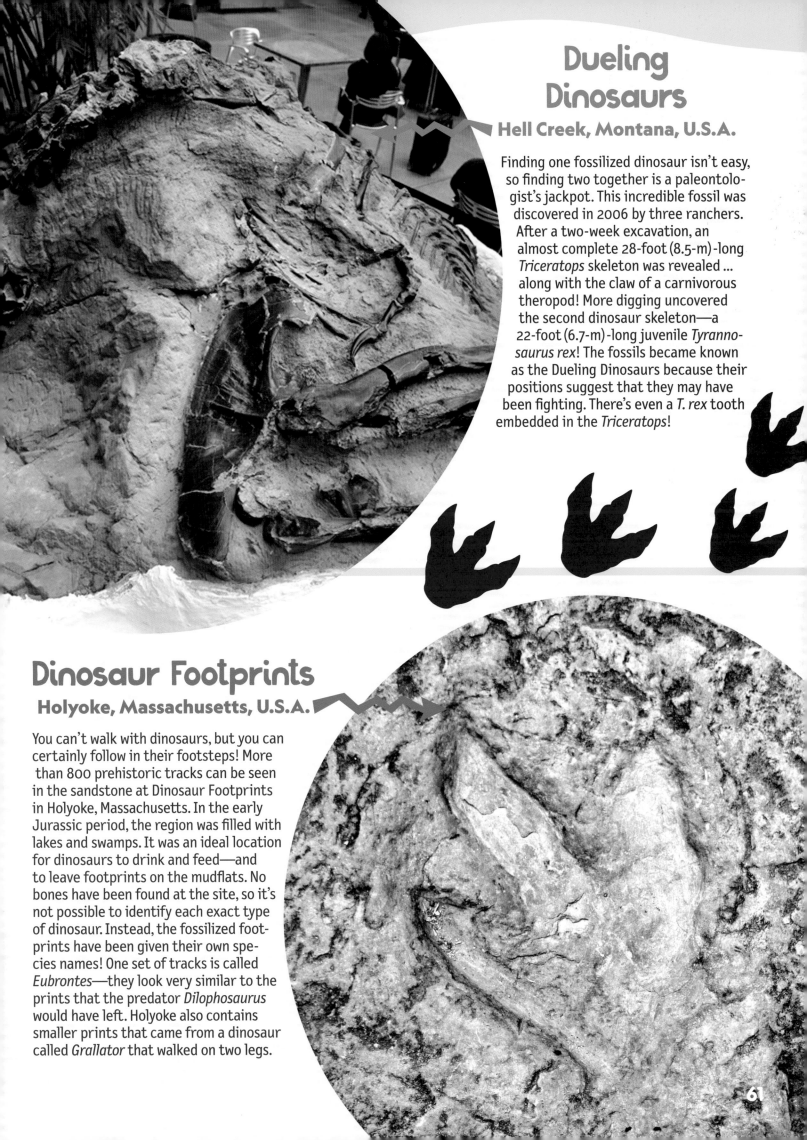

Dueling Dinosaurs
Hell Creek, Montana, U.S.A.

Finding one fossilized dinosaur isn't easy, so finding two together is a paleontologist's jackpot. This incredible fossil was discovered in 2006 by three ranchers. After a two-week excavation, an almost complete 28-foot (8.5-m)-long *Triceratops* skeleton was revealed ... along with the claw of a carnivorous theropod! More digging uncovered the second dinosaur skeleton—a 22-foot (6.7-m)-long juvenile *Tyrannosaurus rex*! The fossils became known as the Dueling Dinosaurs because their positions suggest that they may have been fighting. There's even a *T. rex* tooth embedded in the *Triceratops*!

Dinosaur Footprints
Holyoke, Massachusetts, U.S.A.

You can't walk with dinosaurs, but you can certainly follow in their footsteps! More than 800 prehistoric tracks can be seen in the sandstone at Dinosaur Footprints in Holyoke, Massachusetts. In the early Jurassic period, the region was filled with lakes and swamps. It was an ideal location for dinosaurs to drink and feed—and to leave footprints on the mudflats. No bones have been found at the site, so it's not possible to identify each exact type of dinosaur. Instead, the fossilized footprints have been given their own species names! One set of tracks is called *Eubrontes*—they look very similar to the prints that the predator *Dilophosaurus* would have left. Holyoke also contains smaller prints that came from a dinosaur called *Grallator* that walked on two legs.

Weird VACATIONS

Burning of Zozobra
New Mexico, U.S.A.

Setting Santa Fe alight every year, September's Burning of Zozobra was the brainchild of artist Will Shuster, Jr. He started burning his Zozobra figures (whose name means "worry" in Spanish) in 1924. The gloomy 50-foot (15-m) marionette, said to be the enemy of all that is good, is built of wood, wire, and cloth before being set ablaze along with fireworks for a festival crowd.

Pink Sand Beach
The Bahamas

Need a little color? Soak up some sun at this three-mile (5-km) stretch of sand where everything looks rosy! The pink color of the beach at Harbour Island, the Bahamas, comes from foraminifera, tiny single-celled creatures with red shells. So visitors are actually stepping on sand—and dead insect bodies!

Tree House Hotel
British Columbia, Canada

Tree houses have gotten an upgrade! Free Spirit Spheres offers luxury accommodation in suspended globes in the treetops. Nestled in a coastal rainforest on Vancouver Island, British Columbia, these round rooms offer comfort and composting toilets. Visitors are sure to have a ball!

Mermaid Shows
Florida, U.S.A.

Weeki Wachee is one of the deepest naturally formed underwater caverns in the United States and the perfect home for mermaids. That's right—mermaids. Since 1947, an open-air theater on the site has been putting on mermaid shows with strong swimmers (complete with fish tails) performing underwater acrobatics.

Big Basket Building
Ohio, U.S.A.

Newark, Ohio, has a real basket case to deal with—what to do with the city's wildest building! The Longaberger Company is known for its quality basketware and designed its Ohio headquarters to match the company's best-selling product in 1997. Now the basket-shaped offices are empty and awaiting redevelopment. Fans are hoping a new buyer doesn't get carried away.

Rock City
Georgia, U.S.A.

There's a place in Georgia that's a home for garden gnomes. In the 1900s, Garnet Carter developed Rock City Gardens in Lookout Mountain as a "Fairyland" for his wife, who loved European folktales. Now it's a collection of gardens and mountain trails populated with gnomes and their fairy-tale friends.

CASTLE of the GNOMES

Dog Bark Park
Idaho, U.S.A.

Claiming to be the world's biggest beagle, "Sweet Willy" in Dog Bark Park in Cottonwood, Idaho, is a guesthouse for fans of our four-legged friends. Chainsaw artists and husband-and-wife team Dennis Sullivan and Frances Conklin provide all the wooden doggy decor and doggy treats at this roadside doghouse. Responsible pets are also welcome.

I'M A B&B
DOG BARK PARK.COM

WEIRD WONDERS

It's the hottest place on Earth, a flat desert on the border of California and Nevada where air temperatures can soar to 134.1°F (56.7°C). The area, which is perilous to cross without shade and water, is known as Death Valley. Here, over a crusted, dry lake bed, a mysterious phenomenon seems to move rocks, some hundreds of pounds in weight, of their own accord. These so-called "sailing stones" are too heavy to be lifted by the wind alone. Trails left behind them extend as far as 1,500 feet (450 m). So how are they moving? Mischievous aliens? Superstrong ants? The truth is likely less bizarre. Scientists believe the stones are shifted slowly by winds pushing them over a very thin layer of ice that forms overnight.

SAILING STONES

Death Valley, California, U.S.A.

Some of the moving rocks weigh as much as

700 POUNDS

(320 kg).

HUMAN-MADE MASTERPIECES

Crown Fountain
Chicago, Illinois, U.S.A.

Imagine a fountain. You might picture sculpted fish and cherubs spitting streams of water out of their mouths. Now imagine that instead of a cherub, the creature spitting water into the fountain is you ... and your face is 50 feet (15 m) tall! That's real life for the 1,000 volunteers who were filmed for Chicago's Crown Fountain installation. Their faces are projected onto two video-screen towers, and when they pucker up, water streams out of their mouths. The site, designed by Spanish artist Jaume Plensa, features a long shallow pool between the screens where visitors can splash around.

The Moss Lady
Victoria, Canada

The mega Moss Lady lies tucked under a soft blanket of moss, with living plants sprouting like hair from the top of her head. Snoozing peacefully, she measures 35 feet (10 m) long—that's about as long as a school bus. The sculpture is made from a combination of boulders, wire, concrete, and pipes. It was built in 2015 by an artist named Dale Doebert, who was inspired by a similar sculpture at the Lost Gardens of Heligan in Cornwall, England.

Leaf me alone. I want to sleep!

THE SERPENT'S SPECTACULAR **20-FOOT** (6-M)-TALL MOUTH IS SHAPED BY THE SITE'S BIGGEST CAVE.

Quetzalcóatl's Nest

Naucalpan de Juárez, Mexico

Winding and slithering through trees and bushes, this sensational snake is a size that would put a python to shame. Called El Nido de Quetzalcóatl (Quetzalcóatl's Nest), this snaking series of apartments near Mexico City is named after the feathered serpent deity worshipped by the ancient Aztec. Architect Javier Senosiain designed the complex to fit into the natural landscape. Residents can reach the rooms through a series of tunnels that are connected to natural caves and weave in and out of the rocks into beautifully creative surrounding gardens.

The Golden Mean

Oakland, California, U.S.A.

Do you follow your dreams? Kyrsten Mate did! She woke up one morning with visions of a giant snail car and told her husband, Jon Sarriugarte, that they had to build it! Sarriugarte is a blacksmith, and he set to work finding a car to transform. He bought a 1966 VW bug for $200, removed the body, and steam cleaned what was left. Steel tubing was used for the base of the shell and doors. The vehicle's name refers to the "golden ratio"—a mathematical principle that is represented in the spirals of the giant shell. Sarriugarte is no stranger to art cars, and enjoys installing fire effects in them. The Golden Mean is no different: It shoots flames from its feelers! It also glows in the dark, and its lights can pulse in time to the car's sound system. And thanks to engine enhancements, the Golden Mean doesn't move at a snail's pace!

I've come out of my shell.

ROCKY WONDERS

Pizza Pacaya
San Vicente Pacaya, Guatemala

Some folks will go to extremes for the perfect slice of pizza. For chef Mario David García Mansilla, that means hiking thousands of feet above the village of San Vicente Pacaya in Guatemala with 60 pounds (27 kg) of pizza dough and ingredients to bake using the heat of a volcano. García Mansilla started out by leading tourists up Pacaya volcano to roast marshmallows over the lava. Now he's made a business out of volcano-baked pizza. Pacaya has been active since 1965, with a major eruption in 2010, so García Mansilla has to keep his eye out for lava flows while his mozzarella melts.

Bryce Canyon
Utah, U.S.A.

Say howdy to hoodoos at this hoodoo hot spot! Hoodoos are massive rock spires that exist on every continent in the world. Bryce Canyon is home to the world's largest concentration of them. From the top of the canyon, you can look down in wonder at the mysterious red rock formations. As the sun moves during the day, different patterns and shapes form on the hoodoos, and visitors say they can see unusual figures and faces! A variety of trails take hikers into the canyon, bringing them up close to these breathtakingly beautiful rocks. They might look like they were created by magic, but the bizarre spindly structures have natural origins. For more than half the year, Bryce Canyon can be both above and below water's freezing point in a single day. Snow falls on the rocks, melts, and the water trickles into cracks in the rocks. When the temperature falls again, the water turns into ice and expands, breaking the rocks apart!

Thor's Well
Oregon, U.S.A.

On the Oregon coast near Cape Perpetua, there's a huge hole in the rocks that seems to swallow the Pacific Ocean. Named Thor's Well, after the Norse god of thunder, the hole probably began as a sea cave before its ceiling collapsed, creating a chasm for waves to fill. It only appears bottomless: This "drainpipe of the Pacific" is thought to be about 20 feet (6 m) deep. After the water flows into the well, it's released back into the ocean below sea level.

Fly Geyser
Nevada, U.S.A.

This rainbow-colored wonder in the middle of the Nevada desert is human-made—albeit by mistake! So how did this beautiful accident occur? It all started around 100 years ago when residents were looking for water for their crops. They drilled a well and found 200°F (93°C) boiling water—much too hot for what they wanted—so it was abandoned. Decades later, a geyser (or hot spring) formed at the spot. Then, in 1964, an energy company built another well nearby. But the water wasn't hot enough for what they needed. This well was abandoned, and the hot water burst out to form a second geyser—Fly Geyser. It "stole" the water pressure from the original geyser, and it can fire boiling water five feet (1.5 m) into the air! Fly Geyser is always growing as the minerals from the water solidify into weird shapes.

FLY GEYSER'S VIVID COLORS ARE DUE TO THE ALGAE COVERING IT.

QUIZ WHIZ

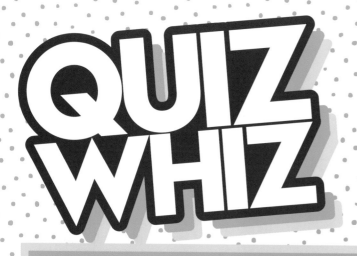

Some answers are weird but true— and others are too weird to be true! Can you separate the facts from the fakes?

1 **Which place has the hottest air temperatures on Earth?**

a. Atacama Desert, Chile
b. Death Valley, California, U.S.A.
c. Oaxaca, Mexico
d. Pink Sand Beach, the Bahamas

2 **In which city would you find this London Underground station?**

a. London, England, of course!
b. London, Canada
c. New York City
d. Mexico City

3 **What is Costa Rica's Restaurante La Oruga shaped like?**

a. A snake
b. A banana
c. A frog
d. A caterpillar

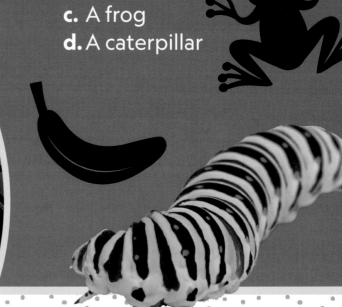

4 What is this blob?

a. A melted piece of candy
b. A beautiful wood-nymph moth
c. A bird dropping
d. Chocolate and vanilla ice cream

5 What is unusual about Pizza Pacaya?

a. It doesn't have tomato sauce.
b. It costs $100 a slice.
c. It is baked on a volcano.
d. It's housed in a museum.

6 Who is this?

a. Weeki Wachee
b. Zozobra
c. Sweet Willy
d. The Flatwoods Monster

7 What can you see at Weeki Wachee?

a. Unicorns
b. Mermaids
c. Dragons
d. Dinosaurs

8 Who built Chichén Itzá?

a. The Maya
b. The Inca
c. The Zozobra
d. The Aztec

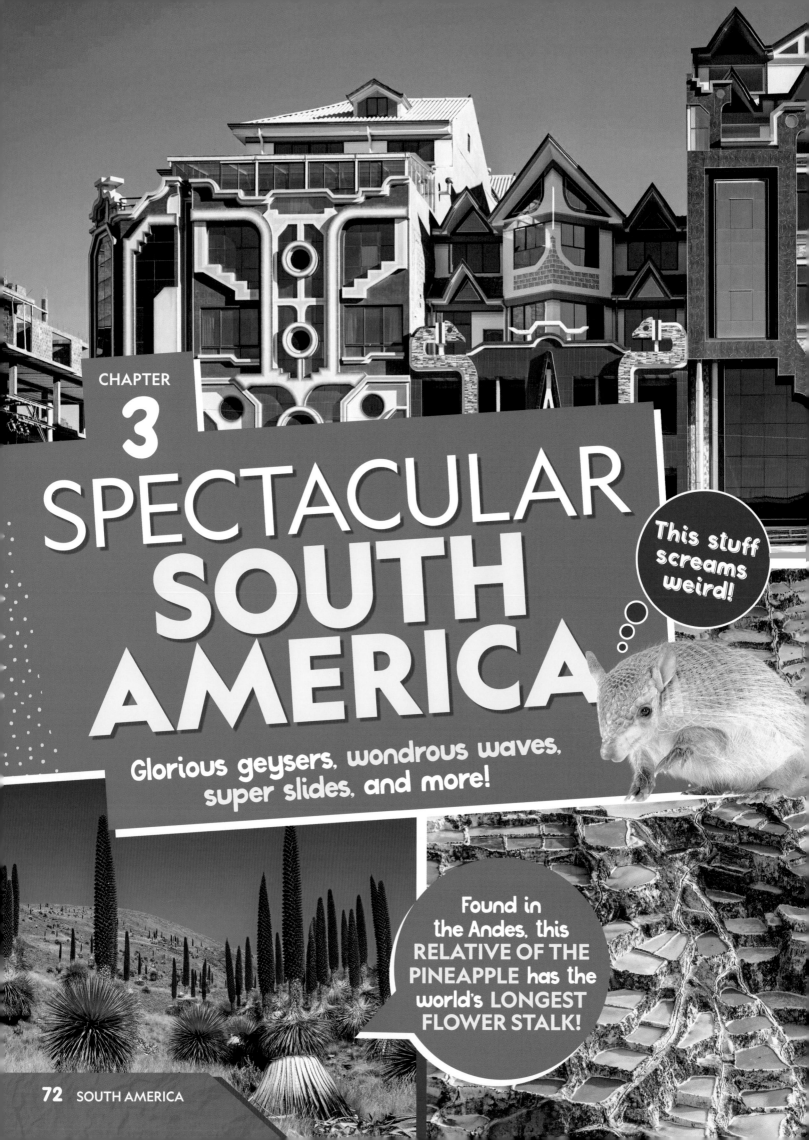

CHAPTER

3
SPECTACULAR SOUTH AMERICA

Glorious geysers, wondrous waves, super slides, and more!

This stuff screams weird!

Found in the Andes, this RELATIVE OF THE PINEAPPLE has the world's LONGEST FLOWER STALK!

WEIRD in the WORLD

Check out some of the WILDEST, WEIRDEST, and MOST MIND-BOGGLING PLACES and ANIMALS across SOUTH AMERICA.

Once a year, you can surf the Amazon River thanks to a sudden rush of ocean water—the waves can travel for miles and last hours!

The smelliest frog in the world is the super-rare Venezuelan skunk frog, which secretes the stink from its skin as a defense.

The waters of the Boiling River in Peru are naturally scorching, reaching temperatures of almost 200°F (93°C).

Caribbean Sea

ATLANTIC OCEAN

French Guiana (France)

SURINAME

GUYANA

VENEZUELA

COLOMBIA

Amazon River

PERU

Boiling River

ECUADOR

Galápagos Islands (Ecuador)

PACIFIC OCEAN

NORTH AMERICA

AFRICA

Atlantic Ocean

SOUTH AMERICA

Pacific Ocean

Southern Ocean

ANTARCTICA

This stuff screams weird!

Suriname has only one movie theater.

The biggest known dinosaur, a 122-foot (37-m)-long titanosaur nicknamed Máximo, was discovered in the Patagonia region of Argentina.

BRAZIL

URUGUAY

PARAGUAY

Falkland Islands (Islas Malvinas) (U.K.)

BOLIVIA

El Jefe geyser

ARGENTINA

Patagonia

CHILE

El Jefe geyser in Chile's Atacama Desert is the most regular in the world, erupting every 132 seconds— only ever differing by two seconds.

Vampire finches are the bloodthirsty birds of the Galápagos that peck large seabirds to drink their blood.

Bolivia has the most official languages of any country in the world: 37.

75

PECULIAR PLACES

Colonia Tovar
Aragua, Venezuela

The town of Colonia Tovar looks like it belongs in Germany. The houses have white walls with dark wooden beams. The restaurants serve bratwurst sausages, apple strudel, and Black Forest cake. But Colonia Tovar isn't actually in Germany—it's west of Caracas, Venezuela! In 1842, a group of settlers left southern Germany to make the long journey to create a home in South America. Originally they stayed isolated from their new neighbors, but now the residents of Colonia Tovar speak Spanish, and the town is a popular destination for weekend visitors from nearby Caracas.

Lençóis Maranhenses National Park
Maranhão, Brazil

Is it a mirage? A computer-generated movie set? Neither. Lençóis Maranhenses National Park is a surreal but natural mix of rolling sand dunes and stunning blue-green freshwater lagoons that stretch as far as the eye can see. The park covers 380,000 acres (154,000 ha)—almost the size of London, England. Its name means "bedsheets" in Portuguese. You can see why—the dunes look like endless white sheets waving in the wind. Scattered among the dunes are hundreds of temporary lakes that fill up during the rainy season (between January and June). The water can't drain away through the impermeable rock below, so the lagoons remain full for many months. Visitors can even take a dip in the beautiful clear water.

The park is home to the **wolffish,** which survives the dry season by **burrowing** into the **mud** and going into a deep sleep!

Caño Cristales
Meta, Colombia

In a remote region of the Serranía de la Macarena, a mountain range in Colombia, an hour's trek into the wilderness, there's a rainbow-colored river that appears for only a few months each year, sometime between June and December. The Caño Cristales, meaning Crystal Channel, includes a variety of vibrant colors, especially a bright pinkish red. That might sound like something out of a sci-fi movie, or perhaps the result of a worrying pollution problem—but it's actually neither. It's completely natural. When the combination of the water level and the warm sunshine is just right, a riverweed that grows in the water blooms bright red. Along with the yellow sand, green mossy rocks, turquoise water, and dark river depths, it creates a breathtaking display known to locals as the "liquid rainbow."

Weirdly Cute!

That's weird!

Screaming Hairy Armadillo

There isn't any mystery to how this curious critter got its name—it's hairy and it screams. That combination doesn't usually equal cute, but this desert dweller is an exception. Its body is covered in a thick armor, like other armadillos, but it has much more hair on its stomach and limbs. These hairs help it to sense its surroundings, which makes up for its poor eyesight. So what's with the "screaming"? It makes a loud squealing noise when it feels threatened. These noisy armadillos live in parts of Argentina, Bolivia, and Paraguay and often build their homes in sand dunes. This means they wind up eating a lot of sand (not by choice!) as they search for food, including plants, insects, birds, and rodents.

EYE-CATCHING ODDITIES

Cuyaba Dwarf Frog

Brazil, Bolivia, and Paraguay

Bottoms up! That's the Cuyaba dwarf frog's approach when it is under threat. Instead of facing off against an opponent or making a run for it, this unusual amphibian turns around and presents its backside! That might sound sort of odd, but this little two-inch (5-cm)-long frog has two black glands with outer white rings on its rear end. When the frog feels threatened, it puffs up its body and lifts itself up, making the glands look like big eyes! If that doesn't scare away its predators, the glands give the frog another defense tactic: They squirt poison!

EDUARDO'S SON LUCA WAS SO IMPRESSED WITH CASA BOLA THAT HE BUILT HIS OWN GLOBE-SHAPED HOUSE!

Casa Bola

São Paulo, Brazil

Eduardo Longo had a ball while working on Casa Bola—or at least, he built one! Longo designed the house as part of a project to build apartment buildings made up of dozens of spherical houses. He started work on Casa Bola in 1974 and spent five years building it himself, despite not having any construction experience. The housing project was never developed further, but this amazing building became Longo's home. Its four levels contain three bedrooms, a dining room, a living room, bathrooms, and a kitchen. Furniture had to be specially created because standard designs would not fit against the curved walls! Much of the interior is white, giving it a futuristic feel, but there is more color on the outside, including a curved yellow slide that can be used to exit the house!

Vinicunca

Andes Mountains, Peru

It's not hard to see why Vinicunca is also known as Rainbow Mountain. This incredible striped peak might look too bizarre to be real, but it's all natural. Vinicunca is made up of 14 different minerals, which create various hues. The red layer, for example, comes from clay, while the yellow band gets its color from sulfur. Until 2015, this weird wonder was totally hidden—completely covered in snow! When that melted, the stripes were revealed. Visitors need to be in good shape because a steep walk is required to reach Vinicunca—but with such a stunning sight as the destination, it's worth it.

Mata Mata Turtle

Ecuador, Venezuela, and Brazil

What's the "mata" with this odd-looking reptile? With its wide, flat neck and triangular head, it looks kind of like it has been squished! But that's just how the mata mata turtle usually looks. It lives in water but isn't a strong swimmer, so prefers to stand in shallow depths, poking its long snout above the surface like a snorkel to breathe. The mata mata has poor eyesight, but it can hear well and has fleshy flaps along its neck, which detect when prey is nearby. The turtle's ridged shell looks like a piece of tree bark—handy camouflage for when it waits motionless for unsuspecting fish and shrimp. When they get close enough, it opens its mouth wide, creating a vacuum to swallow its meal. The mata mata's mouth can't chew, though, so it swallows fish whole!

What's the mata mata with taking it slow?

Mata matas can weigh up to 38 pounds (17 kg)— about the weight of a four-year-old child!

WEIRD WONDERS

This beautiful landscape looks a bit like a patchwork quilt. It's actually a canyon filled with salt pools. Found in the Sacred Valley of the Inca, this ancient site of geometric, human-made pools is still in use today. The area's famous and flavorful pink salt has been harvested here for hundreds of years. There are around 5,000 ponds, and each belongs to a local family—the bigger the family, the bigger their pond. The salt comes from super salty water that streams from a hot spring above the canyon and trickles into the many ponds. Over time, the water evaporates to leave behind a layer of white or pink salt crystals that can be scraped out and sold at market.

SALT MINES OF MARAS

Maras, Peru

The Salt Mines of Maras have been

HARVESTED FOR THEIR SALT

since the 1400s.

WEIRD VACATION DESTINATIONS

Skylodge Pods
Cusco, Peru

If you're scared of heights, look away! To get to this hotel, you have to trek up a 1,300-foot (400-m)-high mountainside and inch your way along a *via ferrata*—a climbing path with metal ladders and cables bolted to the rock to cling on to. When you finally reach your room, it's a see-through metal-and-plexiglass pod fixed to the side of a cliff! The Skylodge Adventure Suites, as they're called, dangle above Peru's Sacred Valley, close to the ancient Inca ruins of Machu Picchu. Each lodge contains a dining area, bathroom, and beds. Of course, the view is fantastic, both down to the valley floor and up to the night sky. Whether you'll be able to relax enough to fall asleep is another matter!

Hotel Unique
São Paulo, Brazil

This trendy hotel is well named: It's not every day you see a building that looks like it's ready to set off to sea! While some people see a boat in the hotel's shape and porthole-like windows, others think it looks more like a slice of watermelon. Whatever you see, the Unique's unusual bowl-shaped design means the floors get wider the higher up in the hotel you go. That means the roof is pretty big—and for good reason! There you'll find a red-tiled rooftop pool with an underwater sound system where a DJ pumps tunes nightly. No wonder the Unique is making waves in São Paulo!

All hands on deck!

Insano

Fortaleza, Brazil

For 10 years, this stomach-turning amusement at Brazil's Beach Park was the world's tallest waterslide. Those daring enough to take the plunge whiz down a slide that's 135 feet (41 m) high—the height of a 14-story building—at 65 miles an hour (105 km/h). There's only one way for a thrill seeker to ride this slide: on their back without any kind of float. But blink and you'll miss it—the experience lasts a grand total of five seconds! The drop is so steep that some riders describe feeling as though they're flying.

BEACH PARK ALSO HAS AN 82-FOOT (25-M) FREE-FALL SLIDE THAT RIDERS DROP INTO THROUGH A TRAPDOOR!

Hostal Las Olas

Copacabana, Bolivia

With bold shapes, bright colors, and intricate embellishments, Las Olas is a complex of 10 stylish villas, or luxury houses, that overlook Lake Titicaca. The idea for the complex came from an ambitious group of friends who wanted to build them using as many natural materials from the region as they could. Their romantic vision blurs the lines between sculpture and architecture. Each hillside suite is a work of art that's different from the next—their shapes are inspired by everything from turtles to snail shells to the wind. To add to the wonder, alpacas roam the grounds.

BY the NUMBERS

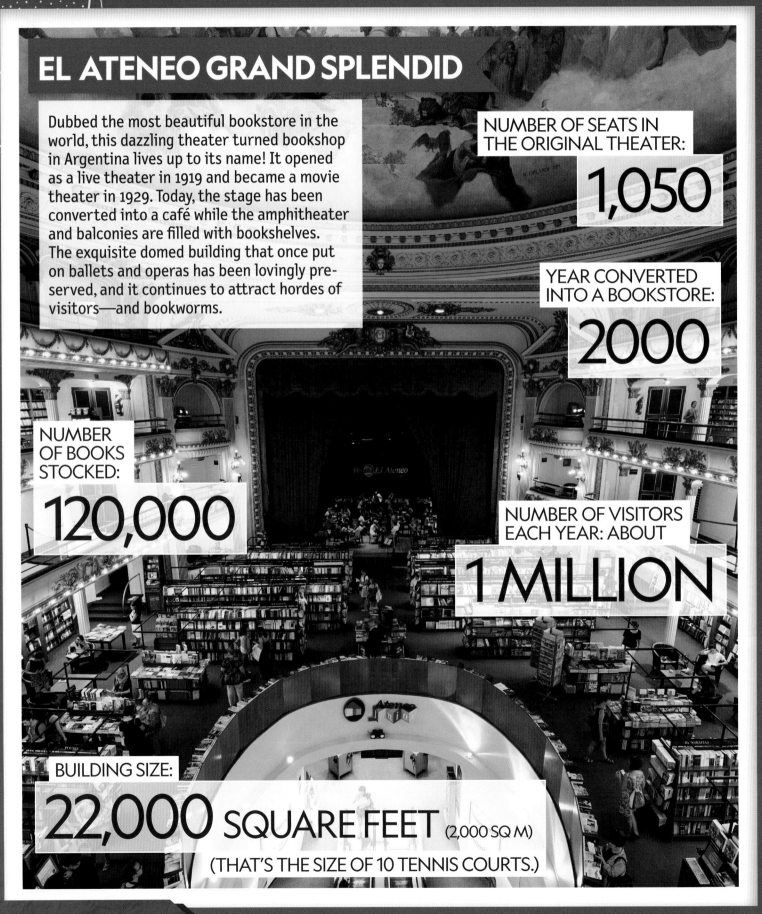

EL ATENEO GRAND SPLENDID

Dubbed the most beautiful bookstore in the world, this dazzling theater turned bookshop in Argentina lives up to its name! It opened as a live theater in 1919 and became a movie theater in 1929. Today, the stage has been converted into a café while the amphitheater and balconies are filled with bookshelves. The exquisite domed building that once put on ballets and operas has been lovingly preserved, and it continues to attract hordes of visitors—and bookworms.

NUMBER OF SEATS IN THE ORIGINAL THEATER:

1,050

YEAR CONVERTED INTO A BOOKSTORE:

2000

NUMBER OF BOOKS STOCKED:

120,000

NUMBER OF VISITORS EACH YEAR: ABOUT

1 MILLION

BUILDING SIZE:

22,000 SQUARE FEET (2,000 SQ M)

(THAT'S THE SIZE OF 10 TENNIS COURTS.)

What's **Weird** About This?

Ever feel like you're in the spotlight?

When you pass by a tower that holds up power lines, you probably don't give it a second glance. But nighttime visitors to Buenos Aires, Argentina, can't help but notice "Coloso." Though it looks like an ordinary transmission tower in the daylight, in the dark, its neon hands, heart, and face transform the metal structure into a giant body that might just make you think robots are taking over the world! Standing at 148 feet (45 m) tall—that's three times the height of the Hollywood sign—"Coloso" is an imposing sight. As its lights change to flash a smiling face, winking eye, and pulsing heart, the enormous sculpture takes on different expressions. "Coloso" was created for an exhibition by a group of artists called DOMA—and thanks to them, we'll never look at a power line tower the same way again!

DRY AS A BONE

Where Rain Never Falls
Atacama Desert, Chile

If you're going for a trek in the Atacama Desert, don't forget a water bottle! This beautiful mountainous desert in northern Chile is the world's driest place, apart from Antarctica. In total, the Atacama receives about half an inch (15 mm) of rain per year. But there are places in the middle where not a single drop has ever been recorded. These areas are so dry that there are no plants, not even cacti—just red, gray, and golden rocks carved into shapes by the wind. Moviemakers often come here to film scenes set on the moon!

The VLT's **huge telescopes** can spot items smaller than a DVD as far away as the **International Space Station.**

Very Large Telescope
Arica, Chile

The aptly named Very Large Telescope, or VLT, is exactly what it sounds like: a telescope with out-of-this-world proportions. It's responsible for many incredible discoveries, including finding R136a1, one of the biggest stars known to humans. (When R136a1 formed, it had a mass 320 times bigger than our sun!) The VLT gets its power from eight telescopes that can work together as one, or separately. Four of them are huge: They have massive mirrors, each 27 feet (8.2 m) across—about the length of a bus! The VLT was built in the Atacama because it's a perfect location for stargazing, with its combination of high altitude, low humidity, and lack of light pollution.

Flowering Desert
Antofagasta, Chile

When you imagine a desert, this floral explosion probably isn't what you think of. The Atacama is one of the driest regions in the world, yet over 200 different types of flowers can be found here during what is known as a superbloom. The colorful carpet of yellow, purple, and pink flowers led locals to nickname it the *desierto florido,* or "flowering desert." This rare phenomenon happens every five to seven years after one of the desert's incredibly rare downpours. When the flowers disappear, the seeds and bulbs remain dormant in the ground. There, they wait years for the next rain so they can sprout once more.

HUMBOLDT PENGUINS OFTEN USE GUANO (BIRD POO!) TO MAKE THEIR BURROW-LIKE NESTS.

Penguins of the Desert
Atacama Desert, Chile

Most penguins make their homes on ice and snow, but this colony lives in the Atacama Desert. Humboldt penguins nest in this hot and barren region, and they take advantage of the plentiful fish in the coastal waters nearby. They hunt for fish in a narrow strip of coast that's home to the Peru Current. Along with keeping the water cool, the current also cools the land closest to the shore, so it's important that the penguins don't stray too deep into the desert.

RIDICULOUS RIDES!

Joseso
Argentina

If good things really do come in small packages, then the Joseso must be one of the best cars ever built. In the 1950s, when resources were scarce after World War II, small vehicles were very popular with motorists in Europe. This inspired Argentine businessman José María Rodríguez to design his own micro-car. The cute little Joseso looked like a toy vehicle scaled up for human use! Its 520-cc engine, which allowed a top speed of about 40 miles an hour (65 km/h), was at the back of the car, with the back seat pushed to one side to make room for it. There was no room for a trunk, but the back seat could fold down to carry luggage. Unfortunately for Rodríguez, the promised support from the government didn't happen—and only 200 cars were built between 1959 and 1960. A few still survive today, occasionally turning heads at classic car shows.

La Garrucha Cable Car
Jardín, Colombia

Wait a minute—is that a floating shed? Not quite! Look closer and you'll see cables holding it up. That's because La Garrucha is a cable car, and it transports passengers over a steep gorge! The town of Jardín is located next to a ravine, and one of the quickest ways to get across it is in La Garrucha. The car is suspended in the air by two steel cables, and a truck engine powers it back and forth every 30 minutes. With the ground hundreds of feet below, some travelers may prefer not to look down. At the top of the valley, a café and amazing views greet those brave enough to make the journey. And for anyone who can't face the return trip, there are other ways to cross the gorge, including a sturdier-looking suspension bridge!

Laguna Garzón Bridge
Rocha and Maldonado, Uruguay

This Uruguayan roadway gives new meaning to the phrase "round trip"! Cars once had to be loaded onto a ferry to cross this lagoon, and a quicker solution was needed. A straight road might have seemed like the obvious choice; instead, this eye-catching bridge is a circle. One of the reasons for the design was to encourage drivers to slow down to appreciate the area's natural beauty. The shape and height of the bridge was an effort to minimize its environmental impact by using as few concrete support columns as possible and reducing the shadow over the lagoon. With pedestrian walkways along both the inside and outside of the curved one-way traffic system, the public is invited to take in panoramic views of this unique coastal landscape. It's even a great spot for bird-watching, fishing, and clam harvesting!

BUILDING THE **LAGUNA GARZÓN BRIDGE** REQUIRED **123,600 CUBIC FEET** (3,500 CUBIC M) OF CONCRETE AND **25 MILES** (40 KM) OF CABLES.

Why did the zebra cross the road?

Traffic Zebras
La Paz, Bolivia

La Paz had a poor record of road safety, and drivers weren't paying much attention to traffic officers. So in 2001 the government decided a new type of authority should hit the streets—zebra educators! At first, 24 costumed citizens were sent out to persuade drivers to obey the traffic laws. Using singing, dancing, and gymnastics, the men and women in full-body striped suits proved to be a big success, with less traffic congestion and fewer collisions. More than 3,000 young people have now been part of the zebra patrol, which is being copied by other South American countries.

Bizarre BUGS!

Orchid Bee

The orchid bee is totally different from the typical black-and-yellow fuzzy kind—it's metallic green and not all that hairy! In fact, its iridescent sheen makes it look more like a beetle than a bee. This flamboyant flying insect is found in the rainforests of South America and has a superlong tongue—up to twice the length of its body!—that can reach deep into narrow flowers to collect scent chemicals. (These flowery perfumes play an important role in the bees' ability to mate.) As their name implies, orchid bees have a special relationship with orchid flowers, in particular. They pollinate more than 700 species of tropical orchids. The flowers lure the bees in with scents of cinnamon, vanilla ... or rotting meat! Pollen then sticks to the bees and they fly off to the next bloom, pollinating along the way.

Peanut-Head Bug

The name says it all! This large Amazon rainforest bug has a head that looks like a giant unshelled peanut. However, scientists think it frightens away predators because to them, it resembles a lizard's head. This makes the bug look bigger and more dangerous than it really is. If that doesn't work, it spreads its wings, revealing an even bigger decoy—a set of scary fake eyes!

Glasswing Butterfly

These incredible insects look almost too delicate to be real, but glasswing butterflies' colorless wings actually help them survive. See-through wings are perfect for blending into surrounding plants, keeping the insects safe from hungry predators. Camouflage isn't their only survival skill, either. They can carry as much as 40 times their own weight and fly fast—up to eight miles an hour (13 km/h). If a glasswing butterfly is caught, it has enough poison to kill a predator!

Wax-Tailed Leafhopper

What does the wax-tailed leafhopper do for protection? It decorates its butt with an elaborate waxy sculpture, of course! The curious critter builds this decorative structure over its rear end for a good reason—to aim and shoot its waste as far away as possible. After feasting on a sugary sap diet, they poop out sticky honeydew. The waxy funnels help them to direct the waste far away from them so they don't drown in their own sticky liquid excrement. Plus, the wax looks a bit like fungus, so it may also put off predators by making the bug look like a dead, decaying animal.

Termites

Termites have built an estimated 200 million cone-shaped mounds over 90,000 square miles (230,000 sq km) in northeastern Brazil. The mounds are arranged in a honeycomb pattern that covers an area the size of Britain, and they are so extensive they can be seen from space. That's pretty extraordinary, considering the termites are half an inch (1.3 cm) long! Each mound is 30 feet (9 m) wide and as much as 10 feet (3 m) tall. But what's visible above the ground is just the leftover dirt dug out by termites building a vast network of underground tunnels. Some of the mounds are a similar age to the Great Pyramids at Giza—more than 4,000 years old!

Bunny Harvestman

What do you get if you cross a rabbit with a spider? Well, the bizarre bunny harvestman might just be the result! In reality, it's neither of those things—this eight-legged wonder belongs to an order of animals called Opiliones, or "daddy longlegs," rather than true spiders. The two yellow spots look like eyes, adding to the illusion, but the arachnid's real eyes are farther down its abdomen!

Leaf-Mimic Katydid

These impressive creatures take the art of camouflage very seriously! As the name suggests, the katydid's body looks like a green leaf. To blend in, these fake leaves look decayed or speckled, and some even have a translucent section resembling a hole! Amazingly, no two leaf-mimic katydids look the same. This makes it very tricky for a potential predator to spot its prey!

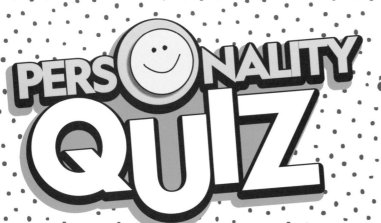

PERSONALITY QUIZ

Which odd South American abode should you call home? Answer the questions to find out.

Think creatively

A time to relax and unwind

When completing a task, you …

A fun day out for you is …

Follow the instructions

Taking a trip to a nature reserve

START

Your perfect vacation is …

Full of nonstop excitement

What? I can't hear you from up here!

Your room is …

Do you like heights?

Physical education

No—I prefer solid ground.

Your favorite subject in school is …

History

Taking a pottery class

Bold and bright

Your favorite colors are ...

Peaceful neutral tones

Bright, calm, and tidy

Chaotic, busy, and full of books

Diving into a pool

Where are you more likely to be found?

At the local library

Your perfect home is: HOSTAL LAS OLAS

You're artistic and lively—so Las Olas is the perfect place to get creative and let the world inspire you. If the twists and turns of your villa don't do the trick, the surrounding nature surely will.

Your perfect home is: CASA TERRACOTA

You're down to earth and a little bit quirky—just like Casa Terracota (see p. 101). Enjoy pottery? Why not live in it! The warm color of this home plus its natural slopes and curves make it a great place to unwind.

Your perfect home is: HOTEL UNIQUE

You're the life of the party, so you need digs that are totally fun. This place is as unique as you are, and with a DJ and rooftop pool, you'll always have something to keep you busy.

Your perfect home is: EL ATENEO GRAND SPLENDID

OK—this isn't a real home. But as a book lover, the Grand Splendid will feel like one. You're curious, smart, and grounded, so you'll love poring over pages in this gorgeous bookstore. Even if you're afraid of heights, you can still enjoy the magnificent balconies from below.

GROOVY GALÁPAGOS

Marine Iguana

The Galápagos Islands are home to the world's only water-loving lizards. Marine iguanas evolved from land iguanas around 4.5 million years ago. And although they spend most of their time out of the water, they head to the ocean to feed. Their blunt snouts are perfect for nibbling algae from rocks, and their long, sharp claws stop them from being washed away. The marine iguana's flat tail is also perfect for swimming. All that ocean dining creates one problem, though—a lot of salt is consumed, too. Luckily, marine iguanas have a special method for dealing with the unwanted sodium chloride: They have developed nasal glands that expel it by sneezing.

When **marine iguanas sneeze,** they sometimes get **hit by their own salty snot,** which forms a **crust on top of their head!**

Sally Lightfoot Crab

This cool crustacean is easy to identify ... and almost impossible to catch! Baby Sally Lightfoot crabs are dark brown or black, which helps them hide on the black rocks formed from lava found on the Galápagos Islands. The crabs molt their shells as they age—and on each newer shell, their red spots get larger until the original black color is completely gone. They no longer need camouflage because they are so agile, able to run in any direction and climb up vertical slopes using the tips of their pointed legs. These extraordinary creatures are so light on their feet that they can skitter across the surface of water! Legend has it that they are named after a Caribbean dancer—and Sally Lightfoot crabs certainly have all the right moves!

Magnificent Frigatebird

Ahoy there, mateys! There be piracy problems in the Pacific! But ain't no gold nor pearls being stolen—'tis fish. Magnificent frigatebirds are nicknamed "pirate birds" because they steal food from other species—even if it has already been eaten! They chase other birds, grab their tail feathers, and shake them violently. The poor victim releases the fish or squid it's holding in its beak or even vomits up recently digested food, which the pirate bird then steals!

THE MALE FRIGATEBIRD'S RED THROAT POUCH, CALLED A GULAR SAC, HELPS IT ATTRACT A MATE AND TAKES 20 MINUTES TO FULLY INFLATE!

Slowly but surely!

Galápagos Tortoise

Jeanne Calment, the oldest known human, lived to be an amazing 122 years old, but humans aren't likely to outlive Galápagos tortoises anytime soon. The oldest on record lived to be 176! Tortoise Harriet was taken from the Galápagos Islands by British naturalist Charles Darwin in 1835 and arrived in Australia in 1842. She lived at the Brisbane City Botanical Gardens for more than 100 years. In 2005, Harriet's 175th birthday was celebrated with cards from around the world and her favorite red hibiscus flowers to munch on!

WEIRD WONDERS

This natural wonder's scenic pillars and high ceilings have earned it the nickname "marble cathedral" by locals. The region was covered by glaciers up until 10,000 years ago, when they retreated, forming General Carrera Lake. Over thousands of years, lake water eroded the nearby cliffs' marble stone, creating striking caves. Unfortunately, erosion means that this amazing phenomenon will one day collapse. Visitors travel by boat to explore the stunning interior but experience something new each time because the caves' appearance keeps changing. Sunlight reflects off the deep turquoise water, and the amount of light entering the caves and the level of the water change dramatically depending on the weather and season, creating different tones and hues on the walls.

MARBLE CAVES

General Carrera Lake, Chile

INCREDIBLE HEAT AND PRESSURE are needed to turn rock **INTO MARBLE.**

PERPLEXING PLANTS

Gran Abuelo Tree

Alerce Costero National Park, Chile

Towering above an ancient evergreen forest, the Gran Abuelo—which means "great-grandfather"—is possibly the oldest living tree in the world. It stands in Chile's Alerce Costero National Park and is thought to be around 5,400 years old. But we cannot know for sure how old the almost 200-foot (60-m)-tall conifer is. When scientists tried to age the tree by taking a sample of its rings, only 40 percent of its massive 13-foot (4-m)-wide trunk could be reached—they suspect the core is rotten. Scientists used a mathematical model to estimate its age instead. If they're correct, Gran Abuelo is at least 500 years the senior of the previous record holder for oldest tree, a California bristlecone pine called Methuselah.

Gran Abuelo is a Patagonian cypress, South America's largest species of tree.

Puya raimondii

Bolivia and Peru

At over 30 feet (9 m) tall, the rare *Puya raimondii*, known as the "Queen of the Andes," is the world's largest bromeliad—a member of the same plant family as the pineapple. It also has the world's longest flower stalk, towering more than 25 feet (8 m) high and containing thousands of flowers. But if you want to see it flower, you could be in for a seriously long wait—these prickly plants don't bloom until they are between 80 and 100 years old! When they eventually do, they are pollinated by birds and bees and then die right after flowering. In the wild, this endangered species can be found growing in the Andes Mountains of Peru and Bolivia.

Shy Plant
Tropical South America

Can a plant be shy? The *Mimosa pudica,* also called the shy plant or touch-me-not plant, has an amazing ability. If you touch it, or just brush past it, the leaves suddenly droop and fold up. This makes it harder for some animals, such as caterpillars, to eat it. Plants aren't known for their speedy moves, so how does the mimosa do this? It has special water-filled cells at the base of each leaf. Touching the leaf makes the cells empty out their water and become floppy, like a deflated balloon—and the leaf collapses. But these plants are smart, too! Scientists have tried playing harmless tricks on mimosas, like sprinkling them with water. At first, they close up, but after the trick is repeated a few times, they learn that there's no danger and stop reacting!

Where's my lipstick?

Hot Lips Plant
Colombia, Costa Rica, and Ecuador

Pucker up! These lips look like they're about to plant a kiss ... but they're a plant! *Palicourea elata,* also known as hot lips, grows in Central and South American rainforests. It's a double deception: Those scarlet smackers aren't flowers, either—they're leaves that open up to let the real white flowers poke through. The leaves' color and shape attract birds and butterflies, which pollinate the plant. Humans are fond of them, too. The Indigenous peoples of the Amazon use the plant to treat a range of illnesses.

STRANGE STRUCTURES

Museu do Amanhã
Rio de Janeiro, Brazil

This enormous futuristic building isn't some gigantic turbine—it's the Museu do Amanhã, or "Museum of Tomorrow." It's a science museum designed by Spanish architect Santiago Calatrava. The eye-catching structure opened in 2015 and features solar spines that move to track the sun. An artful mix of modern tech and nature, the building was inspired by bromeliads—a group of tropical plants. It houses interactive exhibitions about Earth, outer space, and the impact of humans on the planet. Both outside and in, this museum is all about sustainability, and it uses 40 percent less energy than traditional buildings.

New Andean Architecture

El Alto, Bolivia

Self-taught architect Freddy Mamani has sparked the New Andean architecture movement in El Alto with his creative vision to liven up the otherwise monochromatic city. His modern marvels are inspired by his Indigenous Aymara roots, including designs found in the ruins of the ancient city of Tiwanaku and on local textiles known as *aguayo*. This brightly colored, patterned cloth is still woven and worn by the Aymara people. Mamani's stunning buildings are just as exciting on the inside: Think kaleidoscopic patterns and explosions of color from floor to ceiling, with bold zigzagging shapes and jaw-dropping chandeliers. His multilevel designs often include shops on the ground floor. The higher levels are used as everything from galleries to indoor pools. So far, Mamani has completed about 100 buildings like this in El Alto and more throughout Bolivia, inspiring other architects to adopt a similar style.

Casa Terracota

Villa de Leyva, Colombia

You might drink out of a ceramic mug or put flowers in a ceramic vase, but you probably wouldn't imagine something as big as a house could be made out of pottery! Architect Octavio Mendoza Morales didn't want to use ordinary bricks for his house because he thought this traditional material would be too limiting and rigid for how he wanted the building to be constructed and used. So he chose clay instead, which he fired and hardened in the sun to create a ceramic house. The architect began building the house in 1999 and completed the main structure in 2016, but he says he will continue to work on it for the rest of his life. Inside, Casa Terracota has vibrant tile mosaics embellishing the sloping walls. All the furniture is made from clay, too!

Amazon Tall Tower Observatory

Amazon Rainforest, Brazil

Want to take a trip up the tallest tower in South America? Then head to the jungle! Oh, and you'll have to be a scientist, a technician, or a visiting journalist to be allowed up. This skyscraping structure isn't a modern office building in a big city, but a special science research base deep in the Amazon rainforest. Named the Amazon Tall Tower Observatory (ATTO), it was built in 2015 and rises 1,066 feet (325 m) into the sky. Yet it's only 10 feet (3 m) from side to side! It takes an hour to climb to the top. On the way up, there are platforms where scientists can work, as well as a deck right at the summit. The tower is also covered with high-tech sensors for measuring pollution, temperature, humidity, and climate change above the rainforest.

LUCKILY FOR THE EXPERTS WHO WORK ON THE AMAZON'S OBSERVATORY TOWER, THERE'S AN ELEVATOR!

Going up?

KOOKY COLORS!

Escadaria Selarón

Rio de Janeiro, Brazil

When Jorge Selarón began fixing up the crumbling public steps outside his house in Rio, the artist had no idea it would become his life's work—not to mention a global landmark. A painter born in Chile, Selarón ended up spending more than two decades transforming the 400-foot (125-m) staircase into a colorful tribute to his adopted home. While the vibrant green, yellow, and blue of the steps is a nod to Brazil's flag, its 2,000 tiles also feature ceramics sent or hand-delivered from at least 60 countries. The walls are studded with hand-painted portraits and love notes to Brazil written in mosaic form. Today, thousands of tourists scale these 215 spectacular stairs each year—they're a real step up from your average walkway!

THESE ICONIC STEPS HAVE APPEARED IN MUSIC VIDEOS BY SNOOP DOGG AND U2!

Laguna Verde
Altiplano, Bolivia

At Laguna Verde, you can look, but don't touch! This stunning salt lake is a glorious green, although the color can vary because of sediment being stirred up by strong winds. Visitors on different days might experience a bright turquoise or a pale aquamarine. The color comes from large quantities of minerals including sulfur, calcium, lead, and the poisonous chemical arsenic in the water—which make the lake a terrible spot for a swim! The local flamingos have figured this out and won't feed from Laguna Verde.

Laguna Verde is about 40 miles (64 km) south of Laguna Colorada—a red lake!

Weirdly Cute!

Golden Poison Frog

At an average length of one inch (2.5 cm)—about the same as a paper clip—this Colombian amphibian might seem cute and colorful. But it's best not to get too close: It's one of the most poisonous animals on the planet! One tiny frog could have enough venom to kill 10 adults. The local Emberá people smear the frogs' poison on the tips of their blowgun darts for hunting animals. That's why this strangely adorable yet deadly animal is also known as the golden dart frog. The lethal toxins are present in the creatures' skin secretions, and the bright color warns potential predators that this is a snack they don't want to attack!

Weird but true!

MIND-BLOWING FACTS ABOUT

A SWORD-BILLED HUMMINGBIRD'S BEAK is **LONGER** than its **BODY** and **TAIL** put together!

A TOCO TOUCAN'S big beak can quickly **radiate heat away** from **its body** to allow the **tropical bird to KEEP COOL** in hot climates.

THE HARPY EAGLE, ONE OF THE WORLD'S LARGEST RAPTORS, CAN BUILD NESTS AS BIG AS A DOUBLE BED!

The **INCA TERN STEALS FOOD** FROM **SEA LIONS** AND **DOLPHINS—** sometimes right from **THEIR MOUTHS.**

Thanks for the snack!

SOUTH AMERICAN BIRDS

OILBIRDS make nests from **REGURGITATED FRUIT** and **POOP,** high up on **CAVE LEDGES.**

To **attract females,** the **LONG-WATTLED UMBRELLABIRD** waves its inflated wattle and grunts.

HUNDREDS OF MACAWS GATHER EACH **MORNING** along an exposed Amazon riverbank in Peru to **FEAST ON SALTY CLAY.**

QUIZ WHIZ

You've taken an **amazingly weird** tour of South America, but how many freaky facts can you remember? Time to find out!

1 **What's unusual about the termite mounds found in one area of northeastern Brazil?**

a. They have been built in the shape of a star.

b. They smell like pineapple juice.

c. They are so big, they can be seen from space.

d. All 200 million of them were made in just five years.

2 **A cypress in Chile, thought to be the oldest living tree in the world, has a nickname that translates to ...**

a. "Tall uncle"

b. "Great-grandfather"

c. "Super aunt"

d. "Strong grandma"

3 **What did Harriet the tortoise eat at her 175th birthday party?**

a. Cricket salsa

b. Hibiscus flowers

c. Birthday cake, of course!

d. A veggie tray

4 How fast do you drop down the 135-feet (41-m)-high Insano waterslide in Brazil?

a. 65 miles an hour (105 km/h)
b. 4 miles an hour (6 km/h)
c. 18 miles an hour (29 km/h)
d. 32 miles an hour (51 km/h)

5 The country of Suriname has only one ...

a. Restaurant
b. Post office
c. Museum
d. Movie theater

6 What in the mountains of Bolivia and Peru has been nicknamed the "Queen of the Andes"?

a. The world's oldest goat
b. A well-known chinchilla
c. The tip of the tallest mountain
d. A giant bromeliad plant

7 Why does the wax-tailed leafhopper build a waxy sculpture on its rear end?

a. To aim and shoot its poop away from its body
b. To show off to potential mates
c. To give itself something comfy to sit on
d. To help it dig into the ground with its butt

8 What happens in Chile's Atacama Desert once every five to seven years?

a. It gets turned into a water park.
b. It completely flattens in the wind.
c. It blooms with a carpet of flowers.
d. It has displays of southern lights.

Answers: 1. c, 2. b, 3. b, 4. a, 5. d, 6. d, 7. a, 8. c

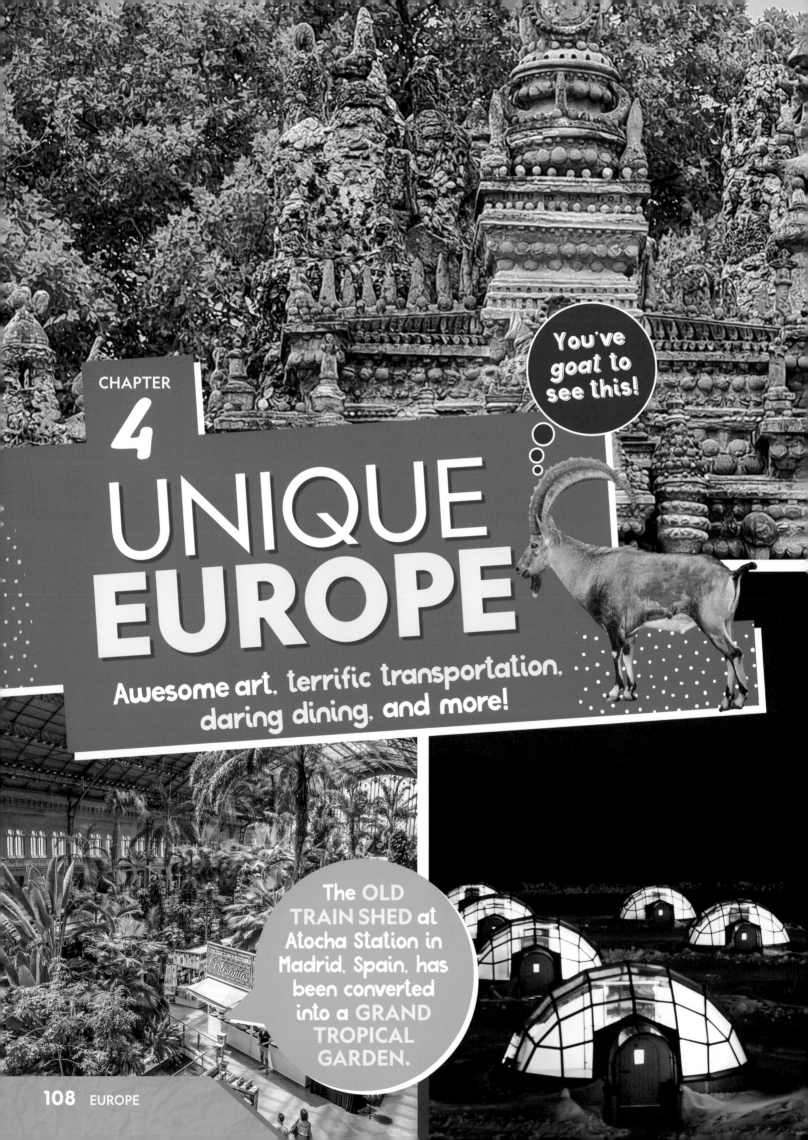

You've goat to see this!

UNIQUE EUROPE

Awesome art, terrific transportation, daring dining, and more!

The OLD TRAIN SHED at Atocha Station in Madrid, Spain, has been converted into a GRAND TROPICAL GARDEN.

MOUNT ETNA, a volcano in Italy that ERUPTS several times a year, is home to two popular SKI RESORTS.

WEIRD in the WORLD

WILLKOMMEN, BIENVENUE, and WELCOME TO EUROPE!

In the **United Kingdom**, you can tell roughly how old a **post box** is by the royal insignia featured on it—the **initials of the monarch** at the time it was made.

Guests at "**Dinner in the Sky**," in Brussels, Belgium, enjoy the creations of top chefs while **dangling from a crane 150 feet (45 m)** in the air.

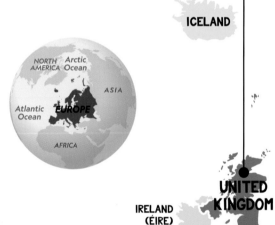

ICELAND

NORTH AMERICA | Arctic Ocean
ASIA
Atlantic Ocean | **EUROPE**
AFRICA

NORWAY
SWEDEN

IRELAND (ÉIRE)
UNITED KINGDOM
North Sea

DENMARK
Baltic Sea
RUSSIA

NETHERLANDS
GERMANY
POLAND

BELGIUM
LUXEMBOURG →
CZECHIA (CZECH REP.)
SLOVAKI

ATLANTIC OCEAN

Bay of Biscay
LIECHTENSTEIN
FRANCE
SWITZ.
Budapest
AUSTRIA
HUNGARY

SLOVENIA
CROATIA

ITALY
SAN MARINO →
BOSNIA & HERZEGOVINA

PORTUGAL
ANDORRA
MONACO
MONTENEGRO
KOSOVO

SPAIN
VATICAN CITY →
ALBANIA

Mediterranean Sea

MALTA

It may be the SECOND SMALLEST of the world's continents, but it's big on STRANGE PLACES, EVENTS, and ANIMALS.

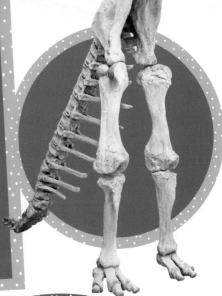

The 17th-century "**Magdeburg Unicorn**" in Germany is a perfect example of fossil reconstruction gone wrong: It has the **legs of a mammoth, horn of a narwhal, and skull of a rhinoceros!**

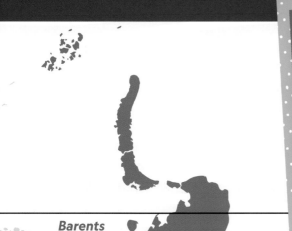

Barents Sea

RUSSIA

FINLAND

ESTONIA

LATVIA

LITHUANIA

BELARUS

KAZAKHSTAN

UKRAINE

MOLDOVA

Caspian Sea

ROMANIA

SERBIA

BULGARIA

NORTH MACEDONIA

TÜRKİYE (TURKEY)

GEORGIA

AZERBAIJAN

Black Sea

GREECE

CYPRUS

While the original stone lion was being renovated in 2022, **a three-ton (2.8-t) Lego lion** sat proudly on the Chain Bridge in Budapest, Hungary.

The world's **longest passenger train**—operated by a **Swiss railway**—was **1.2 miles (1.9 km) long.**

NATURALLY BIZARRE

Ásbyrgi Canyon
Vatnajökull National Park, Iceland

For superstitious travelers, stumbling upon this horseshoe-shaped canyon would be a stroke of luck. Actually, anyone would be lucky to spy this strangely spectacular vista! With a name that means "Shelter of the Gods," Ásbyrgi Canyon is filled with lush greenery and striking waterways with an island of rock in the middle. Its steep, 328-foot (100-m)-high cliffs were first carved out 10 million to eight million years ago—by a flood that was likely caused by a volcano erupting under a glacier! The Viking settlers who discovered it had a different theory, looking to Norse mythology to explain its unusual shape. They believed that the canyon was made by the foot of the god Odin's eight-legged flying horse, Sleipnir. At 2.2 miles (3.5 km) long and 0.7 mile (1.1 km) wide, that's one giant hoofprint!

Legend claims that there is **a golden cave** under Krupaj Spring guarded **by a water spirit called Tartor.**

Krupaj Spring
Milanovac, Serbia

Visiting Krupaj Spring feels like stepping into a fairy tale. But first you have to find this vibrant, tucked-away turquoise lake. Between an old water mill and a hill is a small, easy-to-miss passageway. Take the narrow path through lush forest, past ponds full of fish, and you'll reach the stunning spring. After all that walking, you might be tempted to dive in. But with the water a chilly 50°F (10°C), you might want to think again! Still, there are mysteries to explore under the rippling surface. Scuba divers have discovered a dizzying maze of underwater canals and have given the tunnels nicknames, such as "the Slide" and "the Stomach." It's no wonder this fairy-tale spring has inspired myths and stories.

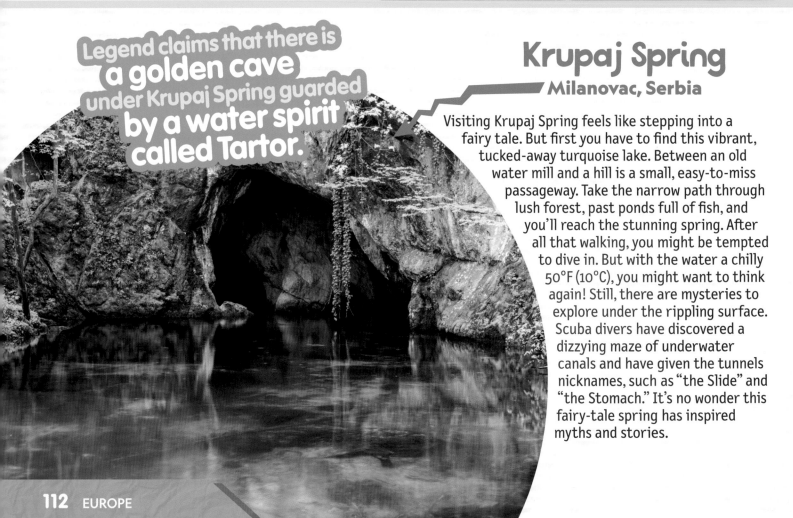

Take a seat and enjoy the view.

Green Lake
Tragöss, Austria

In a mountain village in Austria, you'll find the perfectly clear, small yet beautiful Green Lake, bordered by a pretty park with flowering trees, benches, and a wooden bridge. Well, that's what you'll find if you go during the winter! In the spring, as ice on the surrounding mountains starts to melt, extra water flows into the lake and makes it much deeper. So deep, in fact, that the trees, pathways, benches, and bridge all end up underwater. Scuba divers used to be able to explore the magical world of the park submerged in the clear blue-green water. However, since 2016, diving there has been banned to protect the lake and prevent pollution.

Weirdly Cute!

Eurasian Hoopoe

With a crest of peach-colored feathers, this bird has one distinctive do. Thanks to its long head feathers and the shape of its skinny beak, the hoopoe has been compared to a pickax—a really cute one. When it's excited or senses a nearby predator, the hoopoe fans its crest into a dramatic headpiece. But there's more to this bird than its charming looks. In fact, it's also a little ... gross. The female hoopoe lays pale blue eggs, but they don't stay that color for long. During the breeding season, female hoopoes produce a gooey substance made of oils and wax—and lots of bacteria. Using their beaks, they "paint" their eggs with the bacteria-filled slime, turning them a brown color. To human noses, the fluid is super stinky, but it acts as important protection for the eggs. When it comes to hoopoes, look—but don't smell!

WEIRD SHAPES

Shrinking Sphere
Tartu, Estonia

If you've seen a shape like this before, it was probably brightly colored, made of plastic, and bought from a toy store. It's a Hoberman sphere, a kind of ball that can fold and shrink down to a much smaller shape. Engineer and artist Chuck Hoberman invented it in 1992, and it went on to become a popular toy. But there are also much bigger Hoberman spheres in museums and science centers around the world—and this one, in the AHHAA Science Centre in Tartu, Estonia, is the biggest of them all. It's made of aircraft aluminum and is suspended in midair, where it constantly shrinks and grows. At its full size, it's 19 feet (5.9 m) across—as big as a large classroom!

Human Street Sculpture
 Vienna, Austria

You've probably seen plenty of stone and metal statues of people in city centers, but what about art made up of actual people? This is part of a real-life living, moving artwork created by Austrian artist Willi Dorner called "Bodies in Urban Spaces." To perform the show, a team of dancers, dressed in easy-to-spot, brightly colored sweats, leads the audience through the city streets. Every so often, they suddenly arrange themselves into human patterns, shapes, or surprising positions, sometimes cramming themselves into doorways or onto window ledges, at other times using steps, walls, benches, or even other artworks as part of the performance. It's been performed in Vienna and other cities in Austria and across Europe—with each new location offering new arrangement options!

At Home in a Cube
Rotterdam, Netherlands

Imagine living inside a giant yellow tilted cube perched on top of a concrete stalk. Well, in Rotterdam, you can do just that! These unique homes were designed in the 1970s by famous Dutch architect Piet Blom. Although they're geometric, Blom based the design on a tree. The narrow "trunks" leave plenty of space on the ground, while the cubes on top touch each other like trees in a forest, allowing those inside to bask in the sunshine. One house is open to the public and another is a hotel, so anyone can go see what they're like inside. Don't worry—the floors aren't tilted, too! They're flat, but the walls, ceilings, and windows are all at different angles.

THE CUBE HOUSES FORM A BRIDGE TO CROSS ONE OF THE BUSIEST ROADS INTO THE CITY!

SURREAL SPORTS

Calcio Storico
Florence, Italy

Italians are famous for their love of soccer, which they call *calcio*, or "kick." And once a year, in the city of Florence, they play soccer as it used to be played—an old-fashioned version dating back at least 500 years, called *calcio storico*, or "historic soccer." The rules are very different—in fact, they're almost nonexistent! Pretty much everything you can't do in modern soccer, you CAN do in calcio storico! Each team has 27 players, dressed in medieval jester-style outfits. To get the ball into the net, they can use any body part. They're allowed to wrestle, grab, and elbow their opponents, trip each other up, and even have mass brawls. And the prize for the winners? Traditionally, it's a cow—but these days, they get a free dinner instead.

Strike while the iron's wet!

Extreme Ironing
United Kingdom

Is it a sport, a stunt, or just a joke? No one is sure, but extreme ironing is very popular—and one of the most surreal activities you can imagine. All you have to do is iron something on an ironing board in a ridiculously unlikely or challenging location. It could be a mountaintop, a roof, a rock face, up a tree, while waterskiing, or in countless other silly situations. Extreme ironing is said to date from 1980, inspired by a British man who took his ironing board camping with him. It gradually took off, and now it's spread to other countries and branched out into several different categories, including bungee ironing, high-altitude ironing, and underwater ironing (don't worry, the electricity isn't turned on!). There's even an Extreme Ironing World Championship.

Pumpkin Paddling

Ludwigsburg, Germany

If you love pumpkins—like really, *really* love pumpkins—you need to go to the Ludwigsburg Pumpkin Festival. Held every fall on the grounds of the fabulous Ludwigsburg Palace in southwestern Germany, it lasts more than a month and features over 450,000 pumpkins in hundreds of varieties and sizes. There are biggest pumpkin contests, pumpkin carving contests, pumpkin sculptures, pumpkin-based food stalls, and of course, the pumpkin regatta! Racers paddle their way across the palace lake sitting inside huge hollowed-out pumpkins, which float perfectly (although they are hard to steer). Anyone can take part in the race. Then, at the end of the festival, everyone joins in to smash up the pumpkins.

Bossaball

Spain

BOINGGG!!! Few sports are as lively as bossaball. If you haven't heard of it, that might be because it's pretty new. The sport was invented in Spain in 2004, inspired by the music and martial arts styles of Brazil, and its name means "styleball" in Portuguese. It's similar to volleyball, but it's played while bouncing on a giant inflatable court, with a built-in trampoline on each side of the net. Each four-person team has one player on the trampoline who can bounce up above the net to score points. The fancier the moves they make in midair, the more points they score. Meanwhile, the referee is also a DJ who plays high-energy Latin music to bounce along to!

Extreme ART

Bouquet of Tulips
Paris, France

This giant hand clutching a colorful bunch of flowers emerges from the trees in the garden of the Petit Palais in Paris. If you're wondering about the tulips themselves, well, they're supposed to look like they're made from balloons. The surreal sculpture is the work of American artist Jeff Koons. Standing tall at 41 feet (12.6 m) high, the playful bouquet is made from bronze, aluminum, and stainless steel.

World Living Statues Festival
The Netherlands

On your mark, get set—stay! These performers have made standing still into an art form. Every two years, the World Living Statues Festival brings more than 200,000 visitors to Dutch streets to see 200 artists in very full makeup and costume. With both amateur and professional competitors, this unique event is a showcase for the finest sculpture impersonators on the planet.

Tout Quarry Sculpture Park
Dorset, England

On the Isle of Portland, you can wander around an abandoned quarry from the 1700s, now home to a nature reserve and sculpture garden. Famous artists make their mark at this one-of-a-kind art exhibition. Meandering through mazelike paths, visitors can find 60 different sculptures, each etched into the original quarry stones. The magical 40-acre (16-ha) site has boulders to climb, narrow gaps to squeeze through, and new sights to see all the time as different sculptors add to the ever evolving park.

Wasa Graffitilandia
Vaasa, Finland

What better way to put an abandoned amusement park to use than as a street art gallery? More than 100 artists took part in a volunteer-run project to spray-paint walls, ceilings, arches, pillars, and even trash cans, turning this worn-down site into a thing of beauty.

Chewing Gum Sculptures
Italy

Usually gum in public spaces is a thing to avoid, but not for Maurizio Savini—an artist who has spent the past 20 years using it to sculpt animals, people, and even a chandelier. His work combines fiberglass and chewing gum, producing highly detailed and lifelike creations with the bright pink sticky stuff.

Man at Work Sculpture
Bratislava, Slovakia

Unlike traditional brass sculptures that are grandly placed on tall platforms, this one is as low to the ground as you can get—he's wearing a hard hat and poking out from the sewers! Viktor Hulík is the artist responsible for the mysterious sculpture that nobody seems to know much about ... other than that his name is Čumil.

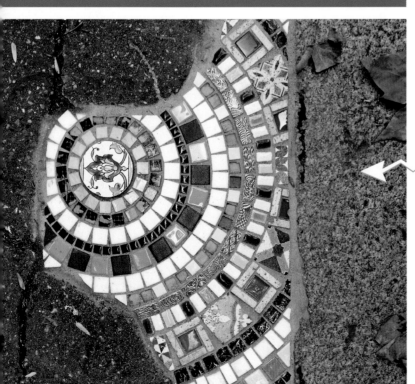

Mosaics to Fix Roads
France

Lyon-based artist Ememem has been fixing potholes and cracked sidewalks by mosaicking over them with colorful tiles. Over 350 of his multicolored, geometric designs decorate the otherwise drab roads, turning problems into pops of literal street art. He's named his work "flacking"—a play on the word *flaque*, which means "puddles."

ROOM WITH A VIEW!

Hotel Ještěd
Mount Ještěd, Czechia

Towering 308 feet (94 m) tall atop a hill overlooking Liberec, Czechia (Czech Republic), is the remarkable Hotel Ještěd. When it comes to combining style and function, this building really makes a point: It was designed by Karel Hubáček in 1963 to be a hotel, restaurant—and TV transmitter! To survive the high winds and harsh winters, the transmitter had to be housed inside the building. Both transmitter and hotel are still operational today, though the cable car that once carried guests the 1,012 feet (308 m) up to the entrance is not. The retro wonder is especially popular in the winter when the nearby ski resort is in full swing. Its 360-degree view is so majestic, you can see two other countries in the distance—Germany and Poland!

Igloo Hotel
Kakslauttanen, Finland

There's no better feeling than being on vacation and pulling back the drapes to a picture-perfect view. Or is there? Deep in the Arctic Circle, Kakslauttanen's glass igloos are all windows, and there are no drapes to obscure the view. Hunkering down in one of these means you can witness the spectacle of the northern lights as you lie tucked up in bed. With it being a teeth-chattering minus 40°F (-40°C) outside, you may think glass walls sound a bit cold. Thankfully, they're made from specially designed thermal glass—keeping the heat in and the glass frost-free for viewing.

What's **Weird** About This?

At first glance this may look like an old ship bobbing around in some icy waters, but this vessel has been frozen into the ice ... **on purpose!** From 2002 to 2015, this 100-year-old ship, the *Noorderlicht*, was deliberately frozen in the ice of the Tempelfjord in winter and used as a hotel. It could take a month of very precise maneuvering to anchor the vessel in the ideal position. It's probably not surprising that it was the only icebound hotel ship in the world. Today, the ship is free to sail the seas, but guests can still book a stay. Aboard there are 10 cabins for up to 20 people to stay at a time while adventuring in the Arctic.

NOORDERLICHT

EYE-CATCHING ODDITIES!

Thumb Sculpture

Puteaux, France

Talk about sticking out like a sore thumb! Pointing up among the skyscrapers of a financial district in France, "Le Pounce" (or "The Thumb") is a 40-foot (12-m)-high, 18-ton (16-t) bronze creation by French artist César Baldaccini. With its discolored facade and organic shape, "The Thumb" is a celebration of nature and imperfection among the pristine, polished business buildings. Baldaccini used a mold of his own thumb to re-create enormously large versions of it. These can be found around the globe in museums and parks, but this one is his most famous work! The artist, who was part of the French 1960s movement called Nouveau Réalisme, played around with the size and shape of everyday objects. We give his style a big thumbs-up!

Le Grand Éléphant

Nantes, France

There's no other ride quite like it! Le Grand Éléphant is 40 feet (12 m) high, 26 feet (8 m) wide, 69 feet (21 m) long and can carry up to 50 passengers at a time for a 30-minute trip. This showstopping invention is found at Les Machines de l'Île, a museum in Nantes that showcases magnificent animals in mechanical form. Their epic elephant is made from 53 tons (48 t) of steel and wood. It travels at a leisurely pace of only up to two miles an hour (3 km/h), so you won't be getting anywhere in a hurry, but you will get there in luxury! This one-of-a-kind creature features an indoor lounge with French doors, balconies, and even a terrace.

TO KEEP IT MOVING, THE ELEPHANT'S METAL BODY MUST BE LUBRICATED WITH 660 GALLONS (2,500 L) OF OIL.

Fire-Breathing Dragon
Kamenka, Lipetsk Oblast, Russia

It's lucky that dragons aren't real—otherwise, seeing this giant, winged monster on top of a hill, spouting flames from its three huge mouths, could be terrifying! It's actually an enormous sculpture in the Kudykina Gora theme park in Kamenka, Russia. Towering over visitors at 50 feet (15 m) tall, it depicts the Zmey Gorynych, a scary super-size dragon from Russian folklore. According to old legends, he had three heads, seven tails, and gleaming copper claws, and was so big that his wings blocked out the sun as he flew. As it gets dark in the evening, the iron-and-concrete sculpture comes to life, letting out a bone-chilling screech and breathing jets of real fire.

Cycling Through Water
Bokrijk, Belgium

Is it a duck? Is it a lost soccer ball? No, it's a cyclist's head! In Bokrijk, Belgium, you can cycle across a lake, from one side to the other, without getting wet—thanks to the Cycling Through Water bike trail. The 650-foot (200-m)-long path is part of a large network of cycle trails in this area, created to encourage people to enjoy the outdoors. It's built right into the lake, creating a dry channel below the water level. Its sides are perfectly level with the surface, so as you ride along, you're close to the water. If you look across the lake from the side, the trail is almost invisible, so all you see are people's heads gliding along!

Talk about riding a wave!

123

Weird but true!

ON **NOVEMBER 5,** IN THE TOWN OF **OTTERY ST. MARY,** ENGLAND, **VILLAGERS CARRY BARRELS OF BURNING TAR** THROUGH THE STREETS **ON THEIR BACKS.**

In 1993, **A POWER OUTAGE** disrupted **NEW YEAR'S EVE** CELEBRATIONS in Bérchules, Spain—so they **POSTPONED** their party **UNTIL AUGUST. (THE TRADITION STUCK!)**

Every spring, **CONTESTANTS** in Gloucestershire, England, participate in an event in which they **RACE DOWN A HILL TRYING TO CATCH A ROUND CHEESE.**

The town of Mohács, Hungary, holds a six-day carnival where men dress up in **DEVIL MASKS** and **SHEEP COSTUMES TO SCARE AWAY THE WINTER.**

WEIRD YEARLY EVENTS

Every **JANUARY**, the people of Shetland, **SCOTLAND**, celebrate the event **UP HELLY AA** by **SETTING FIRE TO A** reproduction of a **VIKING SHIP**.

In one Spanish village, **MEN JUMP OVER ALL THE BABIES BORN** in the past year! The tradition is said to **FREE THEM FROM EVIL.**

DON'T TRY THESE AT HOME!

In Mataelpino, Spain, locals have **REPLACED BULL RUNNING** with *boloencierro,* or "ball running," in which they **RUN WITH A 10-FOOT** (3-m)-wide **BALL THROUGH THE STREETS.**

ANIMAL ANTICS

Kindergarten Wolfartsweier

Wolfartsweier, Germany

If you grow up in the village of Wolfartsweier, Germany, you get to go to kindergarten inside a giant cat! Built in 2011, this cool kitty was created by a team that included the famous children's book author and illustrator Tomi Ungerer, and it's designed with fun in mind. The cat's mouth is the front door, and its big round eyes are upstairs windows. The front paws contain play areas, and at the back of the building, kids can slide down the cat's tail! This kindergarten is definitely a cat, but buildings like this, in the shape of animals or other objects, are actually known as "ducks." Whether a building looks like a cat, an elephant, a shoe, or a basket—it's a duck!

I'm no one-trick pony!

La Balade des Gnomes

Durbuy, Belgium

Here's another great European "duck": a hotel in the shape of a horse! Not just any horse, but the famous Trojan horse of Greek mythology. In the legend, the Greek army hid inside a giant wooden horse on wheels to sneak into the enemy city of Troy. The horse is just one of several guest rooms and cabins at La Balade des Gnomes hotel in Belgium, all with a mythological or adventure theme. (The others include a moon room, a desert island, and a troll's den.) If you stay in the horse, you'll be a lot more comfortable than the ancient Greek soldiers were—it has a TV lounge, three cozy beds, a wooden Jacuzzi, and a coffee machine!

Duck House
Brighton, England

Do you need a rubber duck? How about hundreds of them? In Brighton, England, there's a shop that sells more than 400 varieties of rubber ducks to keep you company in the bathtub. At Duck House, you can find a superhero duck, a *Star Trek* duck, a guitar-playing rock star duck, a queen duck with a crown, and even a spooky ghost, vampire, or zombie duck! Whatever your interest or hobby, favorite sport or TV show, there's a duck for you!

Weirdly Cute!

Slowworm

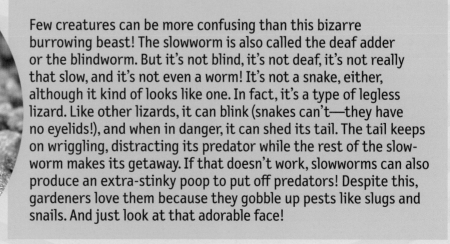

Few creatures can be more confusing than this bizarre burrowing beast! The slowworm is also called the deaf adder or the blindworm. But it's not blind, it's not deaf, it's not really that slow, and it's not even a worm! It's not a snake, either, although it kind of looks like one. In fact, it's a type of legless lizard. Like other lizards, it can blink (snakes can't—they have no eyelids!), and when in danger, it can shed its tail. The tail keeps on wriggling, distracting its predator while the rest of the slowworm makes its getaway. If that doesn't work, slowworms can also produce an extra-stinky poop to put off predators! Despite this, gardeners love them because they gobble up pests like slugs and snails. And just look at that adorable face!

PERSONALITY QUIZ

Answer the questions to reveal your ideal day out!

Which of these jobs would you prefer?

A party planner—meeting lots of people and having a ton of fun!

Which instrument are you more likely to learn?

Home-cooked and familiar

A gardener—spending my days outdoors

Flute

START
What's your food style?

Summer or winter?

You can't beat a cozy winter night.

I love trying new flavors—give me something adventurous!

A loyal puppy who will be my best friend

Are you always hungry?

Which pet are you more likely to have?

A cat—they're independent and quirky.

Green

White

Pick a color.

Something loud like drums!

I feel the need for speed!

An amusement park

With your love of fun, there is no better destination for you than an amusement park. Head to Kernie's Family Park in Germany (see p. 138) to get all the thrills you need at this nuclear power station turned theme park. You'll have a blast!

Fast and ready or slow and steady?

I'm taking it slowly— a vacation is for chilling.

A sculpture trail

Your love of being outdoors on a summer day means this relaxing activity will be perfect for you. Take a slow walk around the streets of France to see the giant thumb sculpture or the road mosaics under your feet—you'll be giving this a thumbs-up!

Pass me the sunscreen and a beach towel!

Volcano skiing

With your love of adventure and busy nature, this wild activity is perfect! Skiing down the slopes of a volcano (see p. 135) might be right up your alley, but if you start to hear any rumbling, you'd better be quick to get off the slopes!

I'm too busy to think about food.

A food tour

You love to experiment with new food flavors and try new dishes. Take a trip to Alton Towers theme park in England, where your food gets delivered by roller coaster (see p. 139), or dare to eat at an ice-cream parlor in Germany where a sundae is not always what it seems (see p. 135)!

I'm already planning my next meal.

STRANGE STATIONS

World's Longest Art Gallery
Stockholm, Sweden

Stockholm's 68-mile (110-km) subway system is said to be the world's longest art gallery. More than 90 of its 100 hundred stations feature unique art on their platforms, stony walls, or waiting hall. The many murals, scenes, and installations were created by 150 artists over the past 70 years. In fact, since 1957, artists have been involved in the design of new stations. Even older stations have been given creative makeovers with sculptures, paintings, and mosaics. Each stop on the line has its own personality and story to tell, often connected to its location. The Royal Institute of Technology station has a futuristic science theme with suspended dodecahedrons, while the King's Garden stop evokes the palace and French gardens that once stood above. It's no wonder that for many tourists the metro is not just transportation but a prime destination!

The ponds here once housed rescued turtles.

Atocha's Tropical Garden
Madrid, Spain

A far cry from chaotic or run-of-the-mill stations, this one in Madrid is more like an oasis. Rather than staring at the usual brick and concrete, at Atocha Station you can escape into this lush indoor jungle. And just in case it's not clear from the picture, we're not talking about a few potted plants here—this 43,056-square-foot (4,000-sq-m) garden is on a grand scale. Its 7,000 plants include more than 260 species from the Americas, Asia, and Australia, everything from Filipino banana trees to Brazilian rubber trees. The garden was started in 1992 in an unused area of the station—with its glazed roof, it was the ideal environment for a greenhouse. Talk about branching out!

BY the NUMBERS

ACROPOLIS

In Greek, *acropolis* means "high city." Built over 50 years in the fifth century B.C., the Acropolis of Athens, Greece, is a cluster of ancient temples that stands proudly over the city on a rocky hill. This ancient citadel (or fortress) was a place to escape to if the city was attacked, and it was also a military base—its high position means it has good views of land and sea. The Parthenon is the most famous building to survive and was built to honor the goddess of wisdom and courage, Athena, for whom Athens is named.

BUILT
2,500
YEARS AGO

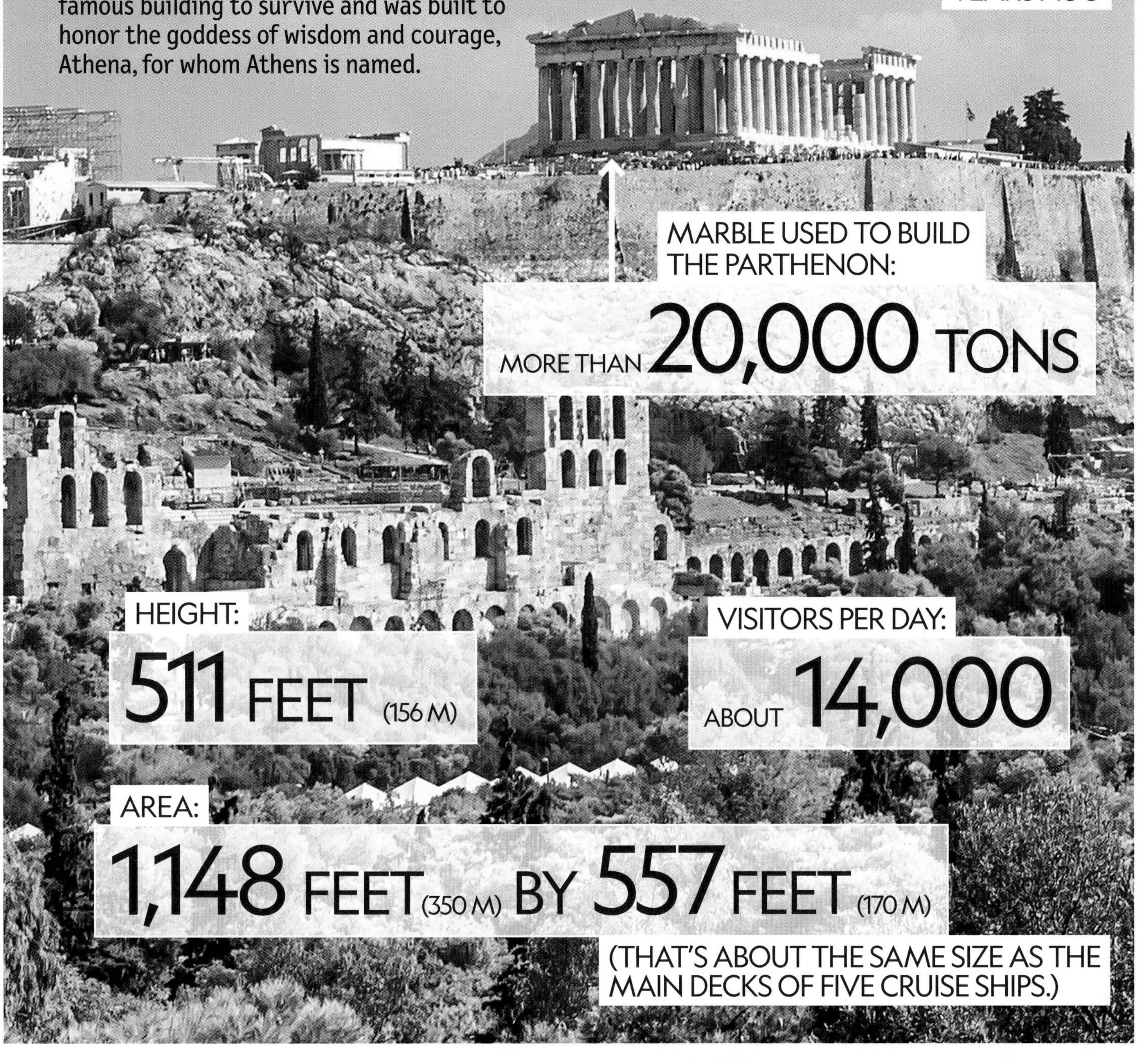

MARBLE USED TO BUILD THE PARTHENON:
MORE THAN **20,000** TONS

HEIGHT:
511 FEET (156 M)

VISITORS PER DAY:
ABOUT **14,000**

AREA:
1,148 FEET (350 M) BY **557** FEET (170 M)

(THAT'S ABOUT THE SAME SIZE AS THE MAIN DECKS OF FIVE CRUISE SHIPS.)

FLOWER FIELDS

The Netherlands

WEIRD WONDERS

Wake up and smell the flowers with this human-made colorful wonder.

Can you tell what these stunning multicolored stripes are made of? Maybe they're part of a vibrant carpet or a traditional woven fabric? Nope! Take a closer look, and you'll see that this is an aerial photograph. It shows the fabulous flower fields of the Netherlands, where flowers such as tulips, daffodils, and hyacinths are important crops. Tourists flock to see the fields in bloom in April and May before the flowers are cut and sent off around the world.

A definite case of flower power!

More than
HALF THE WORLD'S
FRESH CUT FLOWERS
come from the Netherlands.

COLD AS ICE

Frozen Roads
Baltic Sea, Estonia

This might just be the coolest road on the planet! At 15 miles (25 km), Europe's longest ice road takes drivers from mainland Estonia over the frozen Baltic Sea to a nearby island. Needless to say, this is no place for a joy ride—there are strict, special rules for safety. For starters, it won't open unless the ice is at least eight inches (20 cm) thick. Drivers aren't allowed to stop, and they must drive less than 15 miles an hour (25 km/h) or between 25 and 43 miles an hour (40–70 km/h)—not any speed in between those. The middle speed is extremely dangerous because it can cause vibrations that risk cracking the ice. It's also illegal to wear a seat belt! Why? Because if the ice did somehow break, everyone needs the quickest exit possible. It might sound scary, but no serious crashes—or cracks—have happened yet.

Mummified Iceman
Ötztal Alps

Ötzi, also known as "Iceman," is a naturally mummified human preserved for more than 5,000 years. His nickname, Ötzi, comes from the Ötztal Alps on the Austrian-Italian border, where in 1991 German hikers found him sticking out of a glacier. It was originally thought he died of freezing, but x-rays later revealed an arrowhead lodged in his left shoulder. He'd been shot in the back! Of course, the why part remains a mystery. We know a surprising amount of other things about Ötzi, though: He had lactose intolerance, Lyme disease, and 61 tattoos. And we're still learning more: DNA analysis in 2023 revealed that he may have had dark skin and thinning hair, contrary to earlier re-creations. Archaeologists count this amazingly intact iceman—excavated with his clothing, packs, weapons, tools, and even a first aid kit—as one of the greatest finds of the 20th century!

A reconstruction of Ötzi

Volcano Skiing
Mount Etna, Italy

Skiing is a thrill ride as it is—but throw an active volcano into the mix, and things get really exciting! Here, skiers must keep a cool head when the heat is turned up. And this isn't just any volcano: It's Mount Etna—Europe's highest at more than 10,000 feet (3,050 m). Etna also happens to be Europe's most active volcano. It never sleeps and is always spurting lava fountains, giving off gas, or making rumbling noises. Gliding over pristine white snow as volcanic ash rises into the skies makes for a memorable ski.

Ski you later!

Some skiers say the volcano's settled lava makes for an extra smooth ride.

Spaghettieis
Mannheim, Germany

No, that's not a bowl of pasta with tomato sauce—it's ice cream! This iconic German sundae has been impersonating spaghetti since 1969 ... and it still catches people by surprise! The noodle-shaped ice cream with strawberry sauce is an homage to Italy's national dish and was created by Dario Fontanella—an Italian immigrant who owned an ice-cream parlor in Germany. It's made by squeezing vanilla ice cream through a spaetzle press (a device for cutting pasta dough into tube-shaped pieces). The finishing touch is the coconut or white chocolate shavings to look just like Parmesan. Sweet!

135

INTO THIN AIR

International Highline Meeting Festival
The Dolomites, Italy

Most festival-goers sleep in a tent or maybe a camper van. But not at the International Highline Meeting Festival! This meetup, held every year in Italy's Dolomites mountain range, is for fans of highlining—an adventure sport that involves walking along a slack, bouncy tightrope strung between two cliffs or mountaintops. After a busy day of rope-walking—and enjoying festival food and music—the attendees head for bed and snuggle up in tiny hammocks suspended below a highline, dangling hundreds of feet above the ground. Just in case anyone has a nightmare or starts sleepwalking, each person has a safety line attached to the rope as well. Not the easiest setup if you need a midnight bathroom run!

Feva Restaurant
Veneto, Italy

Bored of the same old menu options? In that case, the Feva restaurant in Veneto, in northern Italy, will be like a breath of fresh air. The chefs there have come up with a very light snack, known as *aria fritta*, or "fried air." It's made of very thin layers of tapioca (made from cassava, a potato-like plant), which are deep-fried and dried, forming a puffy ball that looks like a tiny cloud. It's then filled with ozone, a type of oxygen gas, and sprayed with flavorings before being served on a bed of fluffy cotton candy. When you bite into one, it's said to be like breathing fresh Italian mountain air. Delicious! Luckily for the restaurant's customers, it's just an appetizer, and they can get something more filling to follow.

I'm always on top of things.

Climbing Ibex

Mount Etna, Italy

The gravity-defying ibex takes the idea of living on the edge to a whole new level. These brave beasts give any rock climber a run for their money, with no harnesses or safety mats in sight—despite climbing over vertical rocks high up in the mountains! Ibex are big mountain goats that live precariously on the steep sides of the Alps during the winter so that predators can't reach them. Thankfully, their sharp-edged hooves help them jump from one cliff to another. There's also a nutritional benefit to their snowy Alpine retreats. They lick the rocks for salt, an essential part of their diet. During spring and summer, however, ibex return to meadows where there's better food so they can fatten up for the winter months.

Faralda Crane Hotel

Amsterdam, Netherlands

Standing tall in the Port of Amsterdam is what looks like a regular crane. But it's not what it seems. Long gone are its days of hefting around shipping containers and building materials. This 165-foot (50-m)-high crane contains ultra-exclusive luxury accommodations. There are three private suites, and on top of the crane is a spa with incredible views of the Dutch capital. And if simply hanging out so far up isn't epic enough, the Faralda even gives guests the chance to bungee jump off the building.

The Crane Hotel's rooms rotate in the wind, providing different views throughout the day.

Unexpected Theme Parks

Kernie's Family Park
Kalkar, Germany

The only thing this nuclear power plant is capable of fueling is fun! The plant was abandoned before it ever opened, and it was given a mighty makeover. In 2001, hotels, restaurants, and rides sprang up in the building. It has all the classic rides, from teacups to bumper cars to a log flume, but the most popular is the 190-foot (58-m)-high vertical swing, which is found in the former cooling tower.

Puy du Fou
Les Epesses, France

Massive-scale historical reenactments can be found in the 100-year-old forest of Puy du Fou. Visitors of all ages leave the 21st century behind and return to a time in history of their choosing, from the age of the Vikings to World War I.

Montaña Suiza
Donostia-San Sebastián, Spain

The Montaña Suiza (Swiss Mountain) is the oldest working roller coaster that still uses an onboard "brakeman" to control how fast it goes. It runs on railroad-style steel rails that dip and curve along the coast. At points, the seat belt–free wooden carts pass 600 feet (180 m) over the ocean below. It was built by Erich Heidrich in 1928, so it's one of the only pre–World War II roller coasters still standing in southern Europe.

Rollercoaster Restaurant
Staffordshire, England

Food delivered by roller coaster? Sounds like something out of a fantasy movie, right? But Alton Towers theme park in Staffordshire, England, really does have a Rollercoaster Restaurant. Diners sit below the 1,300-foot (400-m) track and watch as their orders race around two loop the loops before shooting 26 feet (8 m) down the "tornado spiral" to their table.

Popeye Village
Anchor Bay, Malta

Hang out with Popeye the Sailor and his friends at Popeye Village—the actual film set featured in the 1980 musical movie *Popeye* starring Robin Williams. The realistic village of 20 buildings was constructed by a crew of 165. Today it is one of Malta's most popular attractions and hosts events and themed parties.

Diggerland
England

Promising "buckets of fun for everyone," Diggerland Parks welcome everyone— even children—to ride, drive, and operate real, full-size excavators. With four locations, each park is packed with over 20 different rides, from dump trucks to mini tractors.

139

BIZARRE BUILDINGS

Seed Stash
Svalbard, Norway

This solitary concrete structure jutting out of the icy wilderness may look like a supervillain's hideaway, but it's a lot more important than that! It's the Svalbard Global Seed Vault, where seeds from all over the world are stored to keep all the species and varieties of plants and crops safe. If any of them are wiped out by disasters or climate change, we can use the stored seeds to get them back. The vault contains more than a million different types of seeds. If you're wondering how they fit them in such a small space, don't worry: This is just the doorway! The vault itself is down a tunnel, deep inside a mountain on the remote Arctic island of Svalbard, to protect it from disasters, wars, weather, and attack.

Postman Cheval's Ideal Palace
Hauterives, France

Beginning in 1879, a postman spent 33 years building a surrealist palace in his vegetable garden. Today, it's internationally admired by surrealist artists and pretty much anyone who knows about it. The mind-boggling historic monument is found within a lush corner of a sleepy French town. Every inch of the building is adorned with intricate carvings of animals and mythological beings, as well as with poems and quotes. Ferdinand Cheval (known as "Postman Cheval") built the astonishing work of art using stones he collected on his rounds. He was inspired by nature, the books he read, and even the postcards he delivered.

Casa do Penedo
Fafe Mountains, Portugal

This "Boulder House" was built between four huge rocks that became the house's walls and ceiling. The unusual dwelling blends in seamlessly with the surrounding landscape and was designed to be used as a family vacation home, complete with a swimming pool carved into one of the granite boulders. However, it attracted so many visitors that trying to have a peaceful getaway there got a bit "rocky." Today, the simple two-story house is a museum instead. It may have no running water or electricity and look like something from the Stone Age, but this bizarre build only dates back as far as the 1970s.

The living room features a concrete sofa that weighs 800 pounds (360 kg).

Fish Out of Water
Headington, Oxford, England

Strolling around the leafy Oxford suburb of Headington, you might be surprised to find an enormous shark statue plunging into the roof of one of the houses. The 25-foot (7.6-m)-long fiberglass shark, known as the Headington Shark, was commissioned in 1986 by the then owner of the house as a political statement. Though neighbors were at first fairly unhappy about the, um, unusual decor, most now agree it's pretty *fin*-tastic.

QUIZ WHIZ

It's hard to keep track of all this weirdness!

See how much you can remember with this quiz. Grab a piece of paper and write down your answers.

1 **What unusual substance does artist Maurizio Savini use to create his sculptures?**

a. Chewing gum
b. Bread
c. Toothpaste
d. Cheese

2 **Why do ibex mountain goats lick rocks in the Alps?**

a. Because they taste sweet
b. Because it helps the goat stick to the rock face
c. To scratch their itchy tongues
d. Because they're covered in nutritious salt

3 **What is the giant hand sculpture in Paris, created by artist Jeff Koons, holding?**

a. A bag of chips
b. A book
c. A bunch of flowers
d. A flashlight

4 What is unusual about the ice cream created by ice-cream parlor owner Dario Fontanella?

a. You don't have to pay for it.
b. It looks like a bowl of spaghetti.
c. Made with a hot cone, it's a race to see if you can eat it before it melts.
d. It's served in bowls shaped like Dario's head.

5 How is food delivered to diners in the Alton Towers theme park restaurant?

a. It shoots around an indoor roller coaster before arriving at your table.
b. It arrives up through hatches built into the floor.
c. Waiters roller-skate your order to your table.
d. Drones fly your order to your seat.

6 What is unique about the igloo hotel in Kakslauttanen, Finland?

a. You have to share the space with the friendly local polar bear.
b. The igloos are balanced high up in the trees.
c. The igloos are made of glass to give you a perfect view.
d. The igloos melt and have to be rebuilt every winter.

8 What unlikely scene will you see inside the Atocha train station in Madrid?

a. A desert, complete with sand dunes
b. A lush indoor jungle
c. A human-made beach with a swimming area
d. A model volcano that spews lava

7 Which body part did French artist César Baldaccini base his sculpture "Le Pounce" on?

a. His knee
b. His foot
c. His nose
d. His thumb

Answers: 1.a, 2.d, 3.c, 4.b, 5.a, 6.c, 7.d, 8.b

Hip-hippo hooray!

AWESOME AFRICA

Astonishing animals, remarkable rocks, secret circles, and more unbelievable surprises!

A very sunny desert in **MOROCCO** boasts the **WORLD'S LARGEST CONCENTRATED SOLAR POWER PLANT.**

During the time of the ANCIENT EGYPTIANS, the Nile River FLOODED every year—on a predictable schedule.

145

WEIRD in the WORLD

With tons of PECULIAR PLACES and EXTRAORDINARY ANIMALS, AFRICA WILL AMAZE YOU again and again!

Uganda's aggressive *Charaxes candiope* butterfly fights other insects and dive-bombs people in its territory.

The world's fastest ant is the Saharan silver ant of northern Africa, which can run 33 inches a second (84 cm/s).

For about 90 years, the Mountains of Kong appeared on maps of West Africa by mistake. They never existed!

Mediterranean Sea

Red Sea

Northern Africa

TUNISIA
MOROCCO
Western Sahara (Morocco)
ALGERIA
LIBYA
EGYPT
MAURITANIA
MALI
NIGER
CHAD
SUDAN
ERITREA
DJIBOUTI
Somaliland (Somalia)
SOUTH SUDAN
ETHIOPIA
SOMALIA
SENEGAL
CABO VERDE
THE GAMBIA →
GUINEA-BISSAU
GUINEA
SIERRA LEONE
LIBERIA
CÔTE D'IVOIRE (IVORY COAST)
BURKINA FASO
GHANA
TOGO
BENIN
NIGERIA
CENTRAL AFRICAN REPUBLIC
CAMEROON

EUROPE
ASIA
AFRICA
SOUTH AMERICA
Indian Ocean
Atlantic Ocean
Southern Ocean

Two dunes in **Ngorongoro, Tanzania,** are made from magnetized volcanic ash—the sand grains stick together, and the dunes have been moving for three million years.

A huge asteroid hit Earth around two billion years ago, creating the 185-mile (298-km)-wide Vredefort crater—the largest known impact structure on our planet.

INDIAN OCEAN

SEYCHELLES

MAURITIUS

Réunion (France)

COMOROS

MADAGASCAR

KENYA

UGANDA

RWANDA

BURUNDI

TANZANIA

Ngorongoro

DEMOCRATIC REPUBLIC OF THE CONGO

MALAWI

MOZAMBIQUE

ESWATINI (SWAZILAND)

LESOTHO

ZIMBABWE

ZAMBIA

CONGO

BOTSWANA

ANGOLA

Namib Sand Sea

Vredefort crater

SOUTH AFRICA

NAMIBIA

GABON

SAO TOME & PRINCIPE

EQUATORIAL GUINEA

ATLANTIC OCEAN

The **Namib Sand Sea** coastal desert is so dry that animals and plants live off water in the fog.

BIZARRE VEHICLES

Traffic Robots
Kinshasa, Democratic Republic of the Congo

You might think you've been transported into a futuristic movie set when driving around Kinshasa! Gigantic aluminum robots fitted with cameras on their shoulders and eyes can be found towering high above the bustling traffic. Designed to tackle serious traffic incidents, the robots' cameras broadcast a live feed to the central police command to help control the road's busy flow. With around nine million residents in the capital city, car accidents were frequent and have now greatly decreased. These solar-powered revolutionary road officers have red and green lights on their hands to signal oncoming traffic. They can even talk or sing to motorists and pedestrians below!

Shipwreck Lodge
Skeleton Coast National Park, Namibia

This beautiful location, complete with rolling sand dunes and waves crashing in the distance, looks idyllic, but the Skeleton Coast in Namibia has a dark side. When the dry air of the desert meets the cold water of the Atlantic, it causes dense fog that can disorient sailors and cause their ships to run aground. Although this is no longer such a regular occurrence, the many wrecks along this coastline were the inspiration behind the design of these isolated lodges. They provide a unique experience for those wanting to bask in the eerie tranquility of the Skeleton Coast.

Microlight Flights
Victoria Falls, Zambia

This breathtaking experience is not for the faint of heart. Daredevils can get the feeling of being "kissed by an angel" as they glide through a mist of water droplets above the colossal Victoria Falls. Swooping over this part of the Zambezi River in a microlight, or lightweight plane, will definitely make you feel small—the water in Victoria Falls drops an incredible 360 feet (110 m). If you can cope with feelings of vertigo, the views are said to be unparalleled, and you may even catch a glimpse of some roaming wildlife on your journey.

VICTORIA FALLS IS CONSIDERED THE WORLD'S LARGEST SHEET OF FALLING WATER.

I'm off to a flying start!

Macrobat
South Africa

Meet the Macrobat! Currently just a concept, this revolutionary design is set to transform personal air travel. Phractyl, a South African start-up company, has shared its vision for an all-electric birdlike aircraft that could tilt its wings, squat down, and even take off and land almost vertically. Currently designed as a one-seater, the plane could be piloted on board or remotely. It has many planned purposes, including as a taxi or to deliver medical supplies. The craft has a maximum travel range of 93 miles (150 km) and would be built to carry a 330-pound (150-kg) load. A prototype is under construction, and it sounds like a soaring success!

Curious CREATURES

Black Rain Frog

It always looks like the black rain frog is having a really bad day, thanks to the permanent frown on its face. Not surprisingly, this annoyed-looking amphibian from South Africa has been nicknamed the "angry avocado"! Usually nocturnal, it retreats into its burrow during the day. It cannot jump or swim, so it crawls around on its short legs instead. That could be a problem for staying safe, but the black rain frog has a different defensive mechanism. It can puff up its body to several times its normal size to scare off predators or make wrestling it from its underground home a tricky task.

Gerenuk

What's worse than a centipede with aching feet? A gerenuk with a sore throat! Its name means "giraffe-necked" in Somali, and it certainly suits this odd-looking creature. The gerenuk has the longest neck of any gazelle. When it balances on its hind legs, it can stand more than six feet seven inches (2 m) tall. This allows it to eat leaves and buds from higher branches. The gerenuk gets most of the water it needs from food and can survive for months or even years without drinking. A shy creature, it may try to avoid being seen by standing still in the shadows. If a predator approaches, the gerenuk may trot away—or stot, a bizarre bounding motion with stiff legs.

South African Springhare

It looks like some kind of "kanga-rabbit," with its long springy back legs that let it leap up high, but this awesome animal is a springhare. Measuring just over one foot (45 cm) in length, this kooky burrowing creature is only slightly larger than an aardvark's tongue! Yet these miniature hoppers can leap more than six feet (2 m). Their curious qualities don't stop there, though—they also glow fluorescent pink and orange under UV light.

Ground Pangolin

This creature might look like it's half reptile and half pine cone, but it's actually a strange, scaly mammal called a pangolin! Pangolins use their impressive scales—which make up about 20 percent of the animal's body weight—as defense against predators. When a hungry animal gets close, the pangolin curls up into a tight ball, and its scales act like tough armor. Pangolins can even close their ears and nostrils to protect themselves from attacks!

Aardvark

This long-nosed super-sniffer is quite the character. With such a prominent snout, it's no surprise that its name translates from Afrikaans as "earth pig." Aardvarks may look strange, but their bodies are perfectly adapted to their sub-Saharan homes. Their incredibly powerful claws mean they can easily burrow and dig up termite mounds— where their favorite food lives. Their thick skin protects them from insect bites, and their long ears disperse heat, helping them to survive in warmer climates. Aardvark sightings are rare because they are nocturnal, spend a lot of time underground, and are solitary animals.

Feasting on termites isn't *aard* with this snout!

Elephant Shrew

This small African animal got its unusual name because of its loooong snout. It uses this fantastically flexible nose to move leaves and soil as it searches for food, such as insects and worms. But, weirdly, another connection to its name has since been discovered. Elephant shrews are not in fact shrews, but they are related to a group of mammals that includes aardvarks—and elephants! The elephant is included in the "big five" group of favorite African safari animals—and the elephant shrew is a member of the "little five"! Other members of the smaller group include the ant lion, rhinoceros beetle, buffalo weaver, and leopard tortoise.

RECORD BREAKERS

Largest Coffee-Grounds Art
Sandton, South Africa

Art can be created from so many different materials: paint, wood, stone ... coffee! That's what artist Percy Maimela used to create an incredible portrait in 2019. A company called BrainFarm had the idea of making a portrait of a South African DJ called Black Coffee, using black coffee! Maimela was excited by the project but wanted to push it even further, making the artwork big enough to set a new world record. It took the artist just four hours to make this astonishingly realistic picture on a white vinyl canvas. Bigger than six king-size beds pushed together, it is the largest picture ever made from coffee grounds. Of course, Maimela doesn't normally work with powdered beans— he is best known for creating portraits with salt!

Largest Uncut Emerald
Kagem Mine, Zambia

Gemstone collectors might go green with envy when they hear about these fabulous finds! In 2021, a massive 7,525-carat emerald was discovered in Zambia. It was named Chimpembele, which means "rhino" in the local Bemba dialect, because the huge gem looks like it has a horn on the top. Carats are used for weighing precious stones, and one carat is equal to .00705 ounce (200 mg). An emerald in a ring might be around two carats; Chimpembele would be 3,762 times heavier than that! At three pounds five ounces (1.5 kg), it is officially the world's largest uncut emerald. Chimpembele seized the title from a 6,225-carat emerald nicknamed Insofu, meaning "elephant," which was unearthed in the same mine. After each was sold at auction, some of the proceeds were donated to conservation efforts to help their namesake animals.

The Big Rush Big Swing
Moses Mabhida Stadium, Durban, South Africa

Brave enough to take a seat? The Big Rush Big Swing sits 348 feet (106 m) above this World Cup soccer arena. As it swings (at a height taller than the Statue of Liberty!), it completes a massive 722-foot (220-m) arc under the stadium's colossal roof. Thrill seekers of all ages can enjoy the ride: There is no age limit—riders as young as eight have taken a swing, as well as some 75-year-olds! If you're in no hurry to experience the "big rush" yourself, you can watch friends and family take the plunge from a viewing gallery in the stadium.

Highest-Altitude Soccer Match
Mount Kilimanjaro, Tanzania

Soccer fans often travel long distances to support their team, but how many would be prepared to climb a mountain? In 2017, two star-studded, multi-international women's teams climbed for six days to Stella Point on Mount Kilimanjaro—the world's tallest stand-alone mountain—to compete in a match. The ascent of 18,885 feet (5,756 m) was followed by a descent into a volcanic crater for the game. The players included Portia Modise, South Africa's record scorer with 101 goals, and U.S. midfielder Lori Lindsey, who won a gold medal at the 2012 Olympic Games. The game was organized by the Equal Playing Field initiative to highlight the lower pay for women in sports compared to men. It is the highest-altitude game of soccer ever played, with the natural arena being 4,515 feet (1,376 m) above the world's highest professional stadium.

EQUAL PLAYING FIELD ALSO HOLDS THE RECORD FOR THE LOWEST-ALTITUDE SOCCER MATCH, WHICH WAS PLAYED AT THE DEAD SEA!

BY theNUMBERS

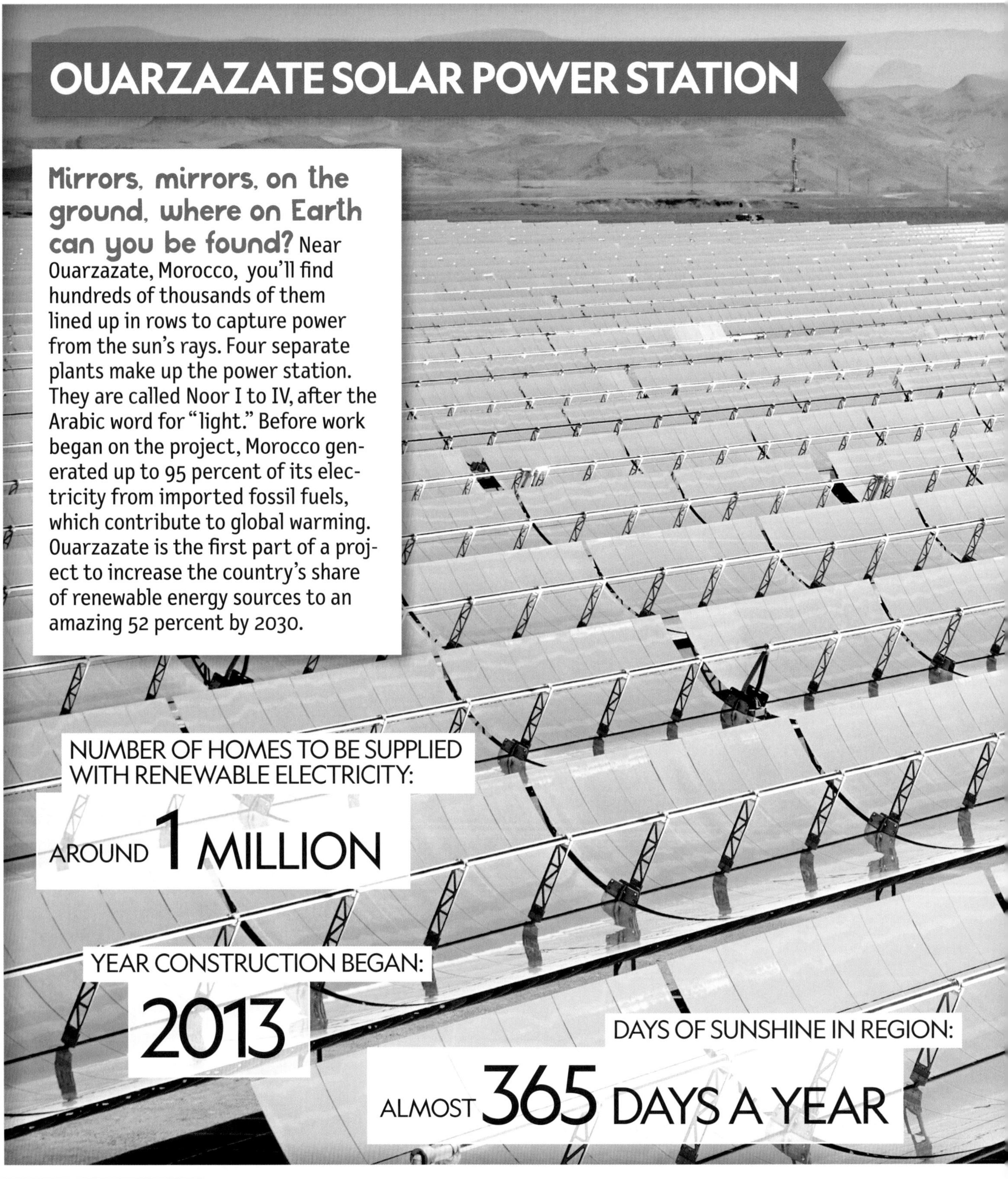

OUARZAZATE SOLAR POWER STATION

Mirrors, mirrors, on the ground, where on Earth can you be found? Near Ouarzazate, Morocco, you'll find hundreds of thousands of them lined up in rows to capture power from the sun's rays. Four separate plants make up the power station. They are called Noor I to IV, after the Arabic word for "light." Before work began on the project, Morocco generated up to 95 percent of its electricity from imported fossil fuels, which contribute to global warming. Ouarzazate is the first part of a project to increase the country's share of renewable energy sources to an amazing 52 percent by 2030.

NUMBER OF HOMES TO BE SUPPLIED WITH RENEWABLE ELECTRICITY:

AROUND **1** MILLION

YEAR CONSTRUCTION BEGAN:

2013

DAYS OF SUNSHINE IN REGION:

ALMOST **365** DAYS A YEAR

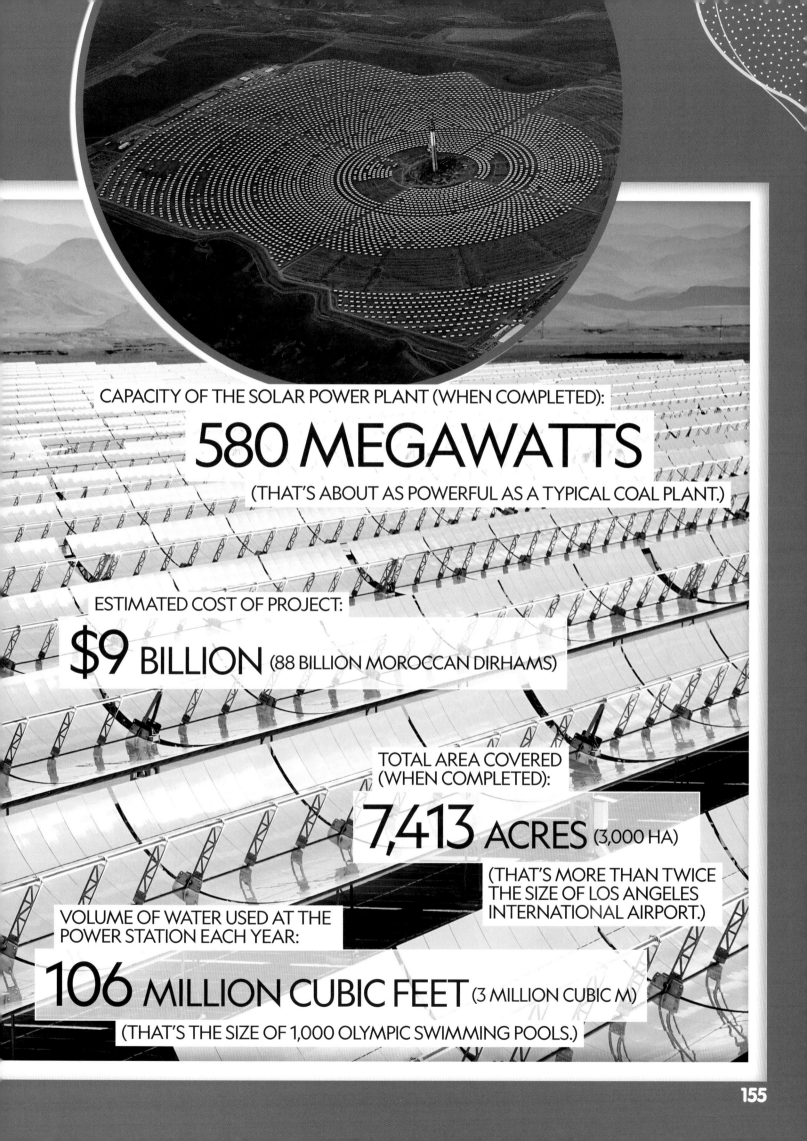

CAPACITY OF THE SOLAR POWER PLANT (WHEN COMPLETED):

580 MEGAWATTS

(THAT'S ABOUT AS POWERFUL AS A TYPICAL COAL PLANT.)

ESTIMATED COST OF PROJECT:

$9 BILLION (88 BILLION MOROCCAN DIRHAMS)

TOTAL AREA COVERED
(WHEN COMPLETED):

7,413 ACRES (3,000 HA)

(THAT'S MORE THAN TWICE
THE SIZE OF LOS ANGELES
INTERNATIONAL AIRPORT.)

VOLUME OF WATER USED AT THE
POWER STATION EACH YEAR:

106 MILLION CUBIC FEET (3 MILLION CUBIC M)

(THAT'S THE SIZE OF 1,000 OLYMPIC SWIMMING POOLS.)

CREATIVE CRITTERS

Elephant Street Art

South Africa

Falko One is a street artist who is making his mark on Cape Town, South Africa—literally! He is the man behind an outbreak of elephants popping up in unexpected places all over the city. His art adorns some weird canvases, including boats, staircases, and even old dumpsters! And quite often the art incorporates elements of the surroundings in unusual ways—one of his elephants might appear to be holding up an air-conditioning unit like a boom box or plucking a piece of fruit from a nearby tree. Falko One began painting when he was 16 years old. After painting an elephant from memory (to hide another picture of chickens), he quickly found his style and has been painting colorful elephants ever since!

Sociable Weaver

Southern Africa

Do you know the expression "There's no place like home"? Well, the sociable weaver, native to the dry savannas of southern Africa, has proven just that. These incredible crafters design the most popular residences around—each nest acts like a huge apartment building for an entire colony. Some of their artsy creations are home to up to 100 different families—that could mean as many as 400 birds in a single nest! Sometimes stretching more than 20 feet (6 m) wide and almost 10 feet (3 m) tall, single nests have been known to be inhabited for up to 100 years. This avian art combines fashion *and* function!

There's room for one more!

I call this "Portrait of the Artist as a Young Pig"!

Pigcasso
Franschhoek Valley, South Africa

Meet Pigcasso, who could trot into a gallery near you! Since being rescued in 2016 by her co-artist, Joanne, Pigcasso has been creating masterpieces that have been admired worldwide. Joanne first encouraged the piggy painter when she noticed the hog's interest in some paintbrushes that had been left lying around. While Pigcasso holds the brush in her mouth and paints across the canvas, Joanne applies colors to the brush. The art they create together has an admirable goal—Joanne hopes it will help people think more carefully about the negative effects of animal agriculture. All the money made from the artwork goes to Farm Sanctuary SA, a nonprofit organization.

Cool CONSTRUCTIONS!

Fairview Goat Tower

In the 1980s, South African cheese- and winemaker Charles Back II was visiting vineyards in Portugal. However, it wasn't grapes that caught his eye—it was a tower built especially for goats. He loved it so much, he knew the 750 goats at his vineyard in Paarl needed one, too. With its spiral wooden staircase and accompanying bridge, the tower is perfect for Fairview's farm animals to climb and play on. The building's fame has spread worldwide and inspired the construction of other goat towers in Argentina, Norway, and the United States. If there's one near you, it's *goat* to be worth a visit!

Villaggio Vista

These landmark buildings, which include the tallest residential tower in West Africa, have an amazing design inspired by their location. If you are into bold colors, then these luxury apartments will be right up your alley. The eye-catching structures are part of Villaggio Vista, an innovative project to create high-rise living in a place where earthquakes and a hot climate have made building upward difficult in the past. Its striking patterns are inspired by kente (Ghanaian textile) weaving patterns. You could even say the buildings are dressed for success!

Jardin Majorelle

It's hard to miss this stunning, electric-blue building surrounded by lush green plants. One of the most visited tourist attractions in Marrakech, Morocco, this was once the home of French painter Jacques Majorelle. It's now home to Le Musée Berbère, a fascinating museum crammed with 600 artifacts showcasing the talents of the Indigenous Berber people. The gardens are also famous—Majorelle loved traveling, and an astonishing 300 different plant species from five continents grow here.

Hotel With Wings

Would you like to stay in a hotel room that sticks out in midair? This amazing hotel is the Hotel du Lac in Tunis, the capital of Tunisia. The floors get longer and longer as you go up, with the top floor measuring twice as long as the bottom floor. It was built in the early 1970s—and not long after that, the makers of the first *Star Wars* movie came to Tunisia to film in the desert. Some say they saw the hotel and it inspired the shape of the sandcrawler, a huge desert vehicle that appears in the movies. Sadly, the hotel is no longer used, so you couldn't stay in it even if you wanted to!

Bibliotheca Alexandrina

It might look like a massive cheese grater, but this vast building is actually a library. An amazing example of modern architecture, it pays tribute to the former renowned ancient Library of Alexandria, which contained hundreds of books, including the original work of ancient Greek poets such as Sophocles and Euripides. The main library was accidentally burned down by Julius Caesar in 48 B.C. when he was helping Cleopatra in her war against her own brother. This modern reimagining of the library sits close to the Mediterranean Sea in the Egyptian city of Alexandria. It was designed by Norwegian architecture firm Snøhetta, which gave the design hidden meaning and purpose: The circular shape reflects the flow of time and knowledge, the windows are designed to let in the light but prevent glare, and the outside walls are carved with characters from all known alphabets.

WEIRD WONDERS

This staggering sight is the colossal sand dunes of Namibia!
The striking, uninhabited peaks almost look like a painting. Situated on the Atlantic coast, the Namib Desert is the oldest desert in the world. The sand gets its rich red color from a coating of iron oxide. Dune 45 (so named because it's located 45 kilometers from the main entrance to Namib-Naukluft National Park, where the dunes are found) is aptly nicknamed "Big Daddy." Although not the highest dune around, it stands 262 feet (80 m) tall and offers spectacular views from the top.

The tallest dune in the Namib Desert measures **1,256 FEET (383 m)**— around the same height as the Eiffel Tower!

JAW-DROPPING SAND DUNES

Namib-Naukluft National Park, Namibia

REMARKABLE ROCKS

White Desert
Farafra, Egypt

In the middle of Egypt's Western Desert, which is part of the Sahara, is a smaller, much stranger desert. It's as white as snow, and covered in tall chalk-white rocks in all kinds of weird shapes. The formations have been compared to mushrooms, meringues, and even modern art. They are made by the wind blasting desert sand over rocks and wearing them away over thousands of years. They're said to look especially magical at sunset and by moonlight—so tourists often come here for an overnight stay and sleep under the stars.

Mount Nyiragongo Volcano
Virunga National Park, Democratic Republic of the Congo

The Nyiragongo volcano, one of the most active in Africa, has erupted at least 34 times since 1882. Despite the constant threat, there are thriving communities residing in towns and cities below. The world's largest lava lake—formed by large volumes of molten lava collecting in a vent, depression, or crater—sits right at the top. You wouldn't want to get too close, though—the bubbling cauldron contains liquid lava that can travel up to 40 miles an hour (64 km/h), gaining speed when traveling down the volcano's steep slope.

Let's sea what's cookin' ...

Balancing Rocks
Michamvi Pingwe Beach, Zanzibar, Tanzania

If you're fishing for a unique dining experience, why not take a trip to one of Zanzibar's finest restaurants, The Rock? Of course, you might have to hail a water taxi to get there—because at certain times this amazing eatery is totally separated from the main island. When the tide is low, customers can walk across the sand at Michamvi Pingwe beach to reach it. But at high tide, it transforms into a small island cut off by the Indian Ocean. Built in 2010, The Rock has an appropriately sea-inspired menu. Its dishes include stewed rock lobster and "Blue Monday"—ravioli filled with blue spirulina (a type of algae) served with crab meat. The Rock also funds swimming lessons for local children—which could be handy if they ever want to visit this unusual diner!

Ol Doinyo Lengai Volcano
Ngorongoro, Tanzania

Most volcanoes erupt with red lava, but this one spews gray or black! Tanzania's Ol Doinyo Lengai is the only volcano on the planet to produce this unique substance, called carbonatite lava. Most magma is made from chains of silicon and oxygen, which makes it viscous, or sticky. The magma inside Ol Doinyo Lengai is missing those chains, so it's the runniest in the world. Instead, carbonatite lava is rich in calcium, sodium, and carbon dioxide. These chains have a much lower melting point, which allows the lava to gush out at half the temperature of other volcano eruptions. The lower temperature and unusual composition give the lava its strange gray color. When it hardens, however, it turns white. Sometimes, the hardened lava will suddenly shatter when there is a rapid change in temperature, making it look like the volcano is sprinkled with snow.

ONE MILLION WILDEBEESTS MIGRATE TO THE VOLCANO EVERY YEAR BECAUSE THE NUTRIENT-PACKED ASH MAKES FOR EXTRA NUTRITIOUS GRAZING!

163

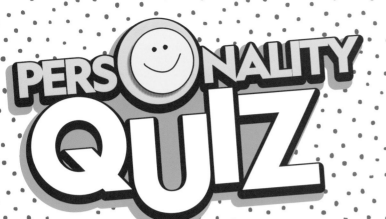

PERSONALITY QUIZ

What is your dream day trip destination? Answer the questions to find out!

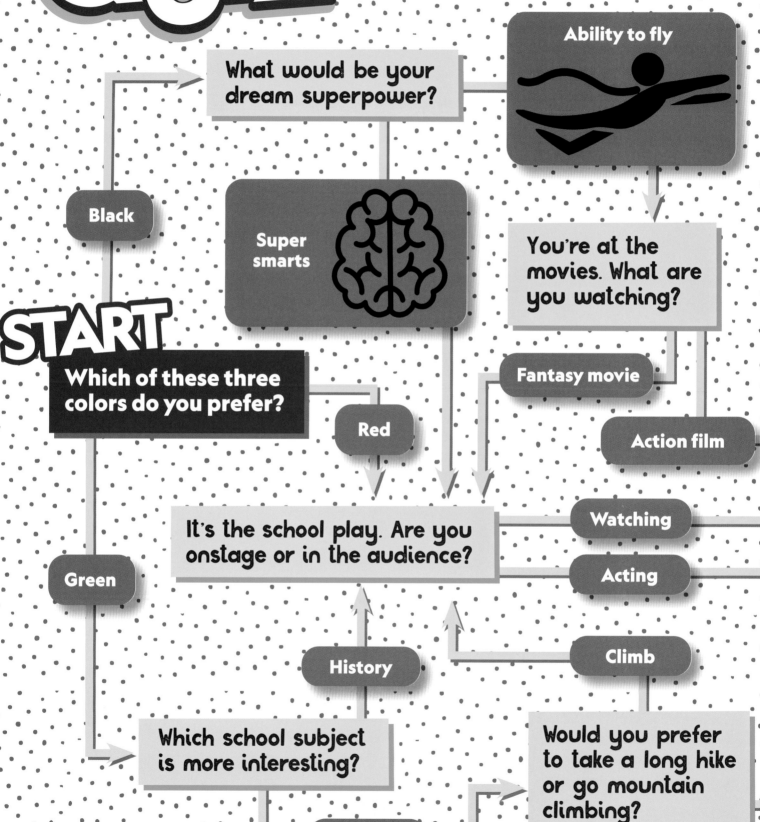

What would be your dream superpower?

Ability to fly

Black

Super smarts

You're at the movies. What are you watching?

START

Which of these three colors do you prefer?

Red

Fantasy movie

Action film

It's the school play. Are you onstage or in the audience?

Watching

Green

Acting

History

Climb

Which school subject is more interesting?

Would you prefer to take a long hike or go mountain climbing?

Science

Lemur

Which animal would it be cool to be?

Wildebeest

No, they're not my favorite.

Are mystery books a fun read?

Yes, I love to puzzle it out.

Hike

The Forest of Knives

Surrounded by lakes and mangrove swamps, this is an astonishing forest (see p. 170) that you don't want to touch! Heavy tropical rainfall has eroded the porous limestone for 200 million years and created these incredible, densely packed rock spires. These "knives" are so sharp, they can slice through skin, so they're best viewed from a distance!

Ol Doinyo Lengai Volcano

An erupting volcano might seem like a place to avoid, but this Tanzanian marvel is one of a kind. Half the temperature of other volcanoes, the lava is black rather than glowing red and turns white when it cools. Don't get too close to Ol Doinyo Lengai, though—a visitor who fell in miraculously survived the ordeal, but it's still more than hot enough to burn.

Namib-Naukluft National Park

You'll be seeing red on your perfect outing—because that's the color of the sand in these massive dunes. The remarkable hue is from iron oxide, with the oldest dunes being the brightest. The area is one of the most sparsely populated in Namibia, but you won't be alone. A variety of wildlife, including kudu, zebras, hyenas, and meerkats, call the park home.

Fairy Circles

These bizarre round patches of earth need to be seen to be believed. Not that you'll get to look at all of them—fairy circles (see p. 172) are spread across 1,100 miles (1,770 km) of southern African grassland. Scientists have spent decades studying them to find the cause. Maybe you'll discover the answer on your day trip ...

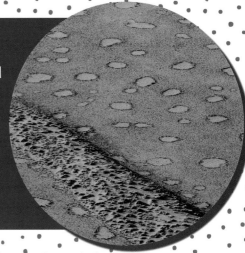

Watch the annual trek of millions of creatures as they journey to find food.

WILDEBEEST MIGRATION

Tanzania and Kenya

Some have referred to it as the greatest show on Earth—and you can see why.

Every year, 1.5 million wildebeests journey about 1,860 miles (3,000 km) in a loop across Tanzania and Kenya. At the end of the rainy season, the wildebeests begin their journey in search of greener pastures following the seasonal rains. Two hundred thousand zebras also join the wildebeests on the journey. The zebras feast on longer grasses, whereas the wildebeests prefer shorter grasses, so they're happy to travel and live together without being in direct competition for the same food.

BY the NUMBERS

THE NILE

It's the longest river in the world ... or is it? Experts have deliberated the question again and again. The Nile is only slightly longer than the world's second longest river, the Amazon. For now, the Nile holds on to the title. But many say it depends on where you classify the start and end points of each river.

THE NILE MEANDERS THROUGH **11 COUNTRIES** ACROSS THE AFRICAN CONTINENT.

95% OF EGYPTIANS LIVE WITHIN A FEW MILES OF THE RIVER.

THE NILE RIVER FLOWS FOR A STAGGERING **4,160 MILES (6,695 KM).** (THAT'S MORE THAN HALF THE DIAMETER OF EARTH!)

THE RIVER HAS A MAXIMUM WIDTH OF **1.7 MILES (2.8 KM).** (THAT'S MORE THAN 37 GREAT SPHINXES OF GIZA LAID OUT IN A LINE!)

THERE ARE 2 MAIN TRIBUTARIES (SMALLER RIVERS THAT FEED INTO A RIVER): THE WHITE NILE (SOUTH SUDAN) AND THE BLUE NILE (ETHIOPIA).

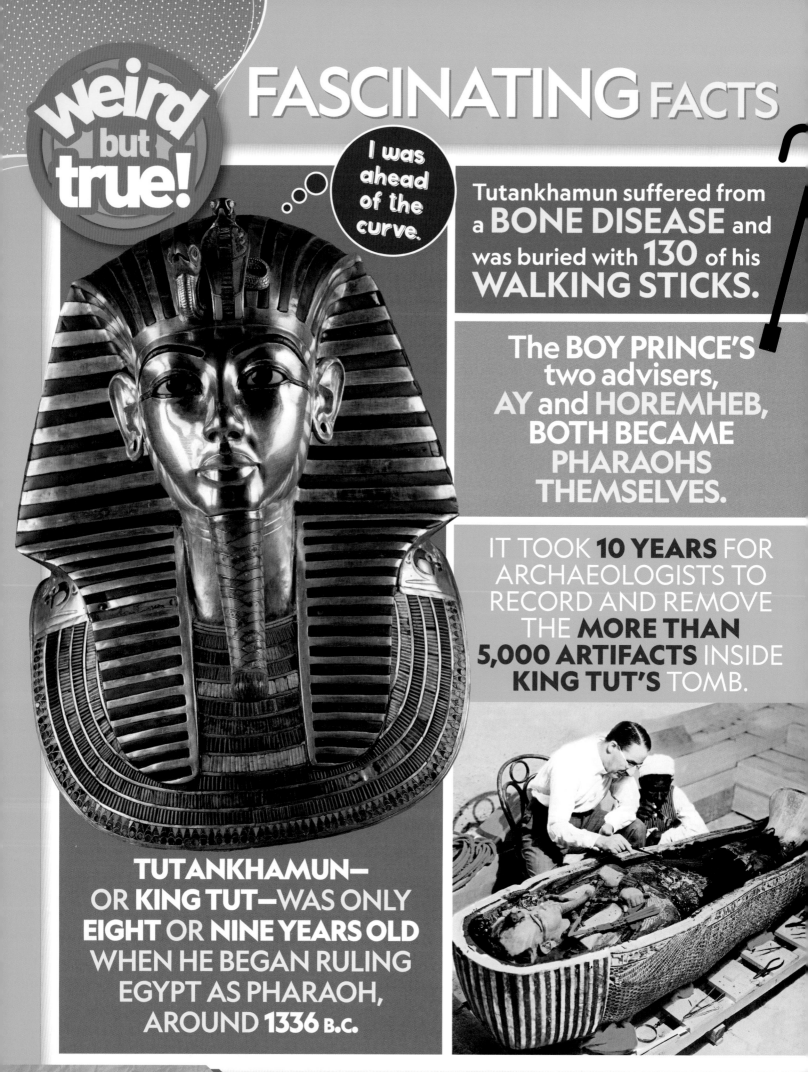

Weird but true!

FASCINATING FACTS

I was ahead of the curve.

Tutankhamun suffered from a **BONE DISEASE** and was buried with **130** of his **WALKING STICKS.**

The **BOY PRINCE'S** two advisers, **AY** and **HOREMHEB**, **BOTH BECAME PHARAOHS THEMSELVES.**

IT TOOK **10 YEARS** FOR ARCHAEOLOGISTS TO RECORD AND REMOVE THE **MORE THAN 5,000 ARTIFACTS** INSIDE **KING TUT'S** TOMB.

TUTANKHAMUN— OR **KING TUT**—WAS ONLY **EIGHT** OR **NINE YEARS OLD** WHEN HE BEGAN RULING EGYPT AS PHARAOH, AROUND **1336** B.C.

ABOUT KING TUT!

PHARAOHS' TOMBS, such as Tutankhamun's, contained **small human statues called** *SHABTIS,* which would **serve the pharaoh in the afterlife.**

Tutankhamun was buried with some of his **clothing,** including **100** **sandals** and **four socks!**

TUTANKHAMUN WAS CALLED TUTANKHATEN AFTER THE **SUN GOD ATEN,** BUT CHANGED HIS NAME TO HONOR **AMUN,** THE EGYPTIAN **GOD OF THE AIR.**

TUTANKHAMUN'S REIGN WAS **QUICKLY FORGOTTEN** AND ANOTHER TOMB, FOR **RAMSES VI,** WAS BUILT **ON TOP OF KING TUT'S!**

TUT'S TOMB CONTAINED **A DAGGER** THAT WAS PROBABLY MADE FROM **METAL TAKEN FROM A** METEORITE.

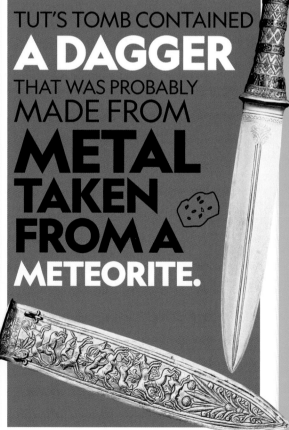

WEIRD WONDERS

If anyone asks what's the point of traveling to Madagascar, they should be directed to the Tsingy de Bemaraha National Park ... there are thousands of points there! The word *tsingy* from the Malagasy language translates to "where one cannot walk barefoot." However, even with your best walking boots on, it is still impossible to cross some regions of this park, which is nick-named "The Forest of Knives." Huge needles of limestone rock rise skyward, some 328 feet (100 m) tall. The lime-stone was formed more than 200 mil-lion years ago, before being raised by the movement of Earth's tec-tonic plates and eroded by mon-soon rains. The gigantic jagged rocks are a no-go area for humans but provide perfect undisturbed shelter for a huge array of wildlife, including chameleons and lemurs.

It's a cut above the rest!

THE FOREST OF KNIVES

Tsingy de Bemaraha National Park, Madagascar

An underground cave system beneath the forest stretches for miles and could be

THE LARGEST

in the world.

FULL CIRCLE!

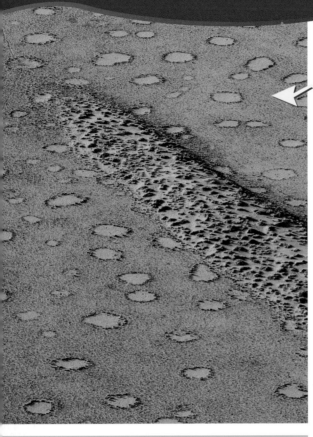

Fairy Circles
Namibia

For decades, bizarre rings of barren ground have appeared in southern Africa's grasslands. These strange circles grow and shrink over time. There have been lots of theories to explain the phenomenon—from the plausible, such as damage by sand termites, to the bizarre, including UFO landings! However, a 2022 investigation suggested a very likely cause—shortage of rainfall. The grasses protect themselves by creating soil-moisture vacuums around their roots, meaning some areas die to let others survive.

Spiral-Horned Antelopes
Sub-Saharan Africa

If you're fascinated by amazing animals, these African bovines offer a bit of a twist. Spiral-horned antelopes have the most incredible corkscrew-shaped headgear. They include species from the bushbuck, the smallest spiral-horned antelope, to the magnificent giant eland, which is the largest of all antelopes. It stands nearly six feet (1.8 m) tall at the shoulder, and those huge horns grow up to 28 inches (71 cm) long. Horns are usually only grown by male antelopes, but female elands have them, too.

Desert Breath
Qesm Hurghada, Egypt

When this bizarre spiral of cones and pits was spotted in the desert near the Red Sea on Google Earth in 2014, it sparked wild theories about its origin. It was even suggested that it might be a gateway to a parallel universe! The truth was soon revealed: It was a piece of land art called "Desert Breath" that had been created 17 years earlier. It consists of 89 cones and 89 pits that span more than a million square feet (100,000 sq m). The large central pit used to contain water, but it has evaporated in the sun. Eventually, "Desert Breath" will disappear, as the artists intended, to show the passage of time.

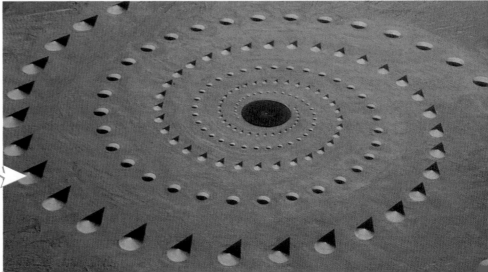

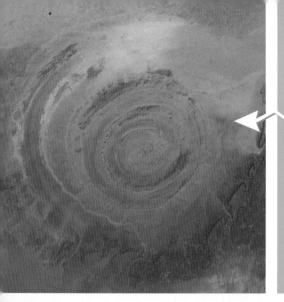

The Eye of the Sahara
Mauritania

If you're on the lookout for the Eye of the Sahara, it might see you first. That's because at ground level it doesn't look like anything special. This 25-mile (40-km)-wide wonder is best appreciated from above—it's even popular with astronauts orbiting Earth. Also known as the Richat Structure, it was initially thought to have been created by the impact from a meteor. It's now known that the Eye is the remnants of a dome rock, which has been eroded over millions of years to reveal flat layers of different rock types, creating a breathtaking bull's-eye effect.

Nabta Playa
Aswan, Egypt

Thousands of years ago, ancient civilizations arranged stones in circles to help record the changing seasons. The stone circle at Nabta Playa in southern Egypt is around 5,000 years old. It is the world's oldest known stone circle, constructed almost 2,000 years before the more famous Stonehenge in England. Part of the Nabta Playa complex includes four pairs of large stones and various smaller stones. Astronomers have now figured out that these acted as a calendar by aligning with the brightest stars in the northern sky—Arcturus, Sirius, and Alpha Centauri. Fortunately, we now have calendars and phones to help us keep track of time, rather than huge stones—especially because recent visitors have moved the rocks, causing some terrible timekeeping!

Marble Berries
Sub-Saharan Africa

If you were asked to think of something naturally shiny, you might imagine a species of beetle or butterfly. But, strangely, the world record for the shiniest thing alive isn't an animal—it's a fruit. The marble berry, *Pollia condensata,* can be found in the forests of many Central African countries. They look tempting to birds and other animals, but they're far from tasty treats. These bright blue spheres are just husks stuffed full of seeds. If munched on, they don't provide any nutrition, but the hungry animal will help disperse the plant's seeds in its poo.

WEIRD WATER

Water Harvesting
Morocco

If you think cloud fishing sounds like a thing of dreams, then think again! This awesome system has been designed to catch water droplets from fog in a collection of large nets. These droplets are then mixed with groundwater and piped into surrounding villages. An incredible 1,660 gallons (6,300 L) are captured daily—that's enough for up to 100 households. The system has transformed lives throughout southwestern Morocco, limiting the need to travel long distances for water.

This process is also called fog catching, fog harvesting, and—oddest of all—fog milking!

Weirdly Cute!
Hippopotamus

A hippo might look like it would be up for a cuddle, but that would be a bad idea. These magnificent, massive mammals are very dangerous. Getting close to one isn't easy anyway—hippos spend most of their lives underwater. Yet, bizarrely, they can't swim or breathe when submerged. Instead, a hippopotamus will rise to the surface about every five minutes to take a breath, even when it is asleep! Hippos like the water and mud because even though their skin is thick, it's very sensitive and can be burned by the hot African sun. To protect itself, a hippo produces a red mucus from its pores that moistens its skin and repels water, but it can look like hippos are sweating blood! Luckily, this incredible, oily liquid also acts as an antibiotic to kill off skin infections.

Guelta d'Archei
Ennedi Plateau, Chad

This permanent desert oasis provides vital drinking water for hundreds of animals. Getting to Guelta d'Archei requires a four-day trip across the Sahara in an off-road vehicle, followed by a lengthy trek on foot, because there are no paved routes that lead directly there. Your arrival at this beautiful location might coincide with one of the many caravans of camels visiting for a drink, but if you're tempted to take a dip, think again! The water there is black—because it's full of camel poo! These droppings encourage the growth of algae, which is eaten by fish. The fish are then feasted on by animals you might not expect to see here: crocodiles. This colony of West African crocs is one of the last remaining in the Sahara region.

Boiling Lake Bogoria
Kenya

Kenya's Lake Bogoria has dozens of springs around the edges, some of them so hot you can actually see areas of water bubbling and boiling. Although the lake is quite hard to get to, tourists come here to eat lunch and use the hot springs to boil eggs for their picnics (taking care not to fall in, of course!). In a nearby river, hot spring water mixes with cooler water, creating the perfect temperature for a warm bath, and it's safe to take a nice relaxing dip.

THERE CAN BE AS MANY AS TWO MILLION FLAMINGOS FEEDING IN LAKE BOGORIA AT ONCE.

175

ANCIENT MYSTERIES

Ruins of Gedi
Malindi, Kenya

Its only inhabitants now are animals such as monkeys and birds, but the Swahili town of Gedi was once a bustling medieval metropolis. The oldest ruins there date back to the 11th century, and Gedi thrived between the 13th and 16th centuries. Besides an outer wall, the town had an inner wall, behind which rich citizens lived. They had special windowless buildings for storing their gold and treasures. A secret door in the roof was the only way to gain entrance! Gedi was advanced for its time, boasting running water and flushing toilets. Located just three miles (5 km) from the Indian Ocean coast, the city traded with places as far away as Asia and Europe. Chinese Ming dynasty vases, Venetian beads, and Spanish scissors have been unearthed there. Mysteriously, the town was abandoned in the 17th century—one theory is that the wells dried up.

Is there water in my ear?

Heracleion
Alexandria, Egypt

In 1933, a pilot flying over the bay of Alexandria, on the coast of Egypt, looked down and saw ruins under the water. Later, divers explored the seafloor and found statues, columns, coins, sunken ships, and the remains of a temple. These ruins were remnants of the city of Heracleion, one of ancient Egypt's most important ports, which stood on islands in the bay 2,500 years ago. At some point, the islands were washed away, and the buildings collapsed and sank into the sea. No one knows exactly when or how. It might have been a tsunami, earthquakes, or rising sea levels, or maybe all of the above! And there's probably much more of Heracleion waiting to be found under the muddy seafloor.

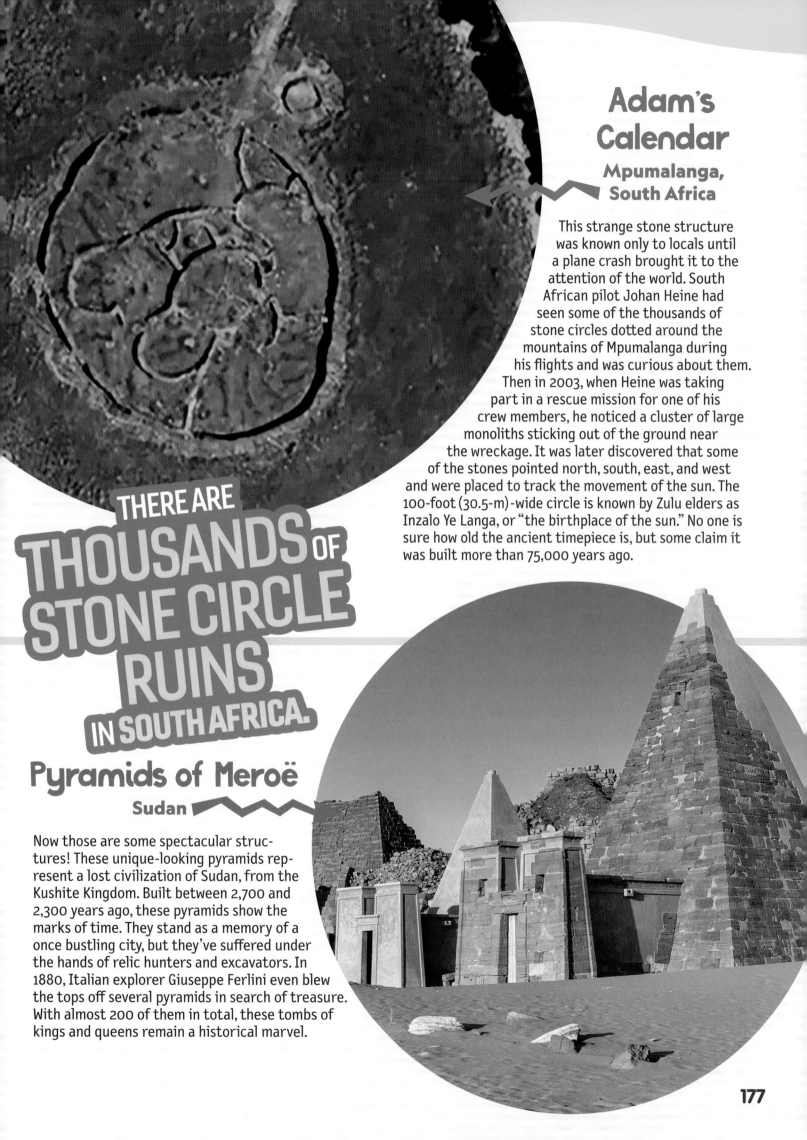

Adam's Calendar

Mpumalanga, South Africa

This strange stone structure was known only to locals until a plane crash brought it to the attention of the world. South African pilot Johan Heine had seen some of the thousands of stone circles dotted around the mountains of Mpumalanga during his flights and was curious about them. Then in 2003, when Heine was taking part in a rescue mission for one of his crew members, he noticed a cluster of large monoliths sticking out of the ground near the wreckage. It was later discovered that some of the stones pointed north, south, east, and west and were placed to track the movement of the sun. The 100-foot (30.5-m)-wide circle is known by Zulu elders as Inzalo Ye Langa, or "the birthplace of the sun." No one is sure how old the ancient timepiece is, but some claim it was built more than 75,000 years ago.

THERE ARE THOUSANDS OF STONE CIRCLE RUINS IN SOUTH AFRICA.

Pyramids of Meroë

Sudan

Now those are some spectacular structures! These unique-looking pyramids represent a lost civilization of Sudan, from the Kushite Kingdom. Built between 2,700 and 2,300 years ago, these pyramids show the marks of time. They stand as a memory of a once bustling city, but they've suffered under the hands of relic hunters and excavators. In 1880, Italian explorer Giuseppe Ferlini even blew the tops off several pyramids in search of treasure. With almost 200 of them in total, these tombs of kings and queens remain a historical marvel.

QUIZ WHIZ

One continent, 54 countries, oodles of facts.

How many can you remember?

1 **Tutankhamun's tomb contained a dagger probably made from ...**

a. Chalk
b. Emerald
c. A meteorite
d. Dinosaur fossils

2 **What does the name of the world's largest emerald, Chipembele, mean?**

a. Chipmunk
b. Elephant
c. Rhino
d. Whale

3 **What is a Macrobat?**

a. A large-winged mammal
b. A one-seater plane
c. A seafood restaurant
d. An ancient stone circle

4 **Who lived inside Gedi's second inner wall?**

a. Gazelles
b. Lawbreakers
c. Reality show contestants
d. Wealthy citizens

5 **What is the world's shiniest fruit?**

a. Glambutan
b. Glossy grape
c. Marble berry
d. Mirror drupe

6 **Which is the largest species of antelope?**

a. Big bushback
b. Giant eland
c. Greater kudu
d. Humongous bongo

7 **Which amphibian has a permanent frown?**

a. Bad day frog
b. Black rain frog
c. Monday morning frog
d. Stubbed toe frog

8 **How do hippos cool down?**

a. Drink coconut water
b. Migrate to mountain slopes
c. Produce red mucus
d. Swim backstroke

6

ASTOUNDING ASIA

Breathtaking bridges, magnificent mammals, fascinating festivals, and more!

Seriously, it's out-sand-ing!

Midnight hikers climb this **INDONESIAN VOLCANO** to see its **BLUE LAVA**.

The dome that tops the famous Taj Mahal is called an "ONION DOME" for its bulbous shape.

WEIRD in the WORLD

WORLD'S BIGGEST CONTINENT,

Asia is the **WORLD'S BIGGEST CONTINENT,** so it's no surprise that it's home to so many unique people, **ANIMALS, PLACES,** and **EVENTS.**

The village of *Houtong* in Taiwan is home to **hundreds of stray cats,** and attracts tourists who feed and photograph them on the weekends.

The weird shapes created by **windblown ice** and **snow** on the trees on Japan's Mount Zaō volcano are called Juhyō, or **"snow monsters."**

ARCTIC OCEAN

PACIFIC OCEAN

Mount Zaō

JAPAN

NORTH KOREA

SOUTH KOREA

R U S S I A

MONGOLIA

CHINA

KAZAKHSTAN

KYRGYZSTAN

UZBEKISTAN

TAJIKISTAN

TURKMENISTAN

AFGHANISTAN

IRAN

(RUSSIA)

GEORGIA

ARMENIA

AZERBAIJAN

TÜRKİYE (TURKEY)

SYRIA

IRAQ

LEBANON

ISRAEL

JORDAN

EGYPT

KUWAIT

SAUDI ARABIA

Mediterranean Sea

Houtong
TAIWAN

Lianhe
Ruins

PHILIPPINES

Mabul
Island

INDONESIA

TIMOR-LESTE
(EAST TIMOR)

South
China
Sea

BRUNEI

Java Sea

VIETNAM
LAOS
THAILAND
CAMBODIA

MALAYSIA

← SINGAPORE

MYANMAR
(BURMA)

Chandipur
Beach

NEPAL
BHUTAN
BANGLADESH

INDIA

Bay of
Bengal

SRI LANKA

INDIAN
OCEAN

MALDIVES

PAKISTAN

Arabian
Sea

QATAR
UNITED ARAB
EMIRATES
OMAN

BAHRAIN →

YEMEN

ASIA

Pacific
Ocean

Arctic
Ocean

EUROPE

AFRICA

Indian
Ocean

AUSTRALIA

An old oil rig off the coast of Mabul Island, Malaysia, has been converted into a luxury hotel for scuba divers.

A 3,000-year-old clay figurine discovered at China's Lianhe Ruins looks just like a pig from the Angry Birds franchise.

At Chandipur Beach in India, the sea goes out up to three miles (4.8 km) at different times every day.

I'm ahead of my time!

183

ANIMAL MAGIC

Muju Firefly Festival
South Korea

Light shows at festivals may be pretty common, but this one is far from average. At the Muju Firefly Festival, the skies are illuminated by tiny beetles. That's right—fireflies, and there's an entire eco-friendly festival dedicated to them. Each year, thousands of visitors flock to Muju, South Korea, for music, storytelling, reenactments of traditional weddings, and more. But the real fun starts after dark, when the fireflies light up the night sky. Muju is a perfect natural habitat for fireflies; because they inhabit only superclean places, these critters represent Muju's unspoiled environment.

Paper Animal Sculptures
Shizuoka, Japan

Stories about animals sometimes make the news—and now the news is being made into animals! On a trip to Zambia in Africa, Japanese artist Chie Hitotsuyama saw a rhinoceros that had been injured by poachers. She says that the encounter made her aware of the life force in all creatures and inspired her to start making 3D animal sculptures. Hitotsuyama's grandfather owned a paper mill and, using the mill's old warehouse as her studio, the artist upcycles strings of unwanted rolled-up newspaper pages as her raw materials. She cuts, glues, and shapes the rolled strips into lifelike art, from huddled snow monkeys to swimming dugongs to watchful rabbits.

Monkey Buffet
Thailand

Food festivals can often resemble an animal feeding frenzy, but none more than this monkey buffet in Thailand. Held within the ruins of a Lopburi temple on the last Sunday of November, a plentiful banquet is provided for the area's thousands of macaques! These fluffy diners are treated to an array of colorful fruits and vegetables. They also get a celebratory dance from their human neighbors, who dress in monkey costumes! The monkeys are seen as good luck—a tradition that traces back more than 2,000 years to an ancient Sanskrit epic. In the tale, the monkey king, Hanuman, and his army help rescue Sita, the beloved wife of Prince Rama, from danger.

Weirdly Cute!
Sand Cat

Sand cats are no pampered pets—these wild animals live in harsh deserts. The small felines' sandy-colored fur is ideal for camouflaging in the sand dunes where they live. And that's not the only reason you aren't likely to spot them in the wild: Sand cats are nocturnal and protect themselves from the strong rays of the sun by digging and living in burrows. These cute carnivores are skilled nighttime hunters. They eat small rodents, birds, insects, and spiders. But they also take on more dangerous targets, hunting venomous snakes with a series of rapid blows to the reptile's body followed by a fatal bite on the neck. But there's one catch—snakes are also one of the sand cat's main predators, so it's a battle that the sand cat cannot afford to lose!

COLOR POP!

Picasso Moth
Southeast Asia

This spectacular insect looks as if its vibrant designs have been carefully hand-painted on its wings by famous artist Pablo Picasso. But this miraculous wonder of nature actually evolved to look this way. Found mainly in northern India and Southeast Asia, the moth's two-inch (5-cm) wingspan is covered in bold, colorful geometric prints. Although moths don't have noses, they have an incredible sense of smell. They use their antennae sensors to pick up chemical cues from their surroundings! What pictures can you see on its wings?

Has anyone seen my moth-er?

Kawah Ijen Volcano
Java, Indonesia

These two weird wonders are like night and day—but they're both found at the same volcano on the island of Java! At nighttime, Kawah Ijen looks like it has electric-blue lava pouring down its sides. However, it's actually liquid sulfur! Pent-up sulfuric gases escape from cracks in the rock at high pressure. With temperatures up to 1112°F (600°C), some gases ignite when they meet the air, causing up to 16-foot (5-m)-tall flames, while some condense into streams of liquid sulfur that light up the night. The other oddity is best admired during the day—a stunningly turquoise lake in the crater at the top of the volcano. The water's vivid hue comes from dissolved metals and hydrochloric acid, a powerful chemical used to make bleach and the toxic gas chlorine. At 3,280 feet (1 km) wide, this is the biggest highly acidic lake on planet.

Village of Color
Kampung, Indonesia

Painted every shade from pastel yellows to vibrant pinks, this village is wall-to-wall color—nothing escaped the paintbrush! Welcome to Kampung Warna Warni Jodipan, or the Village of Color. Today, it might be one of the brightest villages on the planet, but not so long ago, this was a typical-looking Indonesian village. So why did it get a magnificent makeover? Kampung was painted these vivid colors by artists, students, and residents as part of a project to improve the area and bring tourists in. And it worked! Turning this traditional village into a work of art has attracted visitors eager to snap photos and share selfies.

Pink Palace
Jaipur, India

If you want a palace that looks like it's straight out of a storybook, then look no further than the magnificent Pink Palace in Jaipur. The palace's 953 honeycombed windows allow for a gentle breeze to move through it—a welcome relief in the hot climate. The intricate latticework on the windows was also designed so that royal women could watch over the life going on outside of the palace without being seen. This ornate masterpiece is five stories high and built from sandstone, which gives the palace its pink hue. In fact, the city of Jaipur itself is known as the Pink City because so many of its buildings are rose colored.

THE PALACE'S HINDI NAME IS **HAWA MAHAL,** MEANING "PALACE OF THE WINDS."

FANTASTIC FACTS ABOUT

Weird but true!

THE GREAT WALL is called **"THE EARTH DRAGON"** because it seems to snake across the mountains like **A SLEEPING DRAGON.**

STICKY RICE was one of the **MANY MATERIALS** used to **CONSTRUCT THE ORIGINAL WALL!**

Contrary to popular belief, **THE GREAT WALL OF CHINA CANNOT BE SEEN FROM SPACE** with the naked eye—you would need **A HIGH-POWERED TELESCOPE.**

The **Great Wall** winds for over **13,000 MILES** (21,000 km). To cover that **distance** on a **running track,** you'd have to run **52,000 LAPS!**

THE GREAT WALL OF CHINA

A legend suggests that a **HELPFUL DRAGON** marked out the wall's path for the **seventh-century workers** who originally built it.

IN 2019, A **RESTORATION PROJECT** USED **3D MAPPING, DRONES,** AND A **COMPUTER ALGORITHM** TO HELP ENGINEERS FIGURE OUT WHERE THE WALL **NEEDED MAINTENANCE.**

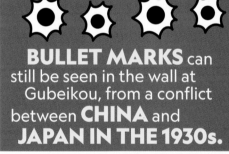

BULLET MARKS can still be seen in the wall at Gubeikou, from a conflict between **CHINA** and **JAPAN IN THE 1930s.**

DURING THE **MING DYNASTY,** SOLDIERS MAY HAVE **BURNED WOLF DUNG** IN THE WALL'S WATCHTOWERS TO CREATE **SMOKE SIGNALS.**

COOL CRITTERS

Bhupathy's Purple Frog
Western Ghats, India

Scientists discovered a new frog in the Western Ghats mountains in 2017—which wasn't easy, considering this little amphibian spends almost its entire life underground! Bhupathy's purple frog, named in honor of an Indian zoologist, has slimy skin, tiny eyes, and a pointy nose. It has hard, spade-like feet perfect for digging, and a long tongue that scoops up tasty termites and ants. The most time these fascinating creatures spend aboveground is at the start of their lives. The frogs mate during monsoon season. Instead of swimming around like most tadpoles, the offspring develop mouths like suckerfish and cling to rocks in the heavy rain. They have tiny teeth and feast on the algae growing there. The tadpoles spend around 120 days clinging on rocks before detaching and disappearing underground.

Saiga
Central Asia

Anyone who *nose* about antelopes will recognize the saiga. It has a large snout with two widely set nostrils. This bizarre body part might look unusual, but it's incredibly useful in a dry and dusty environment. The saiga lives in arid grasslands, and its nose helps filter out dust in the summer. In the winter, the distinctive schnoz warms and moistens the air that the saiga breathes in. During the mating season, it may also amplify the saiga's rutting calls. Unfortunately, this fabulous creature was listed as critically endangered in 2001. There's been good news recently, though. The saiga population in Kazakhstan has been growing; in 2022 it reached more than one million.

What a breath of fresh air!

Saigas can travel more than **50 miles (80 km)** in just one day.

Japanese Spider Crab

Japan

Just how big can a crab be? Well, this one is big enough to fill an average-size living room! The Japanese spider crab has 10 incredibly long, skinny legs and has a leg span of up to 12.5 feet (3.8 m). Its body is relatively small, though— only about the size of a trash can! But don't panic: The spider crab doesn't spin a web, and it's not interested in catching or eating you. Found in the Pacific Ocean around Japan, it's a slow-moving gentle giant, eating only small fish and scavenging dead animals. And if you ever want to spot one of these spider crabs, grab yourself a submarine—they live up to 1,640 feet (500 m) underwater on the seafloor.

JAPANESE SPIDER CRAB EGGS **ARE ONLY 0.3 INCH** (8 MM) LONG—SIMILAR TO **A GRAIN OF RICE!**

Weirdly Cute!

Irrawaddy Dolphin

This unusually expressive round-faced character is the Irrawaddy dolphin. These curious creatures have many distinctive features, but it's their happy faces that most people notice first. Their lips and small beaks often make it look like they're smiling! They can frequently be found waving and slapping the water, but possibly the weirdest thing about these endangered dolphins is how they catch their dinner: They spit at it! These jets of water help them herd their fishy prey, making their meal easier to catch.

BY the NUMBERS

GARDENS BY THE BAY

This breathtaking collection of architecture and gardens is found by the Marina Bay Waterfront in Singapore. Among the attractions are a Flower Dome (a greenhouse busting at the seams with flowers), a Cloud Forest (a mist-filled conservatory teeming with tropical plants), and a Floral Fantasy (a fairy-tale-inspired hanging garden). However, it's more than just a tourist attraction. This park also provides biodiversity and protects endangered species.

THERE ARE OVER

250 ACRES (101 HA)

SPLIT OVER 3 GARDEN AREAS.

THE CLOUD FOREST
CONSERVATORY
TOWERS AT A HEIGHT OF

115 FEET (35 M).

OVER 15,000 PRESERVED BLOOMS HANG FROM THE FLORAL FANTASY CONSERVATORY CEILING.

THE **FLOWER DOME** HOLDS PLANTS AND FLOWERS FROM **5 CONTINENTS,** INCLUDING **1,000-YEAR-OLD** OLIVE TREES.

THE TALLEST SUPERTREE IS EQUIVALENT IN HEIGHT TO **A 16-STORY BUILDING.**

11 OF THE **SUPERTREES** (GIANT VERTICAL GARDENS) HAVE TECHNOLOGY TO PRODUCE ENVIRONMENTALLY FRIENDLY POWER, SUCH AS SOLAR POWER.

A BRIDGE TOO FAR

The Lucky Knot Bridge
Changsha, China

When is a knot not a knot? When it's a bridge! Or rather, when it is three bridges ... The Lucky Knot Bridge is a pedestrian footpath over the Dragon King Harbor River in Changsha, China. NEXT Architects, the company that created it, wanted it to feel more like a playground than a typical crossing. Built in 2016, the Lucky Knot Bridge is 607 feet (185 m) long and 79 feet (24 m) high, allowing boats to travel under it. There are eight different entrances onto the three bridges, and you can change your route while crossing—the walkways overlap at five points, which are called "moon gates." The bridge's name and inspiration come from the Chinese knot, which is said to act as a good-luck charm and scare away evil spirits.

I'm kind of tied up ...

Dragon Bridge
Da Nang, Vietnam

Motorists have to contend with a lot—roadwork, traffic jams, fire-breathing dragons ... OK, maybe that last item isn't a common hazard, but drivers in Da Nang, Vietnam, might just encounter one. The Dragon Bridge across the Han River opened in March 2013. Spanning 2,185 feet (666 m), the crossing has six lanes for cars and two for pedestrians. Of course, the most remarkable aspect of the bridge is its magnificent dragon design. It's impressive during the day but even more incredible at night. At 9 p.m. every weekend night, vehicles are stopped from crossing the bridge as the serpentine creature breathes jets of fire, cheered on by a crowd of onlookers. The steel beast then follows this spectacle by spraying out jets of water. Anyone standing close is guaranteed a soaking!

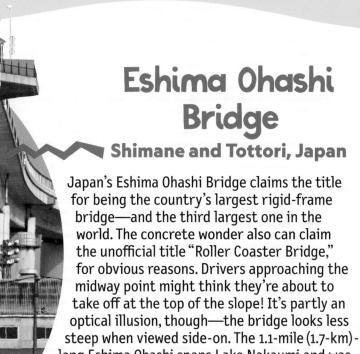

Eshima Ohashi Bridge
Shimane and Tottori, Japan

Japan's Eshima Ohashi Bridge claims the title for being the country's largest rigid-frame bridge—and the third largest one in the world. The concrete wonder also can claim the unofficial title "Roller Coaster Bridge," for obvious reasons. Drivers approaching the midway point might think they're about to take off at the top of the slope! It's partly an optical illusion, though—the bridge looks less steep when viewed side-on. The 1.1-mile (1.7-km)-long Eshima Ohashi spans Lake Nakaumi and was built to replace a drawbridge, allowing ships to pass underneath without disrupting traffic. That's why the new bridge is a giddy 147 feet (44.7 m) tall. It took seven years to build and, at its highest point, provides excellent views of a nearby volcano, Mount Daisen.

Banpo Bridge
Seoul, South Korea

Some bridges won't settle for just one claim to fame! Banpo Bridge over the Han River was the first double-decker bridge to be built in Korea, in 1982. The bottom section is called Jamsu Bridge and was designed to disappear underwater during monsoon season when the river level rises. Once the level drops, mud is cleaned off Jamsu Bridge, and it opens to traffic once again. However, spectators don't come to watch water cover the bridge—the water shooting out of it is the main attraction! Huge jets of water arc into the river from 380 nozzles running along the length of the Banpo's upper level. The bridge is best visited at nighttime when the jets are illuminated by lights synchronized to a hundred different pieces of music, from classical orchestras to brass bands!

AT 3,740 FEET (1,140 M), BANPO IS THE WORLD'S LONGEST BRIDGE FOUNTAIN.

WEIRD WONDERS

PLANK ROAD IN THE SKY

Mount Hua, China

Plank Walk has been called the world's most dangerous hiking trail. It's certainly not for anyone afraid of heights—or for people wearing slippers, which are understandably banned on the rickety-looking planks. Hikers must edge around the 427-foot (130-m)-long walkway circling the tallest peak of Mount Hua, with just a single safety rope for security. In one section, there aren't even any planks, and walkers have to step into holes carved into the cliff face instead. Any tourists who regret taking this route to the peak's panoramic viewpoint won't like the way back, either. The narrow trail does not meet another path, so walkers are forced to return the way they came, navigating around people walking in the opposite direction. Gulp!

The original Huashan Plank Walk was built by a priest 700 YEARS AGO.

STARGAZING

Star Sand Beach
Islands of Japan

Twinkle, twinkle, little star! Have you ever stopped to examine what's beneath your feet while strolling along the beach? Well, if you ever find yourself at Hoshizuna-no-Hama, meaning Star Sand Beach, then make sure you do just that. Unlike other beaches, which are made up of rocks and minerals, this unique coastline has a certain star quality. Scattered within the sand are tiny star-shaped exoskeletons (left by single-celled organisms known as foraminifera). Many refer to it as "living sand," which although not technically accurate, reflects that it was once part of a living organism in the ocean.

星砂浜

竹富島

Five-foot-two (1.57–m) Gagarin was chosen for Vostok 1 partly because he fit into the cramped cockpit!

Yuri Gagarin Monument
Barskoon, Kyrgyzstan

Soviet cosmonaut Yuri Gagarin got closer to the stars than most people ever do. Now he has unexpectedly popped up in Kyrgyzstan! In 1961, Gagarin became the first person to travel into space when he orbited Earth in the Vostok 1 spacecraft. Visitors to Issyk-Kul lake in Barskoon, Kyrgyzstan, can see a large likeness of Gagarin's head, wearing his cosmonaut's helmet, carved into a boulder. A smaller version was later erected on a pedestal nearby. One story claims that Gagarin visited Barskoon after his famous spaceflight and may even have stood on the rock that now features his face. Another local tale claims the statue marks where Vostok 1 actually landed. However, most accounts claim the space capsule's landing site was a long way from Kyrgyzstan, so this explanation is likely a mischievous myth!

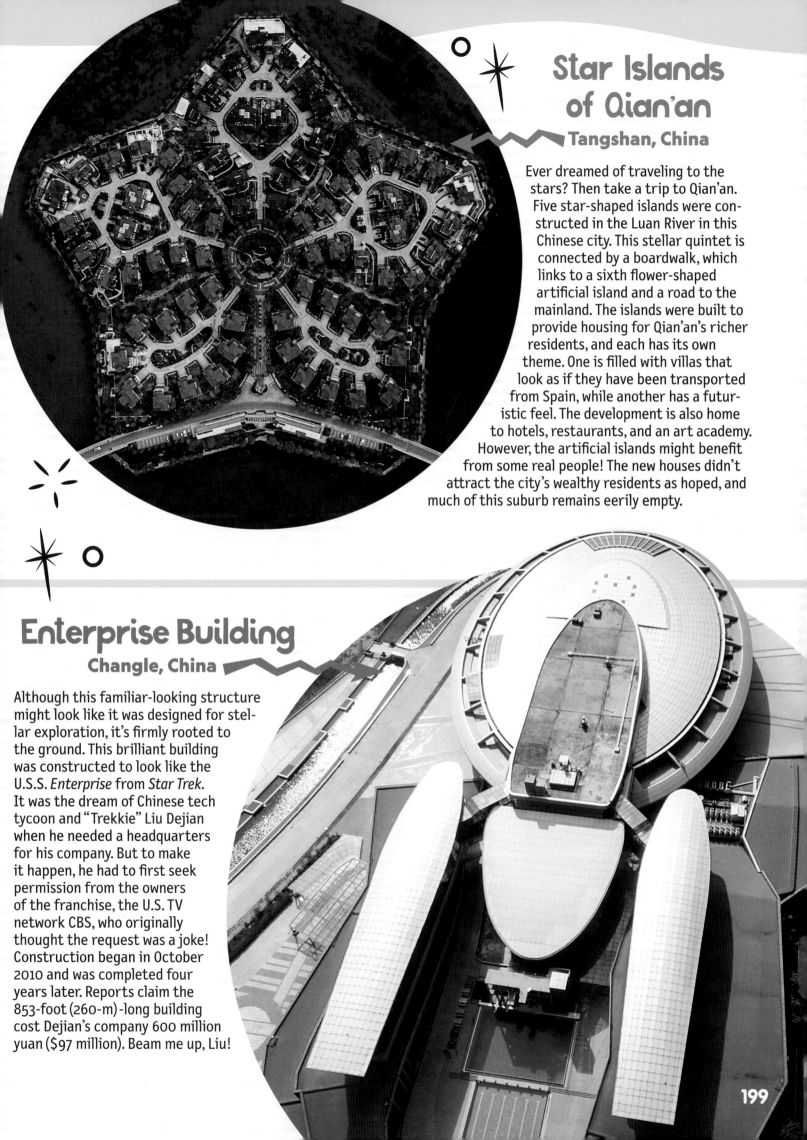

Star Islands of Qian'an
Tangshan, China

Ever dreamed of traveling to the stars? Then take a trip to Qian'an. Five star-shaped islands were constructed in the Luan River in this Chinese city. This stellar quintet is connected by a boardwalk, which links to a sixth flower-shaped artificial island and a road to the mainland. The islands were built to provide housing for Qian'an's richer residents, and each has its own theme. One is filled with villas that look as if they have been transported from Spain, while another has a futuristic feel. The development is also home to hotels, restaurants, and an art academy. However, the artificial islands might benefit from some real people! The new houses didn't attract the city's wealthy residents as hoped, and much of this suburb remains eerily empty.

Enterprise Building
Changle, China

Although this familiar-looking structure might look like it was designed for stellar exploration, it's firmly rooted to the ground. This brilliant building was constructed to look like the U.S.S. *Enterprise* from *Star Trek*. It was the dream of Chinese tech tycoon and "Trekkie" Liu Dejian when he needed a headquarters for his company. But to make it happen, he had to first seek permission from the owners of the franchise, the U.S. TV network CBS, who originally thought the request was a joke! Construction began in October 2010 and was completed four years later. Reports claim the 853-foot (260-m)-long building cost Dejian's company 600 million yuan ($97 million). Beam me up, Liu!

PERSONALITY QUIZ

What awesome activity is most up your alley?

Answer the questions and keep track of your answers to reveal your perfect pastime.

1 **Does getting dirty bother you?**

a. I'd rather keep clean, thanks.
b. I'm usually coated in muck!
c. I don't mind getting my hands dirty.

2 **What would you prefer watching on TV?**

a. An action movie
b. Sports
c. A nature documentary

4 **Which of these is your favorite school subject?**

a. History
b. P.E.
c. Art

3 **Are you a social butterfly?**

a. I prefer small groups of people.
b. Yes, I'm happiest in a big crowd.
c. I'd rather be alone or with one friend.

Mostly A's
Plank Walk, China
Welcome to the high life. You'd have a blast creeping your way around Mount Hua, and you won't even mind all the hiking and standing in line needed to get there. The views are breathtaking, so don't forget to take some photos of your incredible walk ... as long as you don't drop your camera.

5 Which animal would you most like to be?

a. An eagle
b. A dog
c. A monkey

6 How do you feel about waiting in line?

a. If it's worth it, I can wait for hours!
b. I'll hang around ... for a bit.
c. It's not for me.

7 Are you a thrill seeker?

a. Yes—danger is my middle name!
b. A little bit of adventure is great.
c. Not really—nothing wrong with the quiet life!

8 What is your ideal vacation destination?

a. A country cottage for wilderness exploring
b. A beach house to hang ten or hang loose!
c. A staycation with trips to museums and galleries

Mostly B's

Mud Football, South Korea

Squelch on over to the Boryeong Mud Festival (see p. 209), where getting covered in muck is a must. You'll love playing a game of soccer, and you're not afraid to get a little—or a lot—dirty. Here's a challenge: If everyone is coated in mud, how can you tell which side they're on?

Mostly C's

Paper Sculptures, Japan

You're a creative person, so making sculptures would be your ideal activity, especially if they're eco-friendly and use discarded materials. Artist Chie Hitotsuyama carefully constructs detailed likenesses of animals from old newspapers, but you can select anything for your medium and subject matter. Just have fun!

Breathtaking BUILDS!

See-Through Stalls
Tokyo, Japan

There are some occasions where privacy is essential—and using the toilet is high on that list! So a public bathroom with see-through walls sounds like the sort of idea that should be flushed away. However, these rad restrooms in Tokyo cleverly keep you concealed. They are made from glass covered with a material called PDLC, which turns see-through when electricity is applied. When the walls are transparent, it's easy to check that the cubicle is empty and clean before use. When the door is locked, the electric current is turned off and the walls fill with color, so no one can see in or out. Of course, anyone who forgets to lock the door will have to face an audience instead!

Giant Dolls
Manzhouli, China

Dolls are popular toys, but the ones at Matryoshka Square aren't for playtime—one of them is the world's largest, at 98 feet (29.8 m) tall! The plaza is full of hundreds of huge statues based on nesting dolls. Although it's in China, the square symbolizes how the city of Manzhouli is a cultural crossroads, close to the borders of Mongolia and Russia, where the traditional wooden sets are known as *matryoshka*. The ones in Manzhouli have a range of decorations, representing women from different nations or political leaders. Alongside the dolls are brightly painted domed castles, a musical fountain, and a circus!

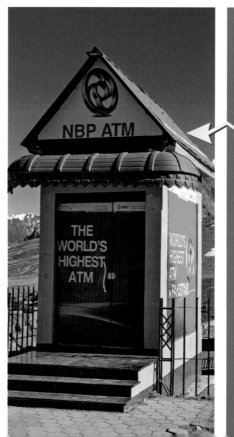

Highest ATM in the World
Gilgit-Baltistan, Pakistan

Way up in Khunjerab Pass sits the highest-altitude ATM in the world. It's found at the dizzying height of 15,396 feet (4,693 m) above sea level—you'd need to trek a long way to get cash out here! So why did the National Bank of Pakistan choose this unlikely location for an ATM? The bank wanted to make an ATM powered by solar panels and wind turbines. The record-breaking ATM opened to the public in 2016.

The Lotus Building
Wujin, China

Completed in 2013, this stunning building looks like it's floating on an artificial lake. The design shows the three stages of the lotus—as a closed-up bud, a new blossom, and a fully opened flower with a seedpod. This beautiful public conference center is also home to the local government's planning department. Constructed over an existing underground building, visitors enter from below to access the airy meeting rooms and exhibition halls inside. At night, the massive metal petals on the building's exterior change color in 30-second intervals. The Lotus Building is extremely energy efficient, with more than 2,500 geothermal piles driven through the base of the lake, allowing the water and ground to help cool or warm the air-conditioning systems.

Meitan Tea Museum
Meitan, China

This towering teapot is really causing a stir. The bizarre building is a hot destination: It set a world record for tallest teapot, at a height of 243 feet (74 m) and with a whopping 54,000 square feet (5,000 sq m) of floor area. The titanic teapot is accompanied by a matching mega teacup, too. The oversize pair celebrate the Meitan region's storied tea culture. With its thriving tea industry, Meitan is a perfect place to have a museum showcasing tea history.

Khan Shatyr Entertainment Center
Nur-Sultan, Kazakhstan

This incredible structure may remind you of a gigantic tent, but if you take a closer look, it's so much more. It is located in Nur-Sultan, Kazakhstan, where the unforgiving climate ranges from minus 31°F (-35°C) in the winter to 95°F (35°C) in the summer! The Khan Shatyr Entertainment Center provides an enclosed world with a steady microclimate no matter what the weather is like outside. It is controlled by a special chemical coating added to the outside of the building that lets sunlight through but protects it from weather extremes. The building provides a year-round sheltered environment where people can enjoy jogging tracks, shopping, movie theaters, and restaurants. It even has a water park with slides and wave pools!

BY the NUMBERS

THE TAJ MAHAL

The world-famous Taj Mahal in India was built in the 17th century on the orders of Emperor Shah Jahan. It was designed to be the final resting place for his wife, Mumtaz Mahal, who died giving birth to their 14th child. The Taj Mahal was built from red sandstone and covered in white marble, which appears to change color depending on the time of day. With Mumtaz Mahal's grave in the center, and matching towers and gardens on either side, its design is almost perfectly symmetrical. However, when Shah Jahan died, he was buried next to his wife, breaking the mirror-image effect.

TIME TO BUILD:
17 YEARS

NUMBER OF WORKERS:
AT LEAST
20,000

HEIGHT:
240 FEET (73.2 M)

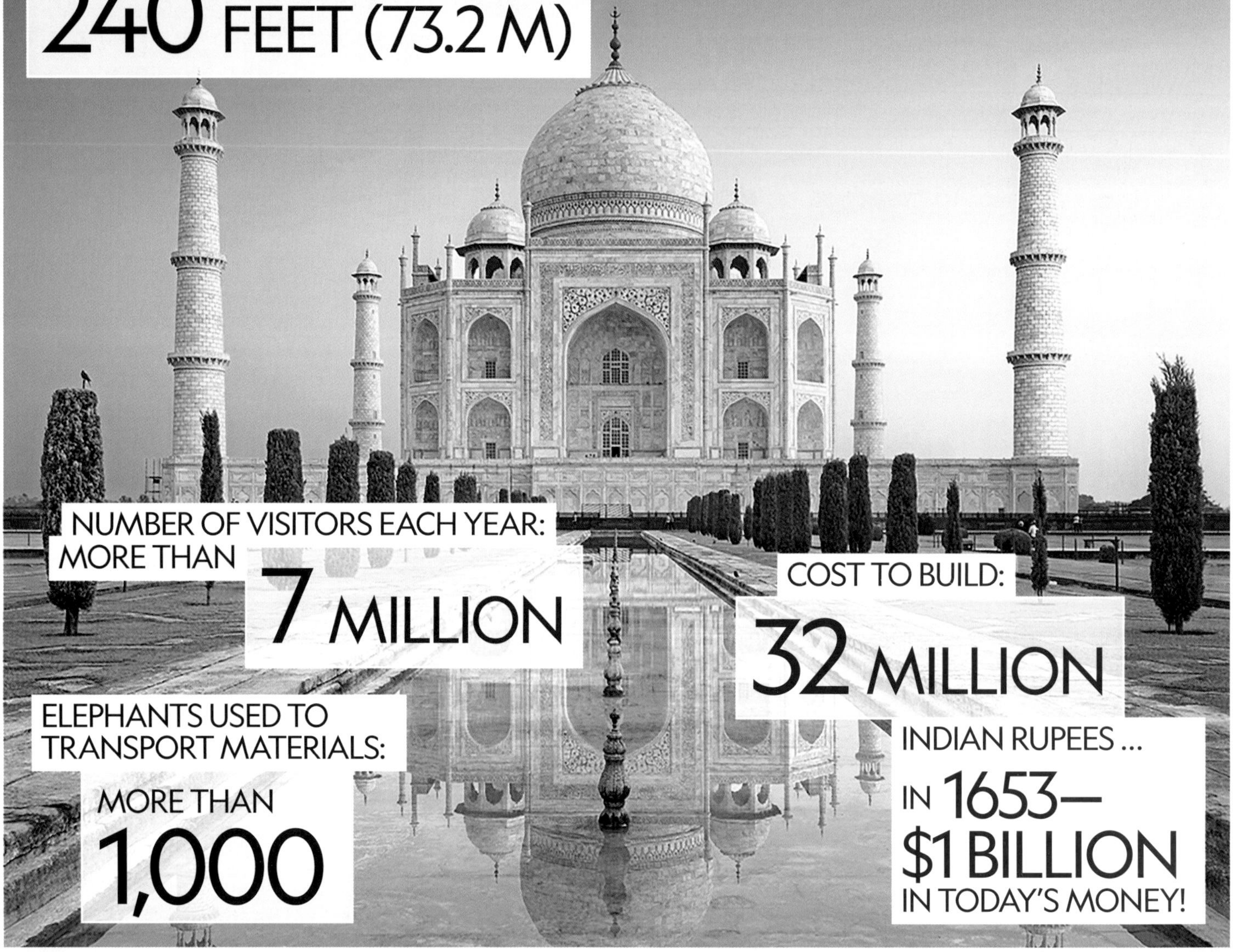

NUMBER OF VISITORS EACH YEAR:
MORE THAN
7 MILLION

ELEPHANTS USED TO TRANSPORT MATERIALS:
MORE THAN
1,000

COST TO BUILD:
32 MILLION
INDIAN RUPEES ...
IN 1653—
$1 BILLION
IN TODAY'S MONEY!

What's **Weird** About This ❓

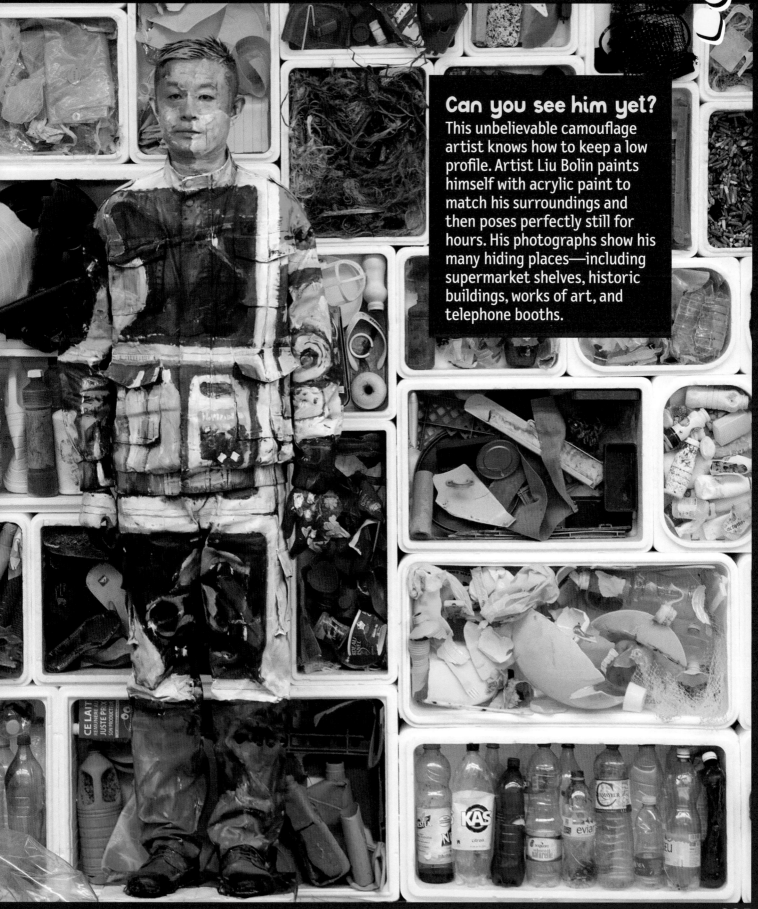

Can you see him yet?
This unbelievable camouflage artist knows how to keep a low profile. Artist Liu Bolin paints himself with acrylic paint to match his surroundings and then poses perfectly still for hours. His photographs show his many hiding places—including supermarket shelves, historic buildings, works of art, and telephone booths.

MAKING A SPLASH

Lake Baikal
Siberia, Russia

Lake Baikal is a record breaker in more ways than one. First, it's been around for a jaw-dropping 25 million to 30 million years, making it the oldest lake in the world. And it's also the world's largest freshwater lake. That's even more special than it sounds—only .007 percent of the world's water comes from freshwater lakes, and Lake Baikal is responsible for 22 percent of that fresh water—more than any other lake on Earth!

300 rivers flow into Lake Baikal, but only one flows away from it—the Angara River.

Rain Vortex
Singapore

Located at the heart of Changi Airport, this record-breaking indoor waterfall is a breathtaking wonder. The water cascades down a whopping 131 feet (40 m). At night, things get even more impressive as a light and sound show are projected onto the waters, bringing them alive. Because Singapore experiences a great number of thunderstorms, all the water is sourced from captured rainwater. That's 10,000 gallons (37,850 L) of reused water getting pumped through every minute!

THERE ARE OVER 200 PLANT SPECIES AROUND THE BASE OF THE WATERFALL.

Deep Dive Dubai

Dubai, U.A.E.

Hold your breath, because you won't believe the depth of this incredible record-breaking dive pool. Deep Dive Dubai holds the current record for the deepest swimming pool for diving—an incredible 196 feet 10 inches (60.02 m). That's as much as 11 giraffes stacked on top of one another! It is filled with 3.7 million gallons (14 million L) of fresh water—the equivalent volume of six Olympic-size pools! But there's more to the pool than its depth: During your dive, you can visit human-made features such as a sunken abandoned city, an arcade with pinball machines, and even an underwater film studio. For those who prefer dry land, Deep Dive Dubai offers a viewing restaurant fitted with large glass windows where diners can peek inside the magical underwater world.

FESTIVAL FUN

Bun Festival

Cheung Chau, Hong Kong

Cheung Chau is big on buns! This fun four-day festival has its origins in the 18th century, when Cheung Chau was threatened by a plague and pirate attacks. According to island legends, local fishermen saved the day by driving away evil spirits with an image of the Taoist god Pak Tai. Celebrating the island's upturn in fortune, this annual event includes dragon dances at Pak Tai temple, a children's parade, and lots of the fluffy (and lucky!) steamed buns that are popular around Asia. The highlight of this unusual festival is the Bun Scrambling competition. At the stroke of midnight, competitors race up one of three 60-foot (18.3-m)-tall columns, which are covered with buns! Climbers must grab as many as they can—the higher on the tower, the more points it scores!

How ice to see you ...

Snow Festival

Sapporo, Japan

Every year, there's a flurry of activity in Sapporo as tourists arrive to marvel at the snow sculptures on display! In 2023, one venue at the Sapporo Snow Festival attracted a humongous 1.75 million visitors. It's hard to believe that this incredibly popular event began in 1950 when some high-school students built just six snow statues. Things snowballed a few years later when trucks and bulldozers were called in to help create giant sculptures. The festival is so big that it now spans three sites. The largest art—up to 50 feet (15 m) high!—is found at Odori Park. Subjects have ranged from dinosaurs and dragons to Darth Vader and Disney characters, and are illuminated at night in an amazing light show. Sapporo's Susukino district is the place to head for ice sculptures while the Tsudome hosts some hands-on winter fun with snow slides and snow rafting.

Mud Festival
Boryeong, South Korea

At Boryeong, mud is marvelous! For two weeks every summer, millions of visitors have flocked to the town to get completely covered in it. There's plenty to do at the festival, from whooshing down the slippery mudslide to taking a dip in the giant mud bath. You can get locked up in the mud prison and have some muck thrown at you. Or if you're feeling competitive, mud wrestling or mud soccer combine sports with sludge! For anybody wanting a souvenir, there are stalls selling skin care products—all including Boryeong mud, of course!

Da Shuhua
Nuanquan, China

In China, fireworks have been used to amaze and amuse for hundreds of years, but originally they were so expensive that only wealthy people could afford them. Five hundred years ago, blacksmiths in Nuanquan decided to create their own more affordable version. They noticed that molten iron produced bright light when poured, so they used a ladle to throw some at a stone wall. The molten iron, heated to 2900°F (1593°C), exploded into thousands of sparks. This fiery spectacle was called Da Shuhua. Today, Da Shuhua takes place once a year as part of the Festival of Lights to celebrate the Chinese Lunar New Year. Aluminum and copper are also now used to introduce green and white hues to the red of the iron. The blacksmiths wear straw hats and sheepskin clothes, claiming protective suits just wouldn't feel "right." Don't try this at home!

With a **still secret** formula, **Da Shuhua** sparks can only be seen in **Nuanquan.**

EXTREME EATERIES

Bird's Nest Restaurant

Koh Kood, Thailand

Ever wondered what it would be like to be a bird? Well, imagine no more. This unique restaurant at Soneva Kiri Resort allows you to dine in a nestlike bamboo pod high above the tropical rainforest of Koh Kood, an island in the Gulf of Thailand. Once you are sitting snug in your pod, you are carefully raised by the staff, high above the spectacular shoreline. The dangling dining rooms are suspended around 16 feet (5 m) above the ground. As you hang around, you can soak up the views of the ocean and take in the rainforest, where you may be lucky enough to spot some local wildlife.

Zauo Fishing Restaurant

Tokyo, Japan

Everyone loves a discount dinner, but there aren't many places where you can save money by catching your own chow. At the Zauo Fishing Restaurant, you can literally fish for your food. You rent your fishing rod, pick your fish, catch it, and let the chef know how you'd like it prepared. And it really is cheaper when you catch it yourself than if you order straight off the menu!

THE DINING AREA AT **ZAUO FISHING RESTAURANT** IS DESIGNED TO LOOK LIKE **BOATS SITTING ABOVE THE LARGE FISH TANK.**

Foodom
Guangzhou, China

When you think of a busy restaurant, you probably imagine crashing pans, flustered chefs, and the odd accidental spill. That's not the case in this radical robot restaurant opened by Qianxi Robotics Group! This eatery is staffed entirely by robots. It has over 20 different types of robot workers, ranging from AI chefs to droid waiters! According to Foodom, the cyber staff can serve up to 600 diners at once and cook a wide range of cuisines, from stir-fry to burgers. Some customers even receive their food less than two minutes after ordering. That's some seriously speedy snacking!

Labasin Waterfall Restaurant
Quezon, Philippines

This restaurant is certainly making a splash! What could be more refreshing than sitting by cascading waters, kicking off your shoes, and cooling your feet in the water that flows below your table? This unusual eatery offers diners the opportunity to feast at bamboo tables submerged at the base of a spectacular rushing waterfall. Despite the fact that you might get drenched as you dine, this experience is not one to be missed. A colorful buffet, served from cooking stations set in the water, offers fresh fish, rice, chicken, and fruit all served on banana leaves. Beyond the waterfall, providing a beautiful backdrop, visitors may also be lucky enough to spot birds peeping out of the surrounding jungle. After dining, many take the opportunity to take a dip in the falling water.

MADCAP MUSEUMS

China Watermelon Museum
Beijing, China

The design of this big building gives a clue to the exhibits found inside. The tapered green roof resembles two massive leaves—and the interior is packed with everything you could ever possibly want to know about watermelons! There are more than 300 photos of the refreshing fruit, as well as books, comics, and poems about them. Watermelons are a popular crop grown south of Beijing, so this is an ideal location for fans of the fruit. The museum has plenty of varieties of watermelons, although they are all models made from wax. Summer is the best time to visit because real ones are grown outside, and hungry visitors can sample them. This attraction is one in a *melon*—in fact, it's the only watermelon museum in the world.

Hair Museum
Avanos, Türkiye (Turkey)

A cave under the Chez Galip pottery workshop in Avanos houses a bizarre collection: locks of hair. Hanging from the walls and ceiling of this underground passageway are thousands of clippings, each attached to the donor's name and address. Owner and local potter Galip Körükçü didn't set out to open a museum. In 1979, one of his friends was leaving Avanos, and Körükçü was so impressed by her hair, he asked for a lock of it as a keepsake. A customer heard the story and offered a clipping, too. The collection kept on growing. Now more than 16,000 locks of hair are displayed underneath the shop. Twice a year, a customer is invited to choose 10 pieces, and the original owners of those clippings are invited back for a free weeklong vacation!

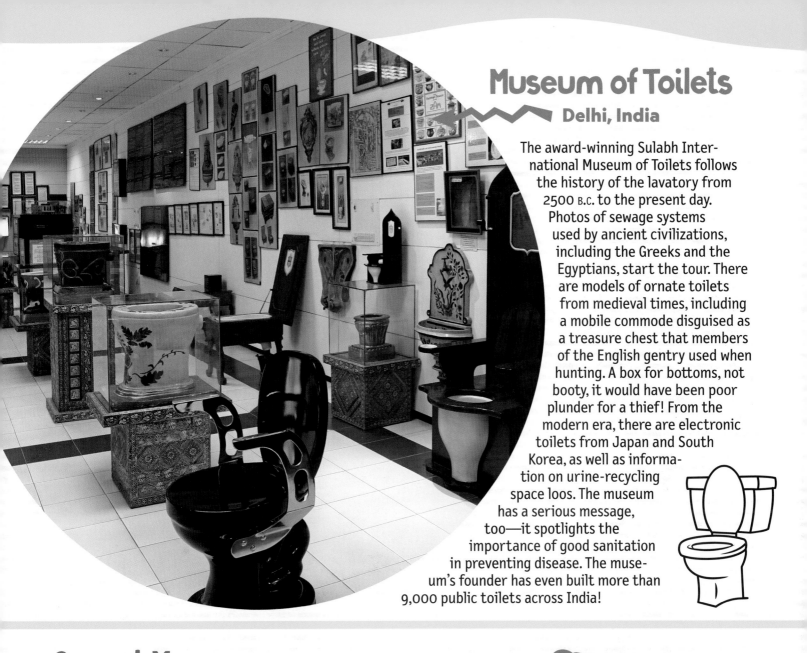

Museum of Toilets
Delhi, India

The award-winning Sulabh International Museum of Toilets follows the history of the lavatory from 2500 B.C. to the present day. Photos of sewage systems used by ancient civilizations, including the Greeks and the Egyptians, start the tour. There are models of ornate toilets from medieval times, including a mobile commode disguised as a treasure chest that members of the English gentry used when hunting. A box for bottoms, not booty, it would have been poor plunder for a thief! From the modern era, there are electronic toilets from Japan and South Korea, as well as information on urine-recycling space loos. The museum has a serious message, too—it spotlights the importance of good sanitation in preventing disease. The museum's founder has even built more than 9,000 public toilets across India!

Camel Museum
Dubai, U.A.E.

Camels play an important role in human life in the United Arab Emirates, from transportation to racing. They're fascinating creatures, able to carry up to 900 pounds (400 kg) for 25 miles (40 km) a day across desert, and able to run at 40 miles an hour (65 km/h). Fortunately, admirers of these amazing animals can further their knowledge of them at Dubai's Camel Museum, which was built back in the 1940s. The info here is way more than skin deep: Visitors can study models of a camel's skeleton and internal organs. There is information about different camel species and how humans have benefited from their wool and milk for thousands of years. The museum is free to enter, so plenty of visitors can always *camel*-long.

CAMELS DON'T BREAK A SWEAT UNTIL IT HITS 106°F (41°C)!

Don't sweat it!

QUIZ WHIZ

Bursting with bizarre info?

Answer the questions to see how much you can remember!

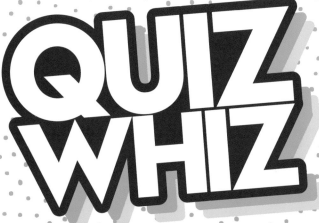

1 What shapes are the human-made islands in Qian'an, China?

a. Banana and oranges
b. Cat and mice
c. Flower and stars
d. Square and triangles

3 How can you avoid being seen in one of Tokyo's transparent bathroom stalls?

a. Line the walls with toilet paper.
b. Lock the door.
c. Pull down the blinds.
d. Turn off the light.

2 What is used to create sparks at Nuanquan's Da Shuhua celebration?

a. Fireworks
b. Lasers
c. Molten iron
d. Static electricity

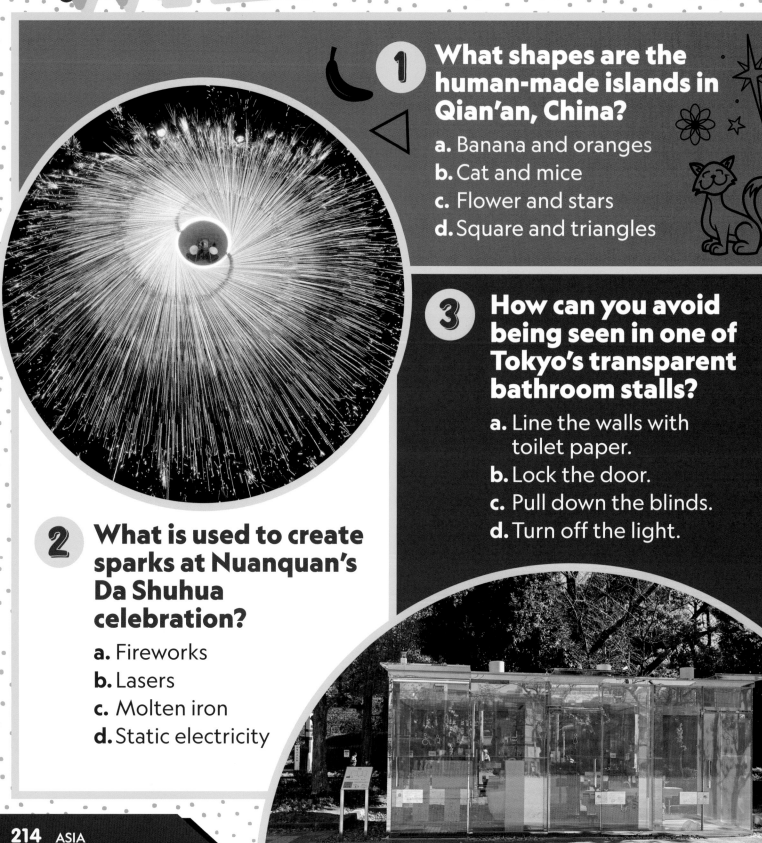

4

What makes the sides of Kawah Ijen volcano appear blue?

a. Acid rain
b. Exploding plums
c. Sulfuric gases
d. Toxic plants

5

How long did it take to build the Taj Mahal in India?

a. 17 days
b. 17 weeks
c. 17 months
d. 17 years

6

What does a saiga NOT use its nose for?

a. Filtering out dust
b. Making loud mating calls
c. Storing termites to eat
d. Warming cold air

7

What does artist Chie Hitotsuyama use to make sculptures?

a. Old balloons
b. Old bridge beams
c. Old buns
d. Old newspapers

8

What is stored under the Chez Galip pottery shop?

a. Hair
b. Hares
c. Hammers
d. Hummus

Answers: 1. c, 2. c, 3. b, 4. c, 5. d, 6. c, 7. d, 8. a

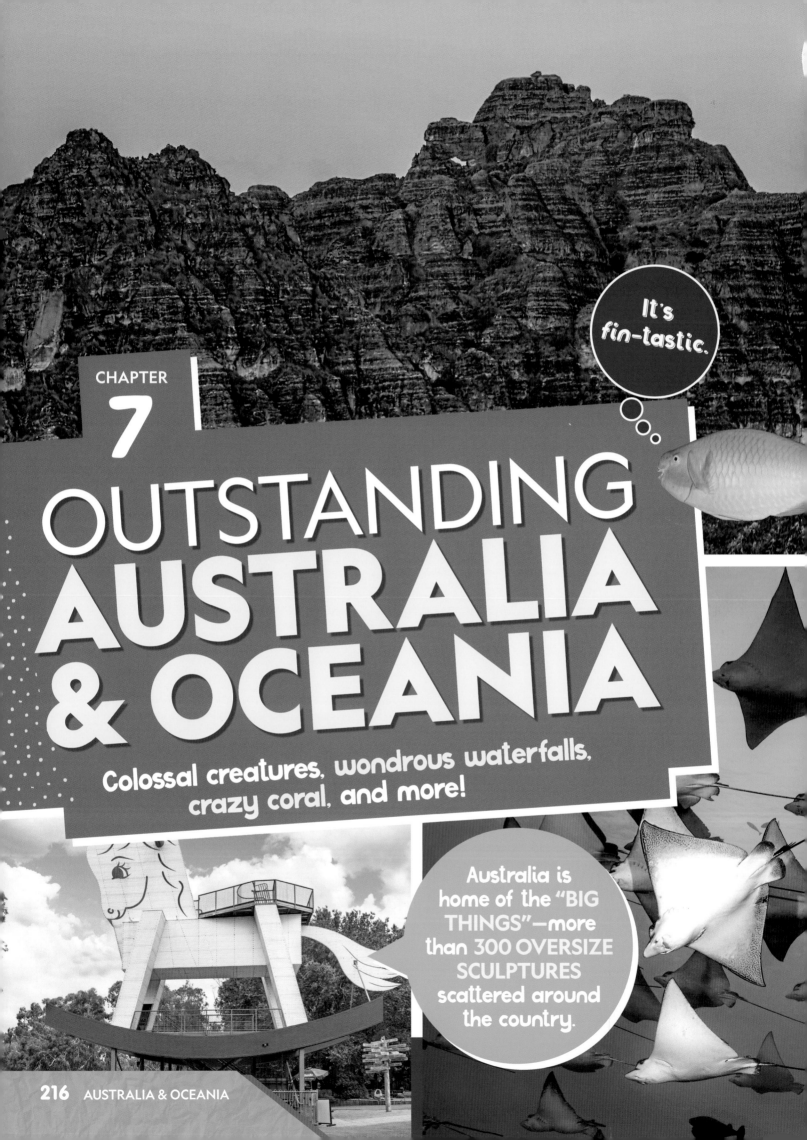

It's fin-tastic.

OUTSTANDING AUSTRALIA & OCEANIA

Colossal creatures, wondrous waterfalls, crazy coral, and more!

Australia is home of the "BIG THINGS"—more than 300 OVERSIZE SCULPTURES scattered around the country.

This THREE-ACRE (1.2-ha) MAZE is made of 14,000 native Hawaiian plants.

STEAMPUNK HQ

WEIRD in the WORLD

With its collection of islands, amazing Oceania is awash with **MARINE MARVELS, FAR-OUT ARCHITECTURE, STRANGE** sculptures, and more!

The world's only preserved colossal squid specimen is on display at New Zealand's Te Papa museum.

That's one beautiful loo!

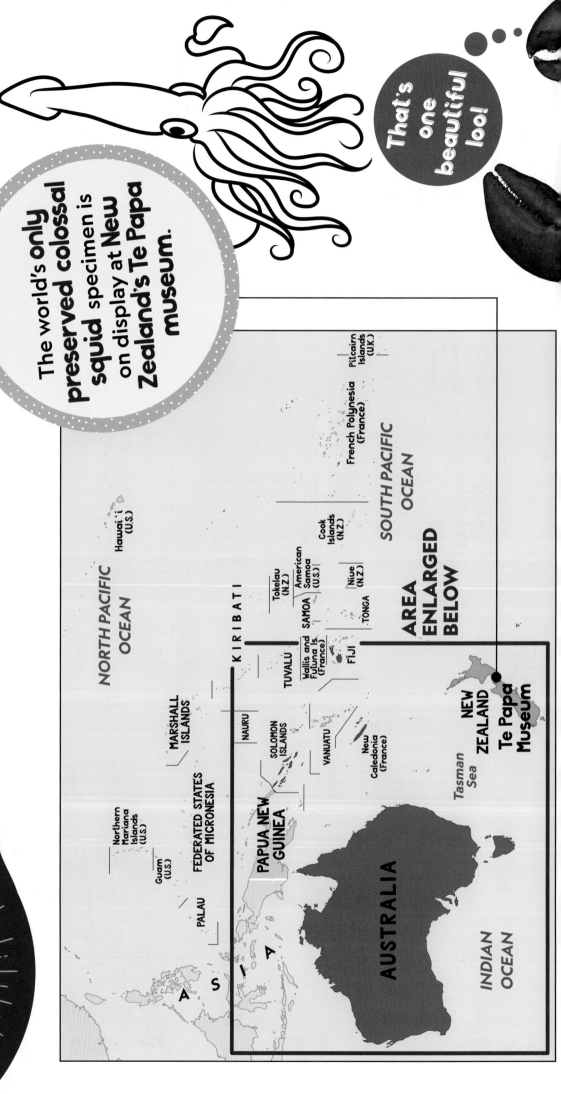

NORTH PACIFIC OCEAN

Hawai'i (U.S.)

Northern Mariana Islands (U.S.)

Guam (U.S.)

PALAU

FEDERATED STATES OF MICRONESIA

MARSHALL ISLANDS

NAURU

KIRIBATI

TUVALU

Tokelau (N.Z.)

American Samoa (U.S.)

SAMOA

Wallis and Futuna Is. (France)

FIJI

Niue (N.Z.)

TONGA

Cook Islands (N.Z.)

French Polynesia (France)

Pitcairn Islands (U.K.)

SOUTH PACIFIC OCEAN

AREA ENLARGED BELOW

SOLOMON ISLANDS

VANUATU

New Caledonia (France)

PAPUA NEW GUINEA

ASIA

AUSTRALIA

INDIAN OCEAN

Tasman Sea

NEW ZEALAND

Te Papa Museum

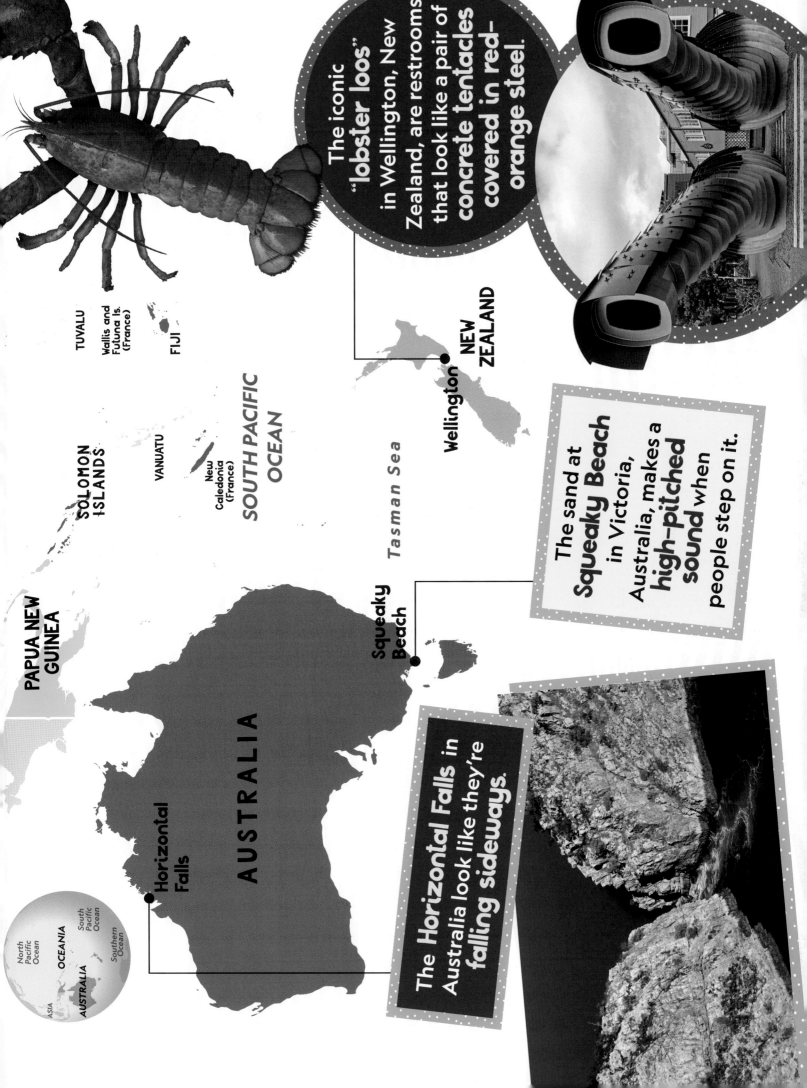

The iconic **"lobster loos"** in Wellington, New Zealand, are restrooms that look like a pair of concrete tentacles covered in red-orange steel.

TUVALU

Wallis and Futuna Is. (France)

FIJI

SOLOMON ISLANDS

VANUATU

New Caledonia (France)

SOUTH PACIFIC OCEAN

PAPUA NEW GUINEA

Tasman Sea

Wellington

NEW ZEALAND

The sand at **Squeaky Beach** in Victoria, Australia, makes a **high-pitched sound** when people step on it.

Squeaky Beach

A U S T R A L I A

Horizontal Falls

The *Horizontal Falls* in Australia look like they're falling sideways.

North Pacific Ocean

OCEANIA

South Pacific Ocean

ASIA

AUSTRALIA

Southern Ocean

ISLAND ODDITIES

Fossilized Coral Forest
Niue

On the remote island of Niue, you will discover astonishing coral formations and fields bursting with greenery. But it's what the roots of these plants and trees are sprouting from that makes it so utterly unique—instead of soil, the ferns, coconut palms, and other big trees grow out of fossilized coral that has been decaying over many years. Standing about 200 feet (60 m) above sea level, this fascinating geological feature is very rare.

NIUE IS ONE OF THE WORLD'S BIGGEST CORAL ISLANDS.

The Island Out of Time
Howland Island

International Date Line West—also called "Anywhere on Earth"—is the time zone of the uninhabited banana-shaped Howland Island. It is one of only two areas in the world (the other being nearby Baker Island) on this special calendar system. Their unique calendar marks that a period of time has ended when that date has passed in every other place in the world. Talk about being late to the party!

Ghost Fleet
Chuuk Lagoon, Micronesia

Lurking below the surface, a sunken "Ghost Fleet" hides in the waters of Chuuk Lagoon, providing a true wreck diver's paradise. Once used as a Japanese naval base during World War II, the atoll—a series of coral islands surrounding the lagoon—in the central Pacific is home to a vast collection of sunken shipwrecks. Remarkably preserved tanks, bulldozers, torpedoes, bombs, motorcycles, and other relics can be found within many of the ships' holds. In 1944, the United States launched Operation Hailstone, which caught Japanese troops off guard. They lost an estimated 50 ships and more than 250 planes in the attack. Amazingly, a reef has grown over these wrecks, and it has become home to a diverse collection of sharks, manta rays, turtles, fish, corals, and more.

I'm hedging my bets ...

Pineapple Maze
Wahiawa, Hawaii, U.S.A.

Lose yourself in the 2.5 miles (4 km) of tangled paths that make up this pineapple-shaped puzzle. Dole Plantation's mega maze stretches across three acres (1.2 ha) with paths crafted from 14,000 colorful native plants. When it opened in 1998, it was the largest plant maze in the world. Eight rest stations help guide the way to the pineapple-shaped garden at the center. The fastest times through the maze are posted on a sign near the entrance. Let's hope this leafy labyrinth doesn't leave visitors feeling prickly!

The **average time** to complete the maze is about **one hour,** but the record time is **seven minutes.**

SURPRISING FACTS ABOUT THE

weird but true!

The **Great Barrier Reef** is the **only living structure** that's **visible** to the naked eye from **SPACE.**

In **2021,** snorkelers found a **400-year-old coral** the size of **a double-decker bus.**

The Great Barrier Reef is made up of more than **1,000 INDIVIDUAL ISLANDS** and **2,900 REEFS.**

133 VARIETIES OF SHARKS AND RAYS SWIM IN THE GREAT BARRIER REEF.

GREAT BARRIER REEF

SIX OF THE WORLD'S SEVEN SPECIES OF **SEA TURTLES** ARE FOUND IN THE GREAT BARRIER REEF.

The corals **all spawn** at the same time each year, releasing **so many eggs** it looks like an underwater blizzard!

THE **GREAT BARRIER REEF** IS THE SAME SIZE AS **70 MILLION FOOTBALL FIELDS.**

A secret reef was found behind the Great Barrier Reef, made from giant **doughnut-shaped rings of algae.**

The 1911 wreck of the **S.S. YONGALA** PASSENGER SHIP has become one of the reef's most impressive **WILDLIFE** SANCTUARIES.

Much of the **SAND FOUND AROUND THE REEF** is from **PARROTFISH** eating soft coral bodies and **POOPING** out the **HARD SKELETONS AS SAND.**

In 2020, explorers discovered a tower of coral taller than the **EMPIRE STATE BUILDING.**

WEIRD WONDERS

I'm seeing red!

This little Australian territory is home to an array of interesting creatures. But none steal the spotlight quite like the Christmas Island red crab *(Gecarcoidea natalis)*—a bright red land crab. These crustaceans are not found anywhere else on Earth. Once a year, they leave their cooler homes in the forest and begin a mammoth trek to the coast. Because their larvae can survive only in water during their first weeks of life, these crimson crawlers must travel to the ocean to breed. This dangerous trek can take up to 18 days. During that time, they swarm the island. The human residents (close to 2,000) do their best to assist—building tunnels and crab crossings to help them navigate dangerous roads.

CRAB INVASION

Christmas Island

There are around

50 MILLION CLAMBERING CRABS

on the island!

Go Big OR GO HOME

The Big Mango

Australia is home to the "Big Things," a collection of supersize sculptures. A monstrous mango made from fiberglass sits outside the Bowen Visitor Information Centre in Queensland. The 32-foot (10-m)-tall sculpture was created to honor the mango orchards in the area. The mouth-watering sculpture caught the attention of someone who thought the fruit was ripe for the picking. That's right—the mango was stolen! The heist turned out to be part of a publicity stunt by the fast-food chicken chain Nando's, and was soon returned.

The Big Rocking Horse

How would you attract visitors to a toy factory? Well, this one in the Adelaide Hills went with a 60-foot (18.3-m)-tall rocking horse! The epic build was finished in 1981 and took eight months and $100,000 dollars to complete. Visitors who aren't afraid of heights are invited to climb a series of ladders (some narrow areas require crawling—you've been warned!) to enjoy a view from the top.

The Big Lobster

Nicknamed "Larry the Lobster," this colossal crustacean has been around for more than three decades. The metal sculpture resides at a roadside restaurant. Made from fiberglass and steel, the lobster is about 55 feet (17 m) tall. Paul Kelly is the designer behind this curious critter, which was created to attract people to the area and its seafood.

The Big Banana

Don't slip up and miss this ap-*peel*-ing stop along the Coffs Coast. The jumbo banana is believed to be the first of the Big Things in Australia and one of the country's most photographed objects. Built back in the 1960s on a banana plantation, the 42-foot (13-m)-long fruit stands next to a milk bar serving banana milk, plus a toboggan track, water park, and mini-golf course.

The Big Bench

Two and a half times the size of a regular bench, the Big Bench is located on top of the mines of Broken Hill in New South Wales. Though many of Australia's Big Things are found along busy roads, this one is in a far more idyllic setting. In fact, this viewpoint has also been chosen for scenes in the movies *Mad Max* and *The Adventures of Priscilla, Queen of the Desert*.

I'm sitting pretty.

The Big Playable Guitar

This plywood sculpture is literally music to your ears! Found at Narrandera Visitor Information Centre in New South Wales, this gargantuan guitar even set a Guinness World Record for its size. Made in 1988 to celebrate country music, the oversize instrument took almost 300 hours to build. It's 20 feet (6 m) long and has strings that you can actually play!

WEIRD DAYS OUT

Steampunk HQ
Oamaru, New Zealand

Step inside and enter the wonderfully wacky alternate world of steampunk. (If you're not familiar with steampunk, it's a type of sci-fi fantasy that imagines what would happen if a futuristic society ran on steam power, like machines of the mid to late 1800s.) In the real world, the little coastal town of Oamaru boomed during the 1800s, so it's packed with Victorian architecture—perfect for Steampunk HQ, which is housed in a big old warehouse. The building is brimming with bizarre contraptions and bonkers machinery, such as vehicles and musical instruments made from copper pipes.

Jurassic Park Experience
Kualoa Ranch, Hawaii, U.S.A.

Buckle up for a bumpy and *roar*-some rainforest trek through the Hakipu'u and Ka'a'awa Valleys, nicknamed the Jurassic Valley. The scenery is spectacular on its own, and it also served as filming locations of the dinosaur thrillers *Jurassic World* and *Jurassic World: Fallen Kingdom*, as well as other movies and TV series. Tours take visitors to the *Indominus rex* paddock, where they can see the actual bunkers and dinosaur cages used in the movie. And if an open-air vehicle with panoramic views isn't quite enough, visitors can opt to experience the Jurassic Valley on e-bikes, on horseback, or above the treetops by zip line!

More than 200 movies and TV shows have been filmed in these epic valleys.

BY the NUMBERS

KANGAROO

Meet the world's largest marsupial. If you're thinking of challenging one to a race, you had better do some hard-core training—their incredibly strong hind legs allow kangaroos to move fast. And you wouldn't want to challenge one to a boxing match, either. Male kangaroos pack a powerful punch and often "box" one another, propping themselves up on their tails and duking it out with punches and kicks.

AVERAGE WEIGHT:

200 POUNDS (91 KG)

HOW HIGH THEY CAN JUMP:

6 FEET (1.8 M)

(THAT'S THE AVERAGE HEIGHT OF A REFRIGERATOR.)

A BABY JOEY STAYS IN ITS MOTHER'S POUCH FOR

2 MONTHS.

LIFE SPAN:

UP TO 25 YEARS

THEY CAN LEAP

25 FEET (8 M)

FORWARD IN A SINGLE JUMP.

SPEED:

35 MILES AN HOUR (56 KM/H)

PERSONALITY QUIZ

Australia is known as the Big Country, home to oodles of oversize objects,
but which of its huge sculptures are you most like?

1 Do you like swimming?

a. Sure, it can be fun sometimes.
b. I love it! I'm like a fish.
c. Absolutely not—keep me on land.

2 Which fruit would you choose?

a. An orange
b. A banana
c. An apple

3 What drink are you most likely to order?

a. Milk
b. Soda
c. Hot chocolate

4 How would others describe you?

a. A friend who's always up for fun
b. A daring explorer
c. A prankster

5 Where is your first stop when you go to the zoo?

a. The insect house
b. The lion enclosure
c. The aquarium

6 What hobby are you most likely to have?
a. Playing an instrument
b. Baking something yummy
c. Relaxing with a book

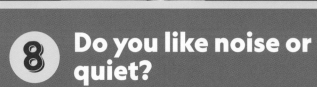

7 How do you feel about trying new things?
a. Fine—I'll try most things.
b. Bring it on—the wilder the better!
c. I'd rather stick to what I know I like.

8 Do you like noise or quiet?
a. I like a bit of both.
b. The louder the better!
c. Peace and quiet is my happy place.

Mostly A's
The Big Guitar
You're a busy bee and always open to new ideas. Always up for trying things and adding a new string to your bow, you are most like the Big Guitar. Visit this giant instrument and have a strum. It might just be the start of a new hobby!

Mostly B's
The Big Banana
With your fun nature and your love of adventure, you're most like the Big Banana! Get yourself some thrills and spills at this banana plantation turned water park. Satisfy your need for excitement on the toboggan track, and test your skills with some mini golf.

Mostly C's
The Big Bench
Your laid-back nature and your quiet, chilled-out attitude makes you most like the Big Bench. Climb aboard this giant chair with a good book and a warm drink. What better place to relax and have a bit of me time.

TAKING FLIGHT

Mataveri International Airport
Rapa Nui

This isolated airport on Rapa Nui (also known as Easter Island) is the most remote airport in the world! Famous for its mysterious stone *moai*, or statues, this island certainly gets a lot of visitors. However, it is a long, lonely 2,336 miles (3,759 km) away from the next nearest airport in Santiago, Chile. That's farther than the distance between Los Angeles and Washington, D.C.! Despite being remote, it draws around 100,000 travelers a year!

Gisborne Airport
New Zealand

If you're a nervous flier, you may want to look away now! Gisborne Airport has to share its runway with the Palmerston North–Gisborne train line. It is one of the few airports in the world to have active train tracks running straight through the middle of its main runway. Although regular passenger and freight trains no longer run on the track, classic locomotive steam trains cross the runway as they travel their short distance of around 10 miles (16 km) from Gisborne to Muriwai.

Flying Coconuts
Samoa

Look into the skies of the Samoan island of Savai'i, and you may see a soaring coconut launching high into the sky. The amazing Alofaaga Blowholes are formed by lava creating underwater caves below the surface. The caves slowly grow toward the surface until they become direct tunnels to the ocean below. The tunnels (named the Taga Tunnels) transport the breaking water at rocketing speeds, sending it erupting into the air. This water can shoot up to 66 feet (20 m) into the sky. For a small fee, locals will toss in a coconut just before the eruption, catapulting the coconut around 100 feet (30 m) into the sky—that's the height of a 10-story building!

Can I have this dance?

Bird of Paradise
Papua New Guinea

Forget angry birds. Here, it's all about the boogie birds. The Vogelkop superb bird of paradise has some serious moves. To impress onlooking females, the male puffs out his chest with his cape flipped up and dances around the female in semicircles. The bird is dressed to impress, too: Its striking blue eyes and vibrant blue breastplate stand out against the blackness of its feathers. Because of its color pattern, though, this bird has been given the nickname "sliding frowny face"!

DISTINCTIVE DWELLINGS

SiloStay
Little River, New Zealand

Want to stay somewhere that goes against the grain? Well, take a look at this unusual accommodation. In the small town of Little River, New Zealand, you can spend the night in one of their converted grain silos (large towers that stored grain). That's right, each of the silos fits a bed, kitchen, living room, and bathroom—all tucked into a metal tower. What's even cooler is that the bathroom toilet and sink are combined! It's not as gross as it sounds: When you flush, fresh water runs into a small sink for washing your hands, and this water then drains directly into the toilet flush tank to be reused. And the environmental thinking doesn't stop there—all the food waste, toilet paper, and poop from the site is used to feed tiger worms (little wrigglers that are experts in turning organic waste into compost).

Korowai Tree Houses

Papua, Indonesia

The Korowai tribe in Papua live in tree houses, most of which are between 20 and 39 feet (6–12 m) off the ground. Some of the buildings are as high as 131 feet (40 m) up in the air! Constructing one involves finding a sturdy tree and removing the top. The building materials all come from the jungle. The frame is made from branches bound together with rattan palms, and the roof is made from large leaves. A ladder carved from a tree trunk hangs from the bottom of the house for access. The tree-top homes sit high above seasonal flood-waters to protect the inhabitants from biting insects at ground level. Over the past few years, many Korowai have moved to live in villages, so this generation may be the last to call the aerial accommodations home.

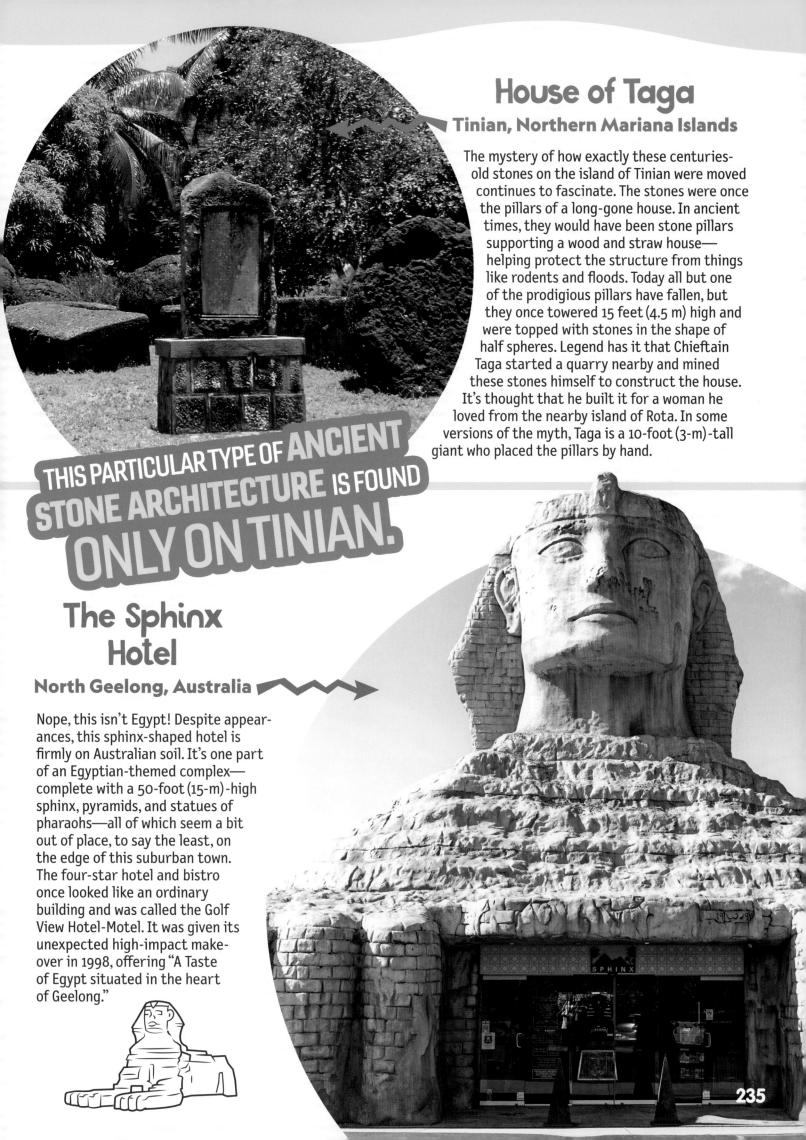

House of Taga
Tinian, Northern Mariana Islands

The mystery of how exactly these centuries-old stones on the island of Tinian were moved continues to fascinate. The stones were once the pillars of a long-gone house. In ancient times, they would have been stone pillars supporting a wood and straw house—helping protect the structure from things like rodents and floods. Today all but one of the prodigious pillars have fallen, but they once towered 15 feet (4.5 m) high and were topped with stones in the shape of half spheres. Legend has it that Chieftain Taga started a quarry nearby and mined these stones himself to construct the house. It's thought that he built it for a woman he loved from the nearby island of Rota. In some versions of the myth, Taga is a 10-foot (3-m)-tall giant who placed the pillars by hand.

THIS PARTICULAR TYPE OF ANCIENT STONE ARCHITECTURE IS FOUND ONLY ON TINIAN.

The Sphinx Hotel
North Geelong, Australia

Nope, this isn't Egypt! Despite appearances, this sphinx-shaped hotel is firmly on Australian soil. It's one part of an Egyptian-themed complex—complete with a 50-foot (15-m)-high sphinx, pyramids, and statues of pharaohs—all of which seem a bit out of place, to say the least, on the edge of this suburban town. The four-star hotel and bistro once looked like an ordinary building and was called the Golf View Hotel-Motel. It was given its unexpected high-impact make-over in 1998, offering "A Taste of Egypt situated in the heart of Geelong."

ANIMAL ANTICS

Peacock Spider
Australia

This little spider, *Maratus banyowla,* is just one of many kinds of colorful, spirited arachnids known as peacock spiders. In fact, the total number of known peacock spiders is up to 108 and counting. These tiny, large-eyed crawlers are only .16 to .24 inch (4–6 mm) in size. Beyond their colorful appearances, peacock spiders are also known for their fancy footwork. Male peacock spiders perform dances to attract a mate, but despite the males' best efforts, sometimes their finest moves just don't cut it. If the females are unimpressed, they have been known to simply gobble up the males right then and there—talk about harsh critics!

Kākāpō
New Zealand

Also known as the "mighty moss chicken" (because of its fluffy plume of green feathers), the kākāpō is the world's only flightless parrot! Its inability to fly could make it vulnerable to attack, but when threatened, it simply freezes, tries to blend into the background, and pretends to be a plant! Recognized as both the world's heaviest and longest-living parrot, the kākāpō can reach an estimated 90 years in age. However, because of habitat loss and the arrival of new predators such as cats and stoats, these birds plunged to seriously low populations. In the 1990s, the total number of kākāpōs was as low as just 50! The good news is that the population of these little fighters has more than quadrupled since then, and many have been relocated to predator-free islands to help conserve them further.

Comb-Crested Jacana
Australia

Now that's a scarily large number of limbs! Or is it? The jacana is well known as a leggy bird with distinct long, spindly toes that allow it to traverse across floating lily pads. These incredibly long toes allow it to spread its weight and stop it from breaking the water's surface tension. So they can literally walk on water! Don't worry, though—the bird's alien-like extra legs actually belong to its chicks. When the father believes that his babies are in danger, he will scoop them up under his wings with only their little legs dangling down! They seem to have plenty of space there, seeing as some have been spotted carrying two chicks under each wing!

THIS BIRD IS ALSO KNOWN AS THE LOTUS BIRD OR LILY TROTTER!

Weirdly Cute!

Matschie's Tree Kangaroo

This incredible creature might not be what you first think of when someone says the word "kangaroo." It doesn't hop around the outback and is much smaller than its red kangaroo cousins, but it sure knows how to live the high life! Found only in the forests of Australia, Papua New Guinea, and West Papua, these kangaroos actually live in trees! Although it is unknown when these mammals evolved into tree dwellers, their bodies are well adapted to it. They have long, gripping claws and a long tail to help them balance. Their thick mahogany fur is perfect for insulating them against damp weather, and it helps them camouflage against predators.

WEIRD WONDERS

The Bungle Bungle Range in Purnululu National Park is famed for its orange-and-black striped rock formations.
Their distinctive domes stretch upward from the savanna planes like oversize beehives. The tallest rocks rise a dizzying 800 feet (250 m) above the ground—about three-quarters the height of Paris's Eiffel Tower. The Bungle Bungles formed over millions of years to create a range so vast that it takes up about 175 square miles (450 sq km). Wind and water have weathered and shaped the soft sandstone rocks into cones and towers. The colorful stripes are found only on the surface of the sandstone. The orange comes from a layer of iron oxide and the black from microbes living on the rock.

BUNGLE BUNGLES

Kimberley Region, Australia

Ancient Aboriginal artwork—dating back

THOUSANDS OF YEARS—

has been found throughout the Bungle Bungles.

AUSSIE ODDITIES

Gnomesville
Ferguson Valley, Australia

An area of land near a roundabout in southwestern Australia is gnome—sorry, home—to a huge collection of tiny statuettes. Gnomesville began in 1995 when the roundabout was being built. First one gnome appeared—although it's unclear whether it was watching over or protesting against the work.) Soon more little folk arrived, distracting drivers from the road. So the statuettes were moved nearby. The collection began to attract visitors who brought their own gnomes to help the tiny town grow, and it wasn't long before gnomes started to arrive from all around the world. The number grows every year. Well, gnome wasn't built in a day, was it?

Hairy Food
Melbourne, Australia

Unless you're looking for a hair ball, you wouldn't want to bite into these delicious-looking dos. Hot dogs, pretzels, and pizzas are just a few of the incredible styles that Mykey O'Halloran has created to raise money for the Make-A-Wish Foundation. Although some creations can take around eight hours to construct, the results are magical! O'Halloran uses a combination of vibrant colors and clever sculpting to make these hairy versions of popular dishes. The stylist has traveled the world using vegan and cruelty-free products on a tour called the Rainbow Road Trip.

O'Halloran has used powdered sugar and hair dye to make toppings for his creations.

Wave Rock
Western Australia

This curved granite cliff face looks like a huge wave about to break ... but it hasn't for millions of years! Wave Rock is the northern face of a granite hill estimated to be around 2.7 billion years old. Water, erosion, and weathering have rounded the rock into this flared shape over the past 130 million years. You can walk along the top or the bottom of the 50-foot (15-m)-high formation—depending on how brave you're feeling! Multicolored stripes run down the curve of the rock, making it look like moving water that's been frozen in time. Water does have something to do with the rock's epic appearance. Its stripes were formed during wet periods when rainwater wore down the granite, dissolving chemicals found within the rock and depositing them over its surface.

Surf's up!

NEARBY IS A ROCK CALLED HIPPO'S YAWN THAT LOOKS LIKE A WIDE, YAWNING MOUTH.

Weirdly Cute!
Mary River Turtle

With its neon green "hair," the Mary River turtle may look ready to front a punk rock band. But it's not actually hair—it's algae! The algae attaches to the rare freshwater turtle because it spends so much of its life submerged. This living mohawk helps the animal hide from river predators. Known as a "breathing turtle," this curiously cute critter uses specialized glands found in its reproductive organs to absorb oxygen underwater, allowing it to stay below the surface for up to 72 hours. As their name suggests, Mary River turtles are found only in the Mary River of Queensland, Australia, where they can live up to an astonishing 100 years of age.

QUIZ WHIZ

It's hard to keep track of all this weirdness! See how much you can remember with this quiz. Grab a piece of paper and write down your answers.

1 **How long can the Mary River turtle stay underwater?**

a. 24 hours
b. 1 week
c. 3 hours
d. 72 hours

2 **The "Big Thing" named Larry is a sculpture of what?**

a. A lobster
b. A llama
c. A ladybug
d. A lemur

3 **What are the Bungle Bungles in Australia?**

a. Twin brothers famous for being clumsy
b. Bats that live in the jungle
c. A series of small one-story houses
d. A range of black-and-orange striped rock formations

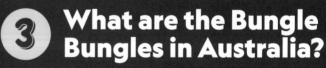

4 **What unexpected shape is a hotel in North Geelong, Australia?**

a. An Egyptian sphinx
b. A giant sunhat
c. A lion's head
d. A cricket bat

5 **In Western Australia, there's a 2.7-billion-year-old rock shaped like ...**

a. A wave about to break
b. A burger in a bun
c. A whale's mouth
d. A sitting cat

6 **What sculpture sits outside the Bowen Tourist Information Centre in Australia?**

a. A robotic koala
b. A giant mango
c. A life-size kangaroo
d. A miniature Sydney

8 **What can be found at the center of the mega maze in Wahiawa, Hawaii?**

a. Snacks and a coffee machine
b. A violin-shaped bench
c. A pineapple-shaped garden
d. A giant stopwatch

7 **What is strange about the giant guitar sculpture in New South Wales, Australia?**

a. It has spaghetti instead of strings.
b. You can play it.
c. It can be heard tuning itself.
d. Nobody knows how it got there.

AMAZING ANTARCTICA

Frozen shipwrecks, millions of penguins, lots of ice, and more!

DECEPTION ISLAND was named by an explorer who in 1820 figured out that it is actually an ACTIVE VOLCANO!

The GIANT ANTARCTIC OCTOPUS has deadly venom that works even at subzero temperatures.

WEIRD in the WORLD

Check out some of the WACKIEST, COOLEST, and DOWNRIGHT WEIRDEST PLACES and ANIMALS across ANTARCTICA!

Lake Vostok is hidden under 2.5 miles (4 km) of ice.

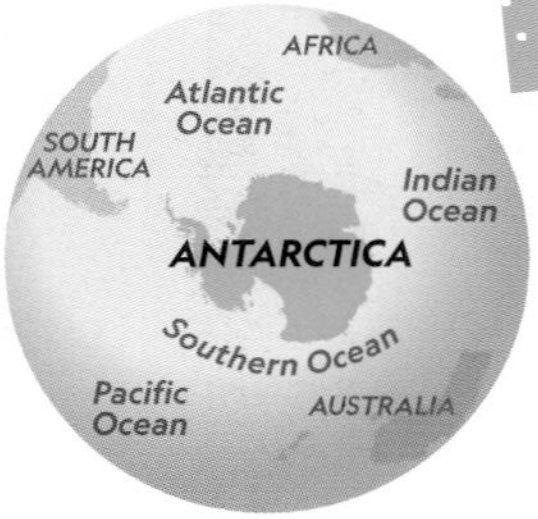

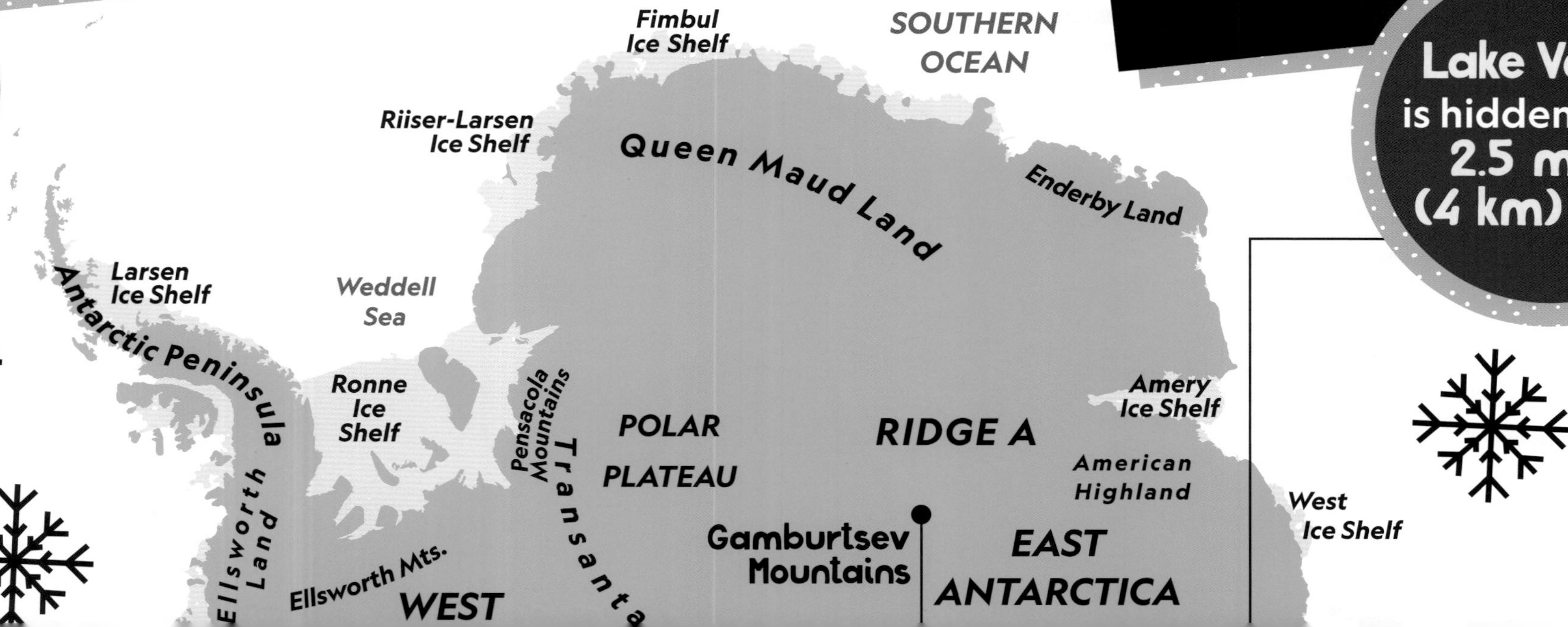

To join the 300 Club, you must leave a sauna heated to 200°F (93°C) to dash around the South Pole marker when it's minus 100°F (-73°C) outside ... wearing only boots!

West Ice Shelf

Enderby Land

Amery Ice Shelf

American Highland

SOUTHERN OCEAN

Queen Maud Land

RIDGE A

EAST ANTARCTICA

Fimbul Ice Shelf

POLAR PLATEAU

Gamburtsev Mountains

Riiser-Larsen Ice Shelf

Pensacola Mountains

T r a n s a n t a

Weddell Sea

Ronne Ice Shelf

WEST

Ellsworth Mts.

Larsen Ice Shelf

Ellsworth Land

Antarctic Peninsula

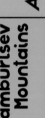

ATLANTIC Ocean

AFRICA

Indian Ocean

ANTARCTICA

AUSTRALIA

Southern Ocean

SOUTH AMERICA

Pacific Ocean

Planes arriving on Antarctica's Ross Island have to land on a runway of compacted snow.

Antarctica's ice may be concealing a river longer than England's Thames, winding its way for 285 miles (460 km) to the Weddell Sea.

Scientists have discovered the DNA of microorganisms that lived a million years ago in samples from the Antarctic seafloor.

No land mammals are native to Antarctica—only marine ones.

The Gamburtsev Mountains, a mountain range the size of the Alps in Europe, are buried 1,970 feet to 3,280 feet (600–1,000 m) of Antarctic snow.

That's weird!

Shackleton Ice Shelf

Wilkes Land

Lake Vostok

rctic Mountains

Victoria Land

ANTARCTICA

Marie Byrd Land

Getz Ice Shelf

Ross Ice Shelf

Ross Island

Ross Sea

SOUTHERN OCEAN

WEIRD WONDERS

Around Antarctica are several huge ice shelves, where thick ice covers the sea. There are also countless free-floating icebergs and ice floes, or flat sections of ice. Although the water is freezing cold, it's not empty: Under the ice, a whole ecosystem of amazing Antarctic wildlife lives in a beautiful blue-green world. Tiny shrimps and krill feed on algae that grow on the underside of the ice, and they in turn become food for sardines, squid, and whales. Penguins zoom and dart around at high speeds to catch fish, chased by hunters such as the fierce leopard seal. There are sometimes humans here, too: scuba divers with cameras explore, spot wildlife, and snap breathtaking shots like this one!

The water temperature around Antarctica can drop AS LOW AS 28°F (-2°C)!

UNDER THE ICE
A Mysterious Underwater Realm

Weird but true!

Norway's **ROALD AMUNDSEN** led the first team to the South Pole in **1911,** with **52 SLED DOGS.**

NOT EVERYONE working in Antarctica is a scientist. There are also lots of other staff: **MECHANICS, ELECTRICIANS, PLUMBERS, MEDICAL STAFF,** and **RADIO OPERATORS.**

ANTARCTICA has an average of **5,000 SQUARE MILES** (13,000 SQ KM) for every person.

About **5,000** international scientists work on bases in Antarctica through **SUMMER,** but only **1,000** brave the **WINTER.**

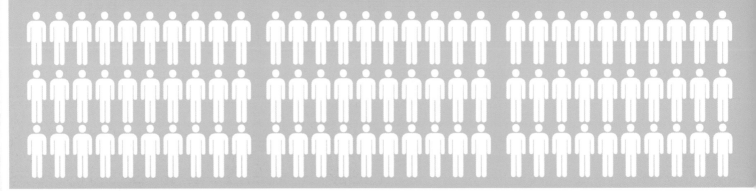

ANTARCTICA

Because Antarctica is so **remote,** the European Space Agency uses it to study how **people cope with darkness** and **isolation.** This helps them plan for future long-distance space journeys.

11 CHILDREN have been born in Antarctica.

Antarctic **SCIENTISTS WITH BEARDS** often find that their **BREATH FREEZES ONTO THEIR FACIAL HAIR,** giving them a face full of **"HAIR-CICLES"**!

RESEARCHERS EAT LOTS OF **CHOCOLATE BARS** FOR ENERGY—THEY HAVE TO BE STUFFED IN A POCKET TO KEEP THEM FROM **TURNING ROCK HARD** IN THE COLD.

The **YOUNGEST PERSON** to trek to the South Pole was the U.K.'s **LEWIS CLARKE,** who reached the pole in January 2014 at age 16.

UNUSUAL UNDERWATER CREATURES

Antarctic Sun Sea Stars

Growing up to 24 inches (60 cm) across, this monster sea star is always on the prowl. It climbs up on top of sponges, rocks, or even human-made underwater equipment and waves its long arms—up to 50 of them—around in the water. Its arms and body are covered in little jawlike grabbers called pedicellariae, which can snap together like a trap to grab prey such as shrimps or small fish. Then it uses its arms to pass the food into its mouth. The tiny traps give this sea star its other name—the "wolftrap" sea star.

Octopuses have blue blood.

Giant Antarctic Octopus

This spooky-looking octopus might be your worst nightmare ... if you happen to be a clam! When it discovers a tasty, shelled sea creature, it uses a row of sharp teeth on its tongue—called a radula—to drill through its prey's shell. It then injects the soft creature inside with venomous saliva to paralyze and slightly dissolve it before gobbling it up. The giant octopus can measure up to 45 inches (115 cm) in length and survive in bone-chilling 28.8°F (-1.8°C) Southern Ocean waters because of a special protein in its blood.

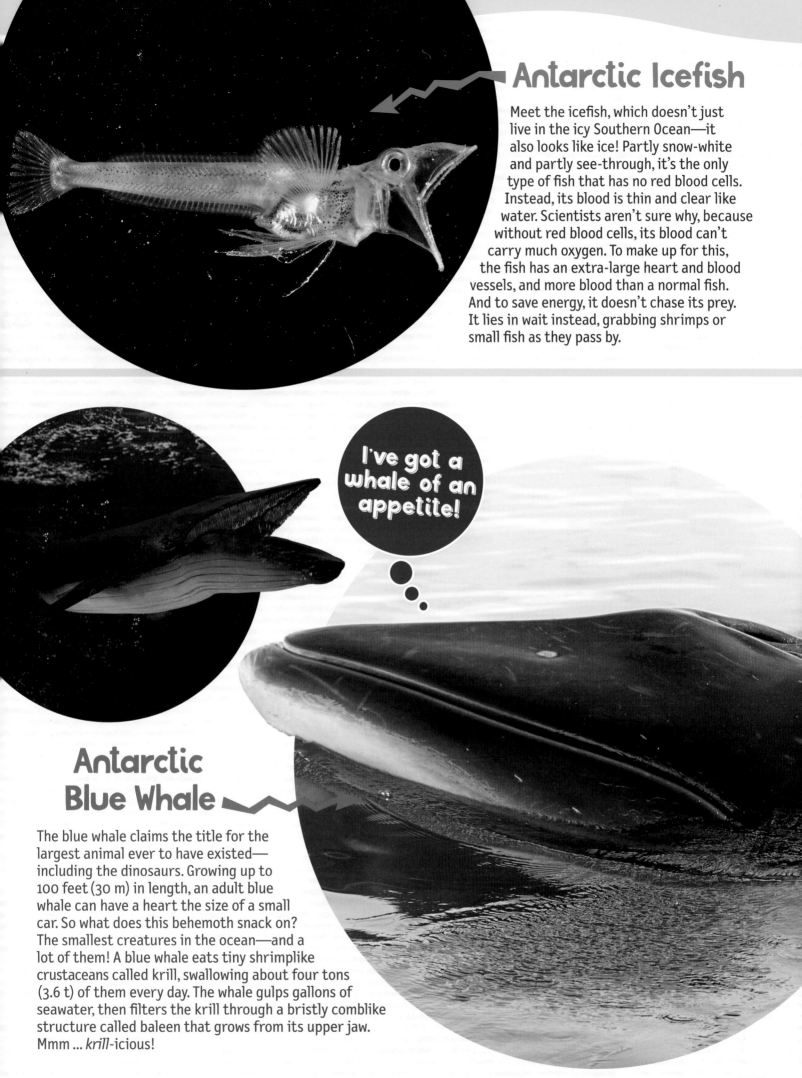

Antarctic Icefish

Meet the icefish, which doesn't just live in the icy Southern Ocean—it also looks like ice! Partly snow-white and partly see-through, it's the only type of fish that has no red blood cells. Instead, its blood is thin and clear like water. Scientists aren't sure why, because without red blood cells, its blood can't carry much oxygen. To make up for this, the fish has an extra-large heart and blood vessels, and more blood than a normal fish. And to save energy, it doesn't chase its prey. It lies in wait instead, grabbing shrimps or small fish as they pass by.

I've got a whale of an appetite!

Antarctic Blue Whale

The blue whale claims the title for the largest animal ever to have existed—including the dinosaurs. Growing up to 100 feet (30 m) in length, an adult blue whale can have a heart the size of a small car. So what does this behemoth snack on? The smallest creatures in the ocean—and a lot of them! A blue whale eats tiny shrimplike crustaceans called krill, swallowing about four tons (3.6 t) of them every day. The whale gulps gallons of seawater, then filters the krill through a bristly comblike structure called baleen that grows from its upper jaw. Mmm ... *krill*-icious!

PERFECT PENGUINS

Adélie Penguin

The Adélie penguin has some impressive leaping skills! Zooming up out of the water to land on sea ice, an Adélie can shoot 10 feet (3 m) into the air—several times its own height! Adélies also live in *enormous* colonies, or groups. In 2018, a new Adélie colony was discovered using satellite images—it was made up of a mind-boggling 1.5 million birds.

Macaroni Penguin

How did macaroni penguins get their name? It's not because they like mac and cheese. (All penguins are carnivores and eat only sea creatures.) Instead, the name comes from the macaronis of 18th-century England, a group of men who wore frilly high-fashion styles—including caps with plumes similar to the macaroni penguin's crest of bright yellow-orange feathers. Despite their stylish looks, though, macaronis don't always have great manners. The males often fight for space in their crowded colonies by slapping one another with their flippers. Grumpy macaronis have been known to give passing scientists a good slap, too!

BY the NUMBERS

THE COOLEST CONTINENT

Antarctica is the coldest, highest, and windiest continent on Earth. It's also the driest—the Antarctic ice sheet is technically the world's largest desert! Want to know exactly how cold, how high, and how dry? Check out these chilling stats about the extreme Antarctic.

COLDEST TEMPERATURE RECORDED:
MINUS 128.6°F
(-89.2°C)

WIND SPEED: UP TO
218 MILES AN HOUR (350 KM/H)

ANNUAL RAIN/SNOWFALL:
2 INCHES (50 MM) A YEAR

AVERAGE ELEVATION:
8,200 FEET (2,500 M) ABOVE SEA LEVEL

HIGHEST POINT:
VINSON MASSIF, 16,050 FEET (4,892 M)

AGE OF OLDEST ICE: 2.7 MILLION YEARS

ICE AND FIRE

Antarctic Hot Pool
Deception Island

There's one place around the Antarctic where you don't have to dress up in several layers outdoors. In fact, many people just wear swimsuits! Deception Island is in the South Shetland Islands, off the Antarctic Peninsula. It's the only place where a ship can sail right into a volcano crater. That's right—Deception Island is an active volcano! The volcano last erupted in 1970 and is now home to tens of thousands of chinstrap penguins and an abandoned whaling station. The gray beach steams with the heat of the volcano and, if you dig yourself a pool, you can enjoy a dip in a hot spring.

Volcano ahoy!

METEORITES ARE METEORS— SPACE ROCKS— THAT HAVE HIT THE GROUND.

Antarctic Meteorites

What comes to mind when you think of Antarctica? Ice? Penguins? And ... meteorites? Millions of chunks of rock left behind from the formation of the solar system fall to Earth every year. The pieces that land are called meteorites. One of the best places to locate them is in Antarctica, where they stand out one the ice and are preserved in glaciers. Hundreds are collected from here every year, giving scientists lots of information on the beginnings of our planet and Earth's nearest neighbors. In 2023, researchers discovered one of the largest meteorites ever on Antarctica, a space rock weighing 16.8 pounds (7.6 kg).

Incredible Ice Towers

Volcanoes in warmer places have fumaroles—vents or cracks in the ground around the volcano where hot volcanic gases and steam shoot out. On Mount Erebus, thanks to the subzero temperatures, fumaroles become huge fumarolic ice towers! These crooked pillars of ice can be between 10 and 12 feet (3–4 m) across and up to 33 feet (10 m) tall. How do they happen? As the boiling hot gas and steam flow out of the ground, they instantly melt the ice and snow above. But then they hit the cold air and freeze onto the ice around the edge of the melted hole. Over time, more and more ice builds up, creating a towering chimney. Once in a while, the top of a tower collapses or topples over—so don't get too close!

MOUNT EREBUS ERUPTS MULTIPLE TIMES A DAY, FIRING OUT AROUND 50 LAVA BOMBS.

Ocean ODDITIES!

Hoff Crab

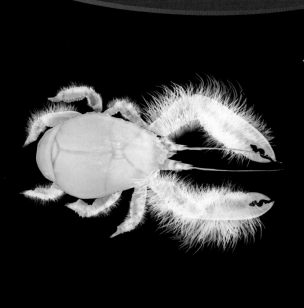

Imagine a small, blind, white deep-sea crab with a very hairy chest, and you have a Hoff crab! This curious creature was discovered in 2010, living in the icy deep seas around Antarctica. It's found near hydrothermal vents, where hot mineral-filled water seeps out of the seafloor. Special vent bacteria live here, and the Hoff crab feeds on them. To make this easier, its underside is covered with hairlike parts that give the bacteria a place to live—and the crab just scrapes a few off whenever it feels like a snack! So why "Hoff"? Scientists gave the crab this name because its hairy-looking chest reminded them of actor David Hasselhoff, known as "the Hoff"—and he was happy to be linked to the cool new discovery!

Orca

Orcas, the largest of the dolphins, have big brains to match, and they're super smart. A bit like humans, they can come up with new ideas to solve problems, then share them and learn from one another. This has happened in Antarctica, where some orcas have invented a way of catching seals that sit on floating ice floes to stay safe. The orcas team up in a group of three or four, then charge toward the ice floe, making a big wave that tips it over or washes the seal completely off!

My lips are sealed!

Leopard Seal

Many people think of seals as cute, chubby, and cuddly creatures who like munching on fish and flopping around on the beach. That's until they see a leopard seal! This seal gets its name because of its spotted coat, but that's not the only way it resembles a big cat. Leopard seals are huge—up to 12 feet (3.6 m) long—and fierce, with their giant jaws full of *T. rex*–style long, sharp teeth. They're streamlined and agile underwater, where they chase and grab penguins, octopuses, squid, and other smaller seals to eat. They can be dangerous to humans, too, and have even been known to chase explorers across the Antarctic sea ice.

Snowy Sheathbill

Meet the birds known as the "garbage collectors" of the Antarctic. Snowy sheathbills, which look like extra-large white pigeons with pink warty faces, get this nickname because they'll eat absolutely anything! Unlike most Antarctic birds, they don't have webbed feet and aren't great swimmers. So instead of diving into the sea to catch fish, they vacuum up any kind of food they can find on land. That ranges from insects and worms to other birds' eggs, animals that have died, and stinky, fish-flavored seal poop! They'll even gang up on penguins to steal whatever food they've caught. And they've also learned to bother humans, hanging around outside research bases, ready to grab snacks from passing scientists!

Krill

It looks like a small, pink, slightly see-through shrimp about the size of your little finger, but this is actually a krill, superstar of the Antarctic seas. To say krill are common in Antarctic waters would be an understatement. There are *gazillions* of them! They form vast shoals called superswarms that are so big that they can be seen from space. In a swarm, a bathtub-size amount of water can contain 20,000 krill! And if you put all the world's krill together, they'd weigh more than all the humans. Krill are also incredibly important, because they are a vital food for countless Antarctic animals—from fish, penguins, and seabirds to squid, seals, and massive whales.

Basket Star

This creepy creature of the Antarctic deep looks like some kind of sci-fi alien monster, but don't panic—it's just a basket star! That's a sea star, or starfish, that resembles a basket because of the way its five main arms divide and branch off into many smaller arm tips (sometimes as many as 5,000 of them!). Its scientific name, *Gorgonocephalus,* means "Gorgon head," after the Gorgon of Greek mythology, who had writhing deadly snakes for hair. But these basket branches don't bite: Instead, the basket star waves them around like a net to catch passing prey, such as small shrimps.

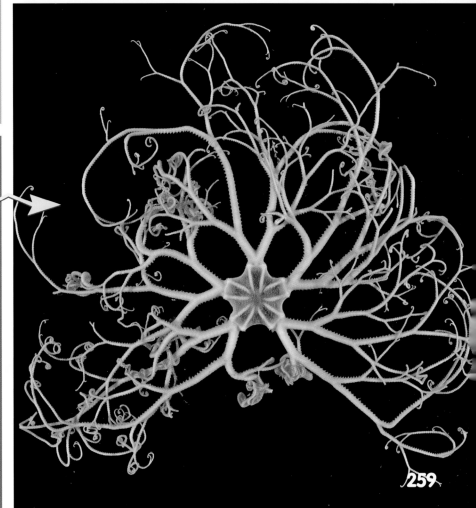

259

ICY TRAVEL

~~~ Making Tracks

Things have moved on a lot since early polar explorers took ponies and dogsleds on their Antarctic adventures more than 100 years ago. Back in the 1960s, a quirky little vehicle could be seen trundling around the polar wilderness: a tiny, iconic Mini car. Instead of driving along on its equally tiny tires, the "Mini-Trac" was given its own caterpillar tracks. Today, scientists mainly get around using planes, trucks, snowmobiles, and Sno-Cats, which have caterpillar tracks for crossing the ice. Over the years, the vehicles have gotten more hi-tech, with eco-friendly models now rolling over the ice.

Bicycling to the South Pole ~~~

As you may know if you've ever tried riding a bike in freezing temperatures, ice and bicycling aren't a great combination. Add in the blasting Antarctic wind and endless snowdrifts, and bicycling from the edge of Antarctica to the South Pole might seem like a definite no-go. But it has been done! In fact, in 2013, three different bicyclists attempted the feat at the same time. The first to make it was British adventurer Maria Leijerstam, who set a record by covering 396 miles (638 km) in 10 days, 14 hours, and 56 minutes. Instead of a normal two-wheeler, she rode a special low-lying three-wheeled bicycle, the ICE Polar Cycle, which she helped design.

What's **Weird** About This?

A legendary ship, crushed by ice and thought lost forever, has been found in the dark depths, swarming with ghostly life!

The ship—called the *Endurance*—has a famous history. It was the ship that carried British explorer Ernest Shackleton and his crew to the Antarctic on the way to the South Pole in 1914. The ship became trapped and pulverized by moving ice, forcing the explorers to cross 800 miles (1,300 km) of rough seas in small boats to get help. Incredibly, Shackleton and his crew all lived to tell the tale. The *Endurance* was discovered by divers in 2022, more than 100 years after it sank. Thanks to the absence of wood-munching marine organisms, the ship is perfectly preserved about 10,000 feet (3,050 m) deep in the Weddell Sea. The wreck is now home to bizarre sea creatures that can survive in perishingly cold waters. Large and pale anemones, sea squirts, and sea lilies have moved in, along with ghostly white crabs and lobsters.

QUIZ WHIZ

Think you're a whiz at weird but true?
Test your knowledge with these quirky questions!

2 **How do planes land on Ross Island, Antarctica?**

a. On the frozen sea
b. On a runway made of compacted snow
c. On a flat iceberg
d. They can't! The island is a volcano.

1 **How do you join the 300 Club?**

a. Live to be 300 years old.
b. Visit the South Pole 300 times.
c. Run around the South Pole wearing only boots.
d. Count 300 penguins.

3 **What is the world's largest desert?**

a. The Sahara in northern Africa
b. The Atacama in Chile
c. The Arabian Desert in western Asia
d. The Antarctic ice sheet

4 What is the *Endurance*?

a. A marathon race across Antarctica

b. Antarctica's largest research station

c. The coldest toilet on Earth

d. A ship that sank off the South Pole

5 What is special about Lake Vostok?

a. It's one of the world's largest subglacial lakes.

b. It's completely frozen.

c. It's home to the world's largest penguin population.

d. All of the above!

6 How many people live in Antarctica?

a. 0

b. 10 to 100 scientists

c. 1,000 to 5,000

d. About 270,000

7 How big is an adult blue whale's heart?

a. As big as a cupcake

b. As big as soccer ball

c. As big as a small car

d. As big as the moon

8 What is unusual about Deception Island?

a. It's completely underwater.

b. It's an active volcano.

c. It has a penguin as mayor.

d. It's covered by ice a mile deep.

The BUBBLE that gives this NEBULA ITS NAME is so big, it's 1.5 TIMES WIDER than the distance between our sun and the next nearest star.

CHAPTER

9

SENSATIONAL SEA & SPACE

Peculiar planets, sensational ships, freaky fish, and more!

I'm over the moon.

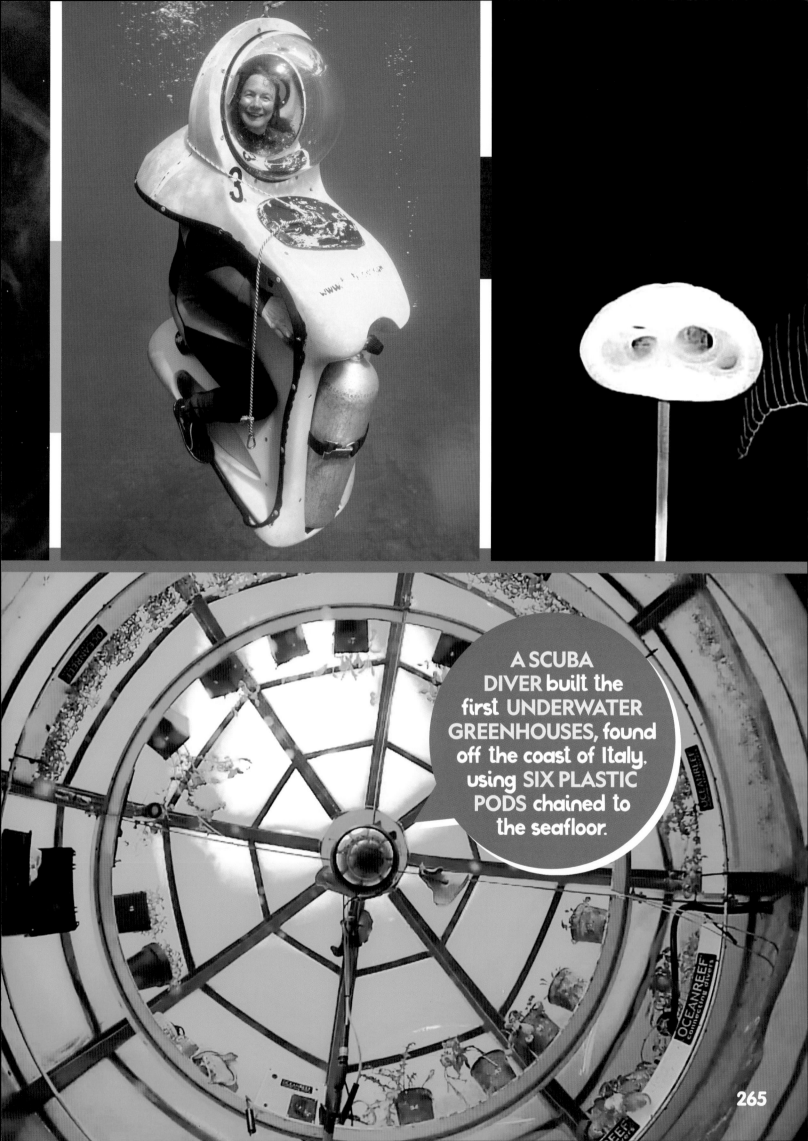

A SCUBA DIVER built the first UNDERWATER GREENHOUSES, found off the coast of Italy, using SIX PLASTIC PODS chained to the seafloor.

WEIRD in the WORLD

Travel beyond the human domain into the DARKEST DEPTHS of the OCEAN and the DISTANT REACHES of OUTER SPACE ...

In 2022, NASA's DART, or Double Asteroid Redirection Test, successfully altered an **asteroid's orbit** by colliding with it.

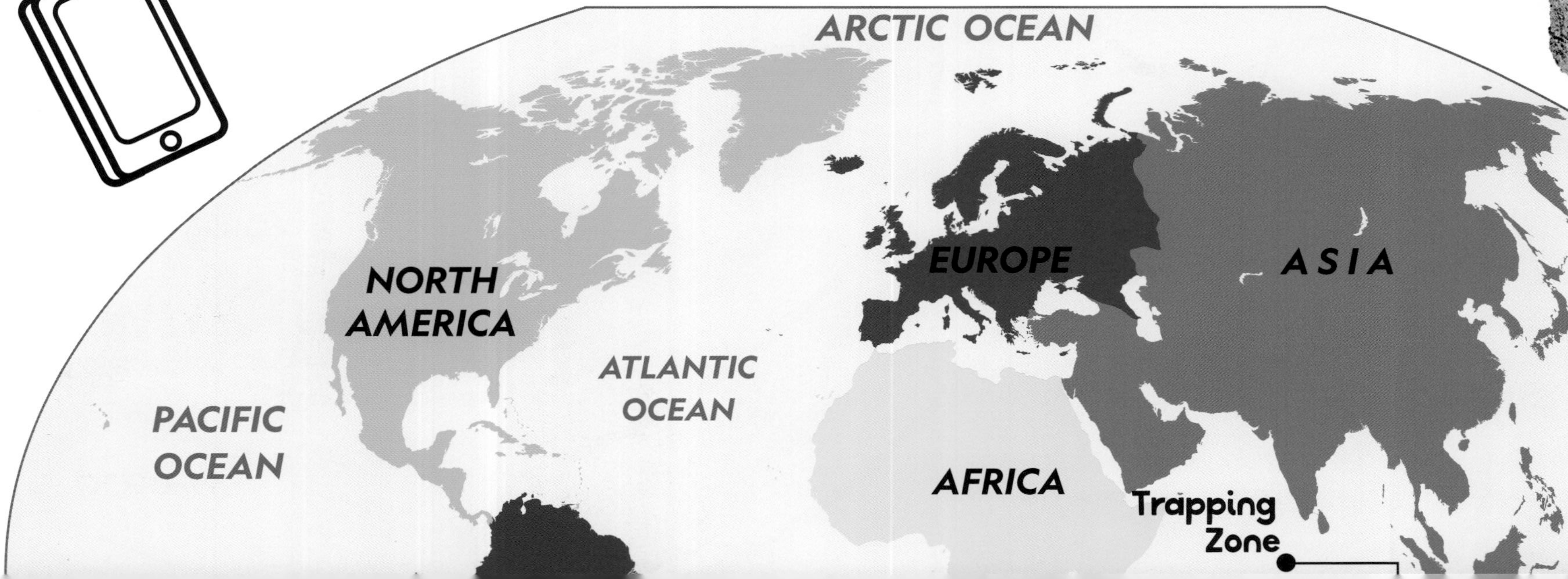

A typical smartphone has three million times more memory than the two Voyager probes—NASA's longest-running space program.

ARCTIC OCEAN

PACIFIC OCEAN

ASIA

EUROPE

AFRICA

ATLANTIC OCEAN

NORTH AMERICA

PACIFIC OCEAN

Trapping Zone

OCEANIA

AUSTRALIA

OCEANIA

INDIAN OCEAN

SOUTHERN OCEAN

ANTARCTICA

SOUTH AMERICA

O-fish-ally cool!

The Trapping Zone is the name of a unique ecosystem in the Maldives where huge numbers of large fish, such as sharks and tuna, feed on tiny organisms called micronekton.

Each mermaid's wineglass alga is one massive cell.

NASA's car-size Parker Solar Probe is the fastest object ever built.

UNDERWATER WEIRDNESS

Fried Egg Jellyfish

Atlantic Ocean, Mediterranean Sea, and Aegean Sea

It's not hard to see how the beautiful and bizarre fried egg jellyfish, from the Cepheidae family, got its name. It can have up to a two-foot (61-cm) diameter, with a bright yellow dome right in its center, making it look like a huge, floating fried egg. Fortunately, its sting has little effect on humans. It is also harmless to crabs and small fish, such as young mackerel, which hide in its tentacles to stay safe. Confusingly, a different jelly from the Phacellophoridae family, which is usually found in colder water, is also nicknamed the fried egg jellyfish. When you're trying to keep track of undersea creatures, that's no *yolk!*

Despite their name, **jellyfish** aren't fish and do not have **fins** or **gills.**

Underwater Fireworks

Eastern Pacific Ocean

Halitrephes jellyfish wouldn't look out of place in the sky on the Fourth of July— hence explorers describing them as "deep-sea fireworks." But despite the jellyfish's big bell, which can reach up to four inches (10 cm), and big burst of colorful tendrils, it would be hard to find in its natural habitat. It lives 4,000 feet (1,200 m) down in the ocean where there's almost no light, so it can be photographed only when a camera light illuminates it.

Pink See-Through Fantasia

Indonesia, Pacific Ocean

This alien-like creature of the deep is a swimming sea cucumber unlike any you've ever seen before. Pink see-through fantasias don't leave much to the imagination—their transparent skin means that their intestines are all on display. One of the coolest things about them is that they light up. They can even shed flakes of their glowing skin to confuse pesky predators—essential for critters this fragile. Their bellies have fingerlike webbing that allows them to swim and move along the seafloor as far down as 8,200 feet (2,500 m) deep.

Forest of the Weird

Johnston Atoll, Pacific Ocean

In 2017, ocean explorers discovered a bizarre collection of sponges and corals 1.5 miles (2.4 km) beneath the surface of the Pacific Ocean on the side of a submerged volcano. The team of scientists likened this underwater ecosystem to an alien landscape before it was dubbed the "forest of the weird"! The explorers spotted glass sponges on long stalks that looked like oval-shaped heads, each with two eyeholes. They nicknamed it the "E.T. sponge," after the character from the 1980s movie. It has only been found in one other place—near the Mariana Trench in the western Pacific Ocean. Adding to the bizarre appearance, all the E.T. sponges were turned in the same direction. Spooky!

THE E.T. SPONGE'S SCIENTIFIC NAME IS *ADVHENA MAGNIFICA*, MEANING "MAGNIFICENT ALIEN."

DOWN TO THE DEPTHS

Deepest Submersible Dive

Mariana Trench, Pacific Ocean

The deepest any human has ever been is 35,872 feet (10,934 m)—almost to the bottom of Challenger Deep in the Mariana Trench. The record was set in 2019 by American explorer Victor Vescovo. He made the trip alone in a deep-sea submersible—a type of small submarine strong enough to resist the deep ocean water pressure. Right at the bottom, he spotted shrimplike sea creatures and, sadly, a plastic bag.

Talk about an all-time low!

Deepest Scuba Dive

Dahab, Red Sea

The world's deepest open-circuit scuba dive reached a staggering 1,090 feet 4.5 inches (332.35 m) down. Open circuit is the most common type of scuba diving and involves using a traditional breathing apparatus called a regulator, which doesn't recycle any of the gas you exhale. Ahmed Gabr set this epic record in the Red Sea in September 2014. The feat required a team of 30 people to support Ahmed, including divers, medical staff, and technicians. A dive like this takes tons of organizing—it took 10 years of preparation but only 15 minutes to descend to the bottom. Coming back up, however, took a whole 13 hours and 35 minutes.

What's **Weird** About This**?**

Greenhouses full of fruits, vegetables, and herbs might not seem particularly weird—until you discover these plants are growing underwater! In 2012, Sergio Gamberini combined his two favorite activities, scuba diving and gardening, to find the ideal conditions for growing basil. Gamberini calls his biosphere domes Nemo's Garden and set them up off the coast of Noli, Italy. In the water, the temperature doesn't change much, and it never gets too dry! The seawater evaporates on the walls of the domes, and fresh water drips down on the plants. During the first experiment, basil plants grew from seeds in just seven weeks.

TIDAL TRANSPORT

Underwater Scooters

Oahu, Hawaii, U.S.A.

If you combined an old-timey scuba suit with a moped, you might get something that looks a lot like a BOB—the "Breathing Observation Bubble." The BOB is a submersible scooter—it floats along under the water's surface, giving tourists an up-close view of colorful fish and underwater eco-systems. BOB riders can breathe easy, too, with their head in an oxygen-filled bubble.

Sorry, got to jet!

Seabreacher

Ending up inside a shark doesn't sound advisable—unless you're in a Seabreacher. The makers of this two-seater, semi-submersible watercraft claim it's the "twisted union of a marine mammal and a high-performance jet!" The Seabreacher is available in three body styles—the Shark, the Killer Whale, and the Dolphin. However, the exterior of each handmade vehicle can be customized by airbrush artists to resemble anything from a raptor to a robot. You'll need serious cash if you want to pilot one of these simulated fish or aquatic mammals, with prices starting at $85,000. This cost includes a supercharged engine capable of zooming 60 miles an hour (100 km/h) on the water's surface. If that's not extreme enough, the Seabreacher can also dive underwater and launch 20 feet (6 m) into the air.

The Manta
Southeast Asia

Every minute, about 17 tons (15.4 t) of plastic waste are dumped into the world's seas—that's roughly the weight of four rhinos. More than 3,000 species of marine creatures have been harmed as a result. Sailor Yvan Bourgnon noticed that the problem was getting worse—in 2015, he even had to abandon a race after his yacht hit garbage in the water. Bourgnon founded the SeaCleaners in 2016 with a mission to protect the oceans and clean up plastic pollution. The company's solution is a giant sailboat called the Manta. Named after the manta ray, which feeds by filtering water, this amazing ship propels itself by swallowing floating plastic waste, which it turns into energy on board. Nonplastic waste is sorted to be taken to the mainland for recycling, and organic matter is returned to the water. Set for its maiden launch in Southeast Asia in 2025, the Manta also houses a state-of-the-art science lab.

The Manta can collect up to 11,000 tons (10,000 t) of plastic every year.

The Schooner Wharf Minimal Regatta
Key West, Florida, U.S.A.

Many different materials can be used to build a boat, but thin plywood and duct tape probably wouldn't be at the top of the list. That's unlucky for the entrants in this wacky regatta race, because those items—along with two struts of wood and some fasteners—are all they can use. Teams of six people compete to construct vessels that can complete the course at Schooner Wharf. Other adhesives are not allowed, but boats can be painted for decoration. Rules aside, the regatta is a festive affair. Past boats have been designed to look like alligators, spaceships, and guitars, and many competitors sport costumes for the occasion. There are also plenty of prizes to win: fastest boat, most creative design, and the one everyone hopes to avoid—the Sinker Award. As duct tape is not the most seaworthy sealant, there are always lots of candidates for that last one!

WEIRD WONDERS

The Great Blue Hole of Belize is a scuba diver's dream. Its pristine waters are bursting with tropical marine life and out-of-this-world coral formations. At its deepest, the underwater sinkhole goes as far down as 400 feet (122 m), so it's not an expedition for the faint of heart. The Great Blue Hole is part of the Barrier Reef Reserve System, which is a World Heritage site. It formed during the last ice age when water filtered through the rock over many, many years, creating stalactites and stalagmites. Over time, these formations caved in on one another. At the end of the ice age, sea levels rose as the ice melted, resulting in the hole becoming engulfed by the Caribbean Sea.

GREAT BLUE HOLE

Belize, Caribbean Sea

The Great Blue Hole is the **BIGGEST NATURAL FORMATION** of its kind in the world.

WHO PUT THAT THERE?

Musical Mermaid
Rudder Cut Cay, the Bahamas

A grand piano is the last thing you'd expect to find at the bottom of the sea. But that's exactly what some lucky divers and snorkelers may encounter on a clear day in the Bahamas. The steel sculpture also includes a life-size mermaid and is nestled near some private islands about 15 feet (4.5 m) down. The wistful mermaid appears to sit on the seafloor, longing for a diver to play her a tune on the piano. The sculpture was sunk to the seafloor to surprise guests enjoying boat trips or snorkeling while staying on the luxury islands.

Sunken Art Gallery
British Virgin Islands

Divers can marvel at the sight of this epic kraken sculpture at the bottom of the ocean. The mighty 80-foot (24-m) kraken was built clinging to an old boat, which was then deliberately sunk. Why? To create a one-of-a-kind reef. The idea behind the underwater art gallery was to create an ideal environment to support endangered marine life. So not only is it lots of fun, but it's also eco-friendly! And it's not just any old ship, either—it's a World War II U.S. Navy fuel barge named the *Kodiak Queen*.

Underwater Pyramid
Yonaguni Jima, Japan

Mystery and controversy surround these stone ruins discovered beneath the waves. Some scholars believe that they are the ancient remains of a Japanese Atlantis that sunk following an earthquake 2,000 years ago. Others say that there's no evidence that the site is human-made. According to their research, the rocks are a natural geological phenomenon. The site was first discovered in 1986 by a local diver. Tourists and researchers continue to dive here today.

Largest Underwater Sculpture
Nassau, the Bahamas

This is the colossal "Ocean Atlas"—a sculpture of a girl carrying the weight of the ocean. It is the biggest sculpture ever constructed underwater, and it's so huge that it had to be put together in sections. The 18-foot (5-m)-tall sculpture stretches from the seafloor to the water's surface. This means that it could be highly hazardous for passing ships, so it has a flag and light at the very top. Besides looking impressive, "Ocean Atlas" is also there to create a reef for creatures to inhabit, while aiming to attract tourists away from polluted reefs to allow time for their recovery.

THIS SCULPTURE IS BASED ON THE ANCIENT GREEK MYTH OF ATLAS, THE GOD WHO HELD UP THE HEAVENS.

Bizarre BEHAVIOR

Stinger Thief

When it comes to resourcefulness, these sea slugs are up there with the best of them. Without shells for protection, aeolid nudibranchs must rely on other ways to stay safe from predators, such as being camouflaged or being brightly colored to signal danger. Besides these run-of-the-mill defense mechanisms, they have their own kind of superpower—they can eat jellyfish and other poisonous sea creatures without being stung. Better still, they can then use the jellyfish tentacles as weapons to fight off their own enemies. Waste not, want not, as they say ... The stinging cells of their prey are digested and stored in the white tips along their backs, ready to be fired out and reused when the time comes.

Rising Rays

What's more spectacular than watching a Munk's devil ray glide through the water? How about seeing thousands of these fascinating fish swimming together? In June and July, large schools of the graceful swimmers can be observed off the coast of Baja California, Mexico. It's not certain why these migratory fish travel here, although it may be to feed, thanks to the large number of zooplankton in the water. It's obvious when the rays arrive because they like to leap vertically out of the water, jumping as high as six feet (1.8 m) before belly flopping back into the sea! Again, no one is sure why—it could be anything from a mating ritual to a way to remove parasites from their skin!

Slime-Time

Any creature with nicknames like "slime eel" and "snot snake" is likely to be good with goo. The hagfish is a master mucus-maker and can produce a bucketful of ooze on demand. This doesn't mean all that gunk is stored in the hagfish's body. Hagfish slime is 99.9 percent seawater, which is mixed with mucus and slime threads. These gooey threads are expelled from around 100 glands running along the animal's body. Once released, they can expand to 10,000 times their original size in a fraction of a second. This sticky substance is released to defend a hagfish from predators and to ward off any fish attempting to steal its food. To avoid getting caught up in its own gunk, the clever hagfish will tie itself in a knot, which it slides toward its tail, scraping off the slime.

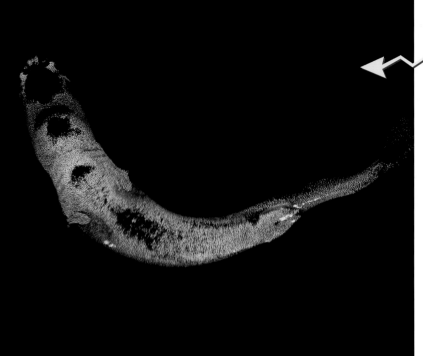

Shark in the Dark

Glowing in the dark might not sound like a bright idea for a predator hoping to sneak up on its prey. That's not the case for the kitefin shark. It isn't the only shark known to emit light, a quality known as bioluminescence. However, at nearly six feet (1.8 m) in length—about the height of a tall man—it is the biggest. The glowing kitefin was discovered at a depth of 2,625 feet (800 m), which is in a layer of water called the twilight zone. Only a small amount of sunlight reaches that zone, so an animal that can produce just enough light to match its surroundings can hide its silhouette. Though kitefins are one of the slowest-moving sharks, surprise attacks could explain how they manage to catch and eat much faster creatures.

Slow Mover

It may sound surprising for an underwater animal, but leafy sea dragons are in fact very bad swimmers—not ideal when hungry predators galore are lurking in the depths. Luckily, leafy sea dragons got it right when it comes to camouflage! They blend in perfectly with their algae-covered environment, thanks to their plantlike tendrils. Surprisingly, they don't use these structures to swim (they're purely for camouflage), but instead rely on two super-thin, transparent fins to move along.

Bubble Bullets

You don't want to get on the wrong side of a pistol shrimp—they're one of the most powerful creatures in existence and can kill their enemies with bubbles. Not just any old bubbles, though—these are 8000°F (4400°C) jet-propelled bubbles! Besides looking threatening, their enormous claws can move as fast as 60 miles an hour (97 km/h). This action creates a serious amount of noise—210 decibels, to be precise, noisier than a gunshot. The sheer speed of this snap makes a bubble shoot out with such force that it often immobilizes and kills the target.

BY the NUMBERS

INTERNATIONAL SPACE STATION

For most people, the idea of space travel feels like a million miles away (literally!). It's hard to picture what living aboard the International Space Station (ISS) would really be like, but these facts and stats should fill in some blanks.

MORE THAN

50 COMPUTERS

CONTROL THE SYSTEMS ON THE SPACE STATION.

NUMBER OF SPACESHIPS THAT CAN BE CONNECTED TO THE SPACE STATION:

8 AT A TIME

SIZE OF THE STATION:

356 FEET (109 M) LONG

(THAT'S ALMOST AS LONG AS AN AMERICAN FOOTBALL FIELD.)

TIME ASTRONAUTS EXERCISE:

2 HOURS A DAY MINIMUM

(THIS KEEPS ASTRONAUTS FROM LOSING TOO MUCH MUSCLE OR BONE MASS IN MICROGRAVITY.)

NUMBER OF TIMES THE ISS ORBITS EARTH:

16 TIMES IN

24 HOURS

7 ASTRONAUTS

LIVE AND WORK ABOARD THE SPACE STATION AT ONCE.

NUMBER OF SPACE AGENCIES OPERATING THE ISS:

5 SPACE AGENCIES FROM

15 COUNTRIES

I'm feeling out of this world!

NUMBER OF ROOMS:

6 SLEEPING QUARTERS

2 BATHROOMS

1 GYM

JOKES IN SPACE

Space Gorilla

U.S. astronaut Scott Kelly took the idea of monkeying around to a whole new level. When his twin brother bought him a gorilla suit for his birthday, Kelly decided to make good use of the unusual gift by taking it aboard the International Space Station. Cue hilarious videos of a big gorilla breaking free from a bag before flying around the station.

Suit-Free Space Walk

One April Fools' Day, three crew members aboard the International Space Station played a prank on Mission Control that would go down in history. The joke was a photograph of all three of them outside the space station, waving through the window. That doesn't sound all that unusual for astronauts until you notice that they're wearing T-shirts and sunglasses ... no space suits in sight! They joked that they were safe, though, because they all had their sunscreen on and couldn't float away because they were tethered to the spacecraft. Now that's an April Fools' prank that's out of this world!

What's **Weird** About This?

You could be left red-faced if you thought you were looking at Mars.
Mars might be nicknamed the red planet, but this is actually a picture of the moon! It's a phenomenon called a blood moon. In a total lunar eclipse, Earth lines up between the moon and the sun. Direct sunlight is blocked from reflecting off the moon. The only light waves that do reach it come from around the edges of Earth. They collide with molecules in Earth's atmosphere that disperse most of the blue light. When the remaining rays hit the surface of the moon, it appears red or orange. Color us amazed!

SPACE ROBOTS

Astrobee

Astronauts have busy schedules and sometimes need assistance with routine duties. In 2019, two robots called Honey and Bumble were sent to the International Space Station, soon followed by a third called Queen. These are the three Astrobees ... which, despite the name, are cube-shaped rather than six-legged critters. The trio are designed to carry out tasks such as recording astronauts' experiments and moving cargo. Each Astrobee has an arm for holding items or grabbing handrails. They also use electric fans for propulsion, so they can fly freely through the space station. During a test simulation, Bumble was even able to locate a blockage in an air vent that was creating a dangerously high level of carbon dioxide. What busy bees they are!

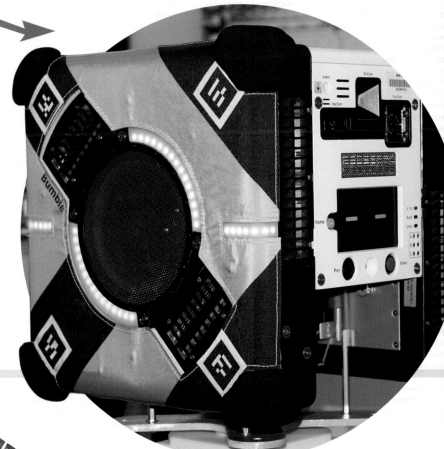

Dextre

When maintenance work is needed outside the International Space Station, the astronauts know who to call. The Special Purpose Dexterous Manipulator, that's who! Luckily, this repair expert also goes by the name Dextre, which is a lot easier to say. It is connected to the end of Canadarm2, which is a massive 60-foot (18.3-m)-long arm that moves supplies around the outside of the ISS. The two-armed Dextre is equipped with lights, video equipment, and a tool platform, and it can perform jobs such as changing batteries and replacing cameras, reducing the number of risky space walks the astronauts have to make. Dextre can be operated from the ground by both NASA and the Canadian Space Agency. The most sophisticated space robot ever built, Dextre is the only one that has repaired itself in space!

RoboSimian

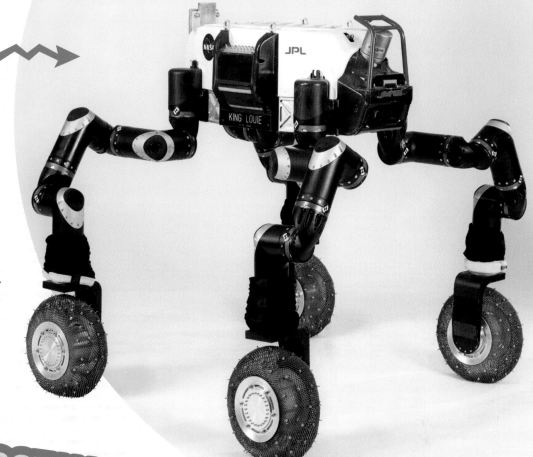

This versatile robot can walk, climb stairs, drive, and use a drill to boot! The RoboSimian has been designed to operate in challenging environments as part of a push to use robots to respond to human-made or natural disasters. One of RoboSimian's strengths is the ability to cope with tough terrain while handling dexterous tasks. It has seven sets of stereo cameras and a lidar (light detection and ranging) device that means it can map its environment in 3D, so that those operating the robot can get a clear idea of the environment it's in.

THE BOT HAS FOUR LIMBS, EACH WITH 28 ARTICULATED JOINTS THAT HELP IT HOLD AND USE TOOLS.

Weirdly Cute!

Kirobo

How cute is this mini space robot? Named Kirobo, Japanese for "hope robot," he's only 13 inches (34 cm) tall and one of the friendliest robots you could meet. Kirobo was actually designed to be a friend—a chatty companion who can recognize your face and keep you company. He went to the International Space Station in 2013 as a companion for Japanese astronaut Koichi Wakata. It was part of an experiment to see how good robots are at helping with loneliness and befriending people—and the answer is, pretty good! In fact, more and more robots are being used this way on Earth as well as in space.

Far, Far AWAY!

Bubble Nebula

Expert bubble blowers can only look on in envy at the Bubble Nebula. This bubble is seven light-years across! A light-year is the distance that light travels in one Earth year—about six trillion miles (9 trillion km). The Bubble Nebula is 7,100 light-years away from Earth and was discovered in 1787 by astronomer William Herschel, who spotted it glowing with his telescope. The bright, four-million-year-old star that "blew" it is 45 times larger than our sun. Its heat turns the gas in the atmosphere into stellar winds, which travel at more than four million miles an hour (6.4 million km/h), expanding the nebula's shell. The bubble will probably burst when its star explodes as a supernova ... but we still have 10 million to 20 million years to marvel at it before then.

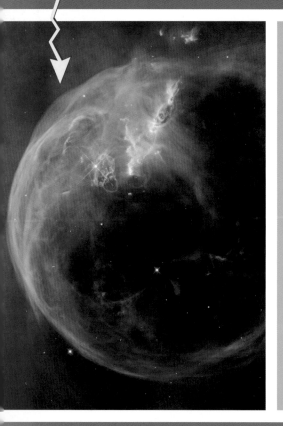

Crab Nebula

Back in 1054, Chinese astronomers noticed a new star that was visible during the daytime for more than three weeks. What they were really watching was a supernova exploding in an expanding wave of gas and dust. Those remnants are now known as the Crab Nebula. Although this *claw*-some nebula is 6,500 light-years from Earth, it is so large that it can be seen using just binoculars. At its center is the rapidly spinning core of the exploded star. This is called a neutron star, and it creates the spectral blue light inside the Crab Nebula. It emits two beams of radiation that make it appear to pulse 30 times a second as it turns—a bit like a celestial lighthouse!

Birthday Tapestry

Created in honor of the Hubble Space Telescope's 30th birthday, this portrait of a nearby galaxy celebrates the incredible imagery that has given humankind a look into the sky. This image was nicknamed the "Cosmic Reef." Hubble has revolutionized astronomy and made it accessible to everyone, forever changing our understanding of the universe around us.

Cosmic Remains

This is the aftermath of a supernova, or explosion of a star—the biggest blast there is in space. These colorful cosmic ribbons of gas, known as DEM L249, are the remains of a Type 1a supernova, which occurs when a white dwarf star dies. Astronomers believe this dwarf star was larger than typical supernovae because its leftover gas was hotter and shone brighter. This probably means that it died earlier in its life cycle, too. White dwarf stars are generally stable and unlikely to explode, but when they are in a binary system where two stars are orbiting each other, they can start sucking matter away from their companions. Sooner or later, the white dwarf steals so much gas that it explodes!

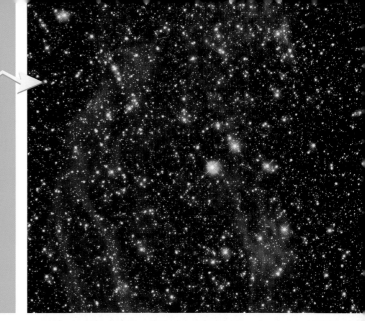

Rare Rings

The Hubble Space Telescope captured these super-rare Einstein rings—the most complete ever discovered in our universe. The unusual shape is because of gravitational lensing, a process that was accurately predicted by scientist Albert Einstein more than 100 years ago. It happens when light shining from far away is pulled and distorted by the gravity of another object before it reaches us.

New Perspective

The first full-color images and spectroscopic data from the James Webb Space Telescope were released during a televised broadcast on July 12, 2022. NASA's telescope is the biggest and most powerful space telescope in existence. So it's not surprising that it's already taken the sharpest images of the universe so far.

Fiery Hourglass

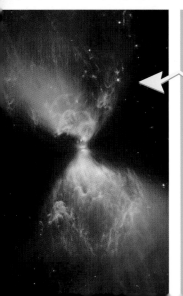

A star is born ... and NASA's James Webb Space Telescope was there to capture it. In the middle of this hourglass shape is a protostar (a mass of gas in the early stages of becoming a star) with light leaking out above and below it. The image was taken on the telescope's near-infrared camera, as the colored clouds are only visible in infrared light, which can't be seen with the human eye. The lower region appears blue because there is less dust between it and the camera than in the orange area. The protostar has been named L1527 and is about 100,000 years old. That's a youngster compared to the sun, the star at the center of our solar system, which is 4.5 billion years old. Eventually, L1527 may have its own solar system, too.

UNLIKELY ITEMS IN SPACE

Luke Skywalker's Lightsaber ∿∿➤

In 2007, the space shuttle *Discovery* launched with the original prop lightsaber from the original 1977 *Star Wars* movie. The Jedi weapon was taken to the orbiting post and back as a way to mark the 30th anniversary of the franchise. Astronaut Jim Reilly greeted R2-D2 and collected the lightsaber before it was taken to the Kennedy Space Center. As you'd expect from hard-core *Star Wars* fans, plenty of people came dressed as their favorite characters to give it the send-off it deserved. The iconic lightsaber then spent two weeks in orbit.

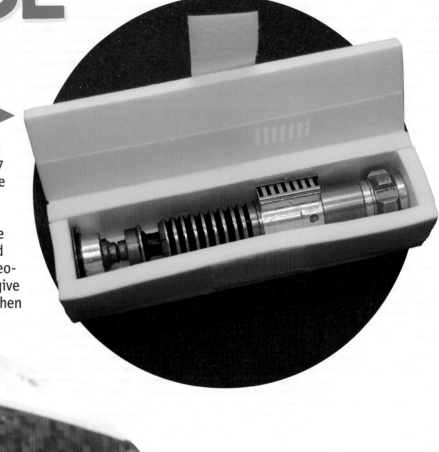

To infinity ... and the ISS!

Buzz Lightyear

Toy Story's favorite spaceman, Buzz Lightyear, went to the International Space Station. The iconic Pixar character was part of NASA and Disney's mission to encourage more children to go into careers in science. The Buzz Lightyear toy took off in 2008 and spent a total of 15 months in space before returning to Earth.

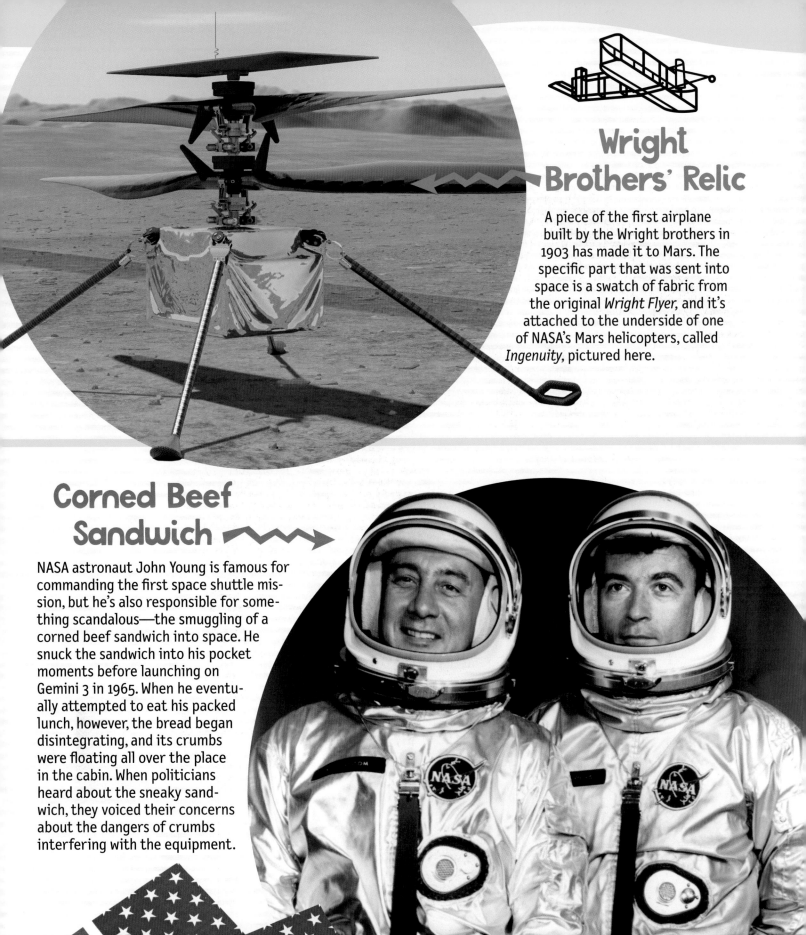

Wright Brothers' Relic

A piece of the first airplane built by the Wright brothers in 1903 has made it to Mars. The specific part that was sent into space is a swatch of fabric from the original *Wright Flyer*, and it's attached to the underside of one of NASA's Mars helicopters, called *Ingenuity*, pictured here.

Corned Beef Sandwich

NASA astronaut John Young is famous for commanding the first space shuttle mission, but he's also responsible for something scandalous—the smuggling of a corned beef sandwich into space. He snuck the sandwich into his pocket moments before launching on Gemini 3 in 1965. When he eventually attempted to eat his packed lunch, however, the bread began disintegrating, and its crumbs were floating all over the place in the cabin. When politicians heard about the sneaky sandwich, they voiced their concerns about the dangers of crumbs interfering with the equipment.

Weird but true!

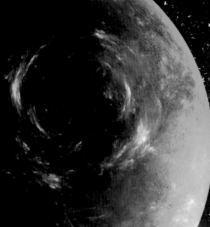

The **WINDS ON NEPTUNE** blow at more than **1,100 MILES AN HOUR (1,770 KM/H)**—1.5 times **FASTER** than the **SPEED OF SOUND.**

MERCURY is the **SMALLEST PLANET** in our solar system—and it's **SHRINKING.**

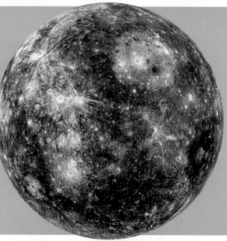

VENUS is the **HOTTEST** planet in our **SOLAR SYSTEM**—the **AVERAGE TEMPERATURE** of its surface is about **870°F (466°C).**

Astronomers think there could be a **GIANT PLANET BEYOND NEPTUNE**—it has been called **"PLANET NINE,"** but it may be a **BLACK HOLE THE SIZE OF A GRAPEFRUIT!**

JUPITER has at least **92 MOONS.**

AMAZING INFO ABOUT PLANETS

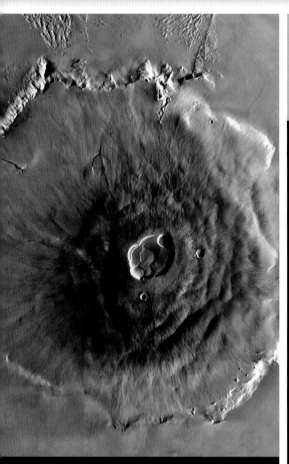

SATURN'S north pole has a **HUGE STORM** that has been raging for decades—it has **SIX SIDES** and is nicknamed **"THE HEXAGON."**

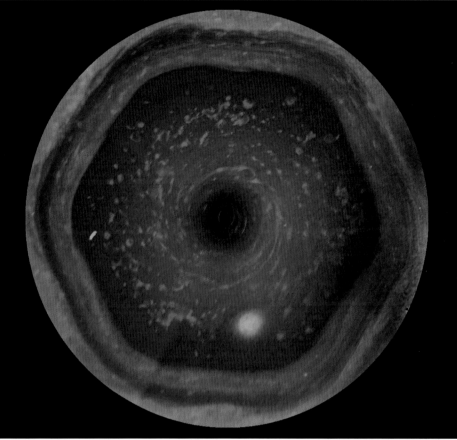

The volcano **OLYMPUS MONS** on **MARS** is **100 TIMES LARGER** than **MAUNA LOA,** the largest active volcano on Earth.

Planets **OUTSIDE OUR SOLAR SYSTEM** are called **EXOPLANETS.**

SEASONS on **URANUS** last **21 EARTH YEARS** each.

More than **1,300 EARTHS** could fit inside **JUPITER.**

QUIZ WHIZ

You've read tons of weird facts about sea and space. The question is, can you remember them all?

1 **How does the hagfish defend itself?**
a. By producing slime
b. By puffing itself up
c. By stinging
d. By biting with venomous fangs

2 **Where is basil grown underwater?**
a. Captain Jack's Pasture
b. Crusoe's Greenhouse
c. Nemo's Garden
d. Dory's Field

3 **What is the biggest sculpture ever constructed underwater?**
a. A girl
b. A lost suitcase
c. A musical instrument
d. A sea monster

4 What is a Seabreacher?

a. A broken dam
b. A glow-in-the-dark shark
c. An undersea volcano
d. A semi-submersible watercraft

5 What is the hexagon on the planet Saturn?

a. A six-sided concert hall
b. A long-lasting storm
c. A massive volcano
d. A lake of molten iron

6 When does a blood moon appear?

a. During a total lunar eclipse
b. Every Halloween
c. In a meteor shower
d. When the moon is closest to Earth

7 Which of these is NOT a robot Astrobee?

a. Bumble
b. Buzz
c. Honey
d. Queen

8 What is the Crab Nebula?

a. An astronaut's fancy lunch
b. A new solar system
c. A white dwarf star
d. The remains of a supernova

INDEX

Boldface indicates illustrations.

A

Aardvarks 151, **151**
Aboriginal art 239
Acropolis, Athens, Greece 131, **131**
Adam's Calendar, South Africa 177, **177**
Adélie penguins 254, **254**
Aeolid nudibranchs 278, **278**
Africa 144–179
Air, fried 136, **136**
Air travel 39, **39**, 149, **149**, 232, **232**, 247, **247**, 289
Alaska, U.S.A. 49, **49**
Alerce Costero National Park, Chile 98, **98**
Alexandria, Egypt 159, **159**, 176, **176**
Algae 241, **241**, 248, 267, **267**
Aliens 14, **14**, 21, 53, **53**
Alligators 50
Alofaaga Blowholes, Samoa 233, **233**
Alps, Europe 134, **134**, 137, **137**
Alton Towers theme park, England 129, 139, **139**
Amazon animals 90, **90**, 105, **105**
Amazon River, South America 74, **74**
Amazon Tall Tower Observatory, Brazil 101, **101**
American Visionary Art Museum, Baltimore, Maryland, U.S.A. 52, **52**
Amsterdam, Netherlands 137, **137**
Amundsen, Roald 250
Amusement parks *see* Theme parks
Ancient world
    calendars 173, **173**, 177, **177**
    Chichén Itzá, Mexico 56–57, **56–57**
    China 183, **183**
    Egypt 145, 159, 168–169, **168–169**, 173, **173**, 176, **176**
    Greece 15, 131, **131**
    ice cream 15
    Indian board game 19, **19**
    mysteries 176–177, **176–177**
    nit comb 34, **34**
    pyramids 56–57, **56–57**, 177, **177**, 277, **277**
Andes Mountains, South America 72, **72**, 79, **79**
Anemones 26–27, **26–27**
Angry Birds 183, **183**
Animals, weirdest 24–27, **24–27**
Antarctic blue whales 253, **253**
Antarctic icefish 253, **253**
Antarctic sun sea stars 252, **252**
Antarctica 244–263
Antelopes 28, **28**, 172, **172**, 190, **190**
Ants 60, **60**, 146
Arabs, ancient 15
Archibald, Bruce 60
Architecture *see* Buildings
Area 51, Nevada, U.S.A. 21
Argentina 75, **75**, 77, **77**, 84, **84**, 85, **85**, 88, **88**, 93, **93**
Armadillos 77, **77**
Art
    ancient Aboriginal 239
    camouflage paintings 205, **205**
    from coffee grounds 152, **152**
    corn mural 45, **45**
    "Desert Breath" (land art) 172, **172**
    displayed upside-down 34, **34**
    Doodle House 30, **30–31**
    elephant street art 156, **156**
    extreme art, Europe 118–119, **118–119**

    from junk 38, **38**, 44, **44**, 59, **59**
    museum 52, **52**
    Pigcasso 157, **157**
    in subways 130, **130**
    video fountain 66, **66**
    see also Sculpture
Ásbyrgi Canyon, Iceland 112, **112**
Asia 180–215
Asteroids 147, 266, **266**
Astrobees (space robots) 284, **284**
Astronaut cow sculpture 39, **39**
Astronauts 198, **198**, 251, 281, 285, 288, 289, **289**
Atacama Desert, Chile 75, **75**, 86–87, **86–87**
El Ateneo Grand Splendid, Argentina 93, **93**
Athens, Greece 131, **131**
ATM, highest-altitude 202, **202**
Atocha Station tropical garden, Spain 108, **108**, 130, **130**
Austin, Texas, U.S.A. 44, **44**, 59, **59**
Australia 216–243
    "Big Things" sculptures 216, **216**, 226–227, **226–227**, 231, **231**
    birds 237, **237**
    Bungle Bungle Range 238–239, **238–239**
    Great Barrier Reef 222–223, **222–223**
    Horizontal Falls 219, **219**
    kangaroos 229, **229**, 237, **237**
    oddities 240–241, **240–241**
    peacock spiders 236, **236**
    rugby 18, **18**
    Sphinx Hotel 235, **235**
    Squeaky Beach 219
    swimming with crocodiles 16, **16**
    turtles 241, **241**
    Wave Rock 241, **241**
Austria 113, **113**, 114, **114**, 134, **134**

B

Back, Charles, II 158
Bahamas, the 62, **62**, 276, **276**, 277, **277**
Baikal, Lake, Russia 206, **206**
Bald cypress trees 50, **50–51**
Baldaccini, César 122
Balloons 19, **19**
Baltimore, Maryland, U.S.A. 52, **52**
Banana sculpture 227, **227**, 231, **231**
Banpo Bridge, South Korea 195, **195**
Basket-shaped building 63, **63**
Basket stars 259, **259**
Bastille Day 20, **20**
Batfish 35
Beaches
    Antarctica 256, **256**
    Insano waterslide, Brazil 83, **83**
    pink sand, Bahamas 62, **62**
    Squeaky Beach, Australia 219
    Star Sand Beach, Japan 198, **198**
    tides 183
Beards 251
Bees 90, **90**
Beetles 184, **184**
Belgium 110, **110**, 123, **123**, 126, **126**
Belize 274–275, **274–275**
Bench sculpture 227, **227**, 231, **231**
Berber people 159
Bhupathy's purple frogs 190, **190**

Big Rush Big Swing 153, **153**
"Big Things" sculptures, Australia 226–227, **226–227**, 231, **231**
Bikes and biking 123, **123**, 260, **260**
Bioluminescence 279, **279**
Birds
    birds of paradise 233, **233**
    blue-footed boobies 25, **25**
    chickens 54, **54**
    comb-crested jacanas 237, **237**
    Eurasian hoopoes 113, **113**
    flamingos 175
    kākāpōs 236, **236**
    magnificent frigatebirds 95, **95**
    moth shaped like bird poop 48, **48**
    penguins 18, **18**, 87, **87**, 248, **248–249**, 254, **254**, 256
    sarus crane attacking antelope 28, **28**
    snowy sheathbills 259, **259**
    sociable weavers 156, **156**
    South America 75, **75**, 95, **95**, 104–105, **104–105**
    vampire finches 75, **75**
Bird's Nest Restaurant, Thailand 210, **210**
Birthday Tapestry (galaxy) 286, **286**
Birthdays 34, **34**
Black holes 290
Black rain frogs 150, **150**
Blom, Piet 115
Blood moon 283, **283**
Blowholes 233, **233**
Blue-footed boobies 25, **25**
Blue whales 253, **253**
Boats 117, **117**, 270, **270**, 272, **272**, 273, **273**
BOB (Breathing Observation Bubble) 272, **272**
"Bodies in Urban Spaces" (sculpture) 114, **114**
Bogoria, Lake, Kenya 175, **175**
Boiling River, Peru 74
Boiling lake 175, **175**
Bolivia
    Cuyaba dwarf frogs 78, **78**
    Laguna Verde 103, **103**
    languages 75
    New Andean architecture 100, **100**
    road safety 89, **89**
    screaming hairy armadillos 77, **77**
    snail-shaped villas 73, **73**, 83, **83**, 93, **93**
Bollywood 55, **55**
Boobies (birds) 25, **25**
Bookstores 84, **84**, 93, **93**
Borda, Adrian 29
Boryeong Mud Festival, South Korea 201, **201**, 209, **209**
Bossaball 117, **117**
Bouis, Sasha and Tara 40
Bourgnon, Yvan 273
Brazil
    Amazon Tall Tower Observatory 101, **101**
    colorful staircase 102, **102**
    Cuyaba dwarf frogs 78, **78**
    globe-shaped house 78, **78**
    Hotel Unique, São Paulo 82, **82**, 93, **93**
    Insano waterslide 83, **83**
    Lençóis Maranhenses National Park 76, **76**
    mata mata turtles 79, **79**
    Museu do Amanhã (Museum of Tomorrow) 100, **100**
    termites 91, **91**

Brazilian treehopper 25
Breathing Observation Bubble (BOB) 272, **272**
Bridges 89, **89**, 111, **111**, 194–195, **194–195**
British Columbia, Canada 60, **60**, 62, **62**, 66, **66**
British Virgin Islands 276, **276**
Bromeliads 98, **98**
Bryce Canyon, Utah, U.S.A. 68, **68**
Bubble Nebula 264, **264**, 286, **286**
Buenos Aires, Argentina 84, **84**, 85, **85**
Bugs *see* Insects
Buildings
    Africa 158–159, **158–159**
    Asia 187, **187**, 199, **199**, 202–203, **202–203**
    Australia & Oceania 234–235, **234–235**
    basket-shaped 63, **63**
    "Boulder House" 141, **141**
    cat-shaped 126, **126**
    colorful 187, **187**
    cube houses 115, **115**
    dog-shaped 63, **63**
    doll-shaped 202, **202**
    Europe 140–141, **140–141**
    globe-shaped 78, **78**
    horse-shaped 126, **126**
    North America 44–45, **44–45**
    pyramids 56–57, **56–57**, 177, **177**, 277, **277**
    shark diving into roof 141, **141**
    snail-shaped 73, **73**, 83, **83**, 93, **93**
    snake-shaped 67, **67**
    South America 73, **73**, 78, **78**, 83, **83**, 92–93, **92–93**,
        100–101, **100–101**
    surrealist palace 140, **140**
    teapot-shaped 203, **203**
    tree houses 234, **234**
Bun Festival, Hong Kong 208, **208**
Bungle Bungle Range, Australia 238–239, **238–239**
Bunny harvestmen 91, **91**
Bushbuck 172
Butterflies 37, **37**, 43, **43**, 90, **90**, 146, **146**

C

Cable cars 88, **88**
Caddo Lake, Texas and Louisiana, U.S.A. 50, **50–51**
Caesar, Julius 159
Calatrava, Santiago 100
Calendars 14–15, **14–15**, 18, 173, **173**, 177, **177**, 220
California, U.S.A.
    Death Valley 36, **36**, 64–65, **64–65**
    Echo Park Time Travel Mart 41, **41**, 59, **59**
    Google's offices 38, **38**
    Hollywood 54–55, **54–55**
    snail-shaped car 67, **67**
    Snoopy drone 34, **34**
    Wall of Frogs 48, **48**
Camel Museum, Dubai, U.A.E. 213, **213**
Camels 175, **175**, 213
Cameron, James 55
Camouflage
    glasswing butterflies 90, **90**
    leaf-mimic katydids 91, **91**
    leafy sea dragons 279, **279**
    mata mata turtles 79, **79**
    Matschie's tree kangaroos 237, **237**
    moths 48, **48**
    paintings 205, **205**
    Sally Lightfoot crabs 94, **94**

    sand cats 185, **185**
Canada 43, **43**, 49, **49**, 60, **60**, 62, **62**, 66, **66**
Canada lynx 49, **49**
Canadian Space Agency 284
Candy *see* Chocolate
Caño Cristales, Colombia 77, **77**
Capitol Records Tower, California, U.S.A. 54
Careers 58–59, **58–59**
Carnivals 124, **124**
Cars 67, **67**, 88, **88**, 148, **148**
Carter, Garnet 63
Casa Bola, Brazil 78, **78**
Casa do Penedo, Portugal 141, **141**
Casa Terracota, Colombia 93, **93**, 101, **101**
Cat-shaped kindergarten 126, **126**
Caterpillar, restaurant shaped like 44, **44**
Cathedral of Junk, Austin, Texas, U.S.A. 44, **44**, 59, **59**
Cats, stray 182, **182**
Cats, wild 49, **49**, 185, **185**
Caves 17, **17**, 67, **67**, 96–97, **96–97**, 171
Cellos 29, **29**
Cerro Negro, Nicaragua 46, **46**
Chad 175, **175**
Challenger Deep 270, **270**
Chandipur Beach, India 183
Charaxes candiope butterflies 146, **146**
Cheese 15, **15**, 33, **33**, 124, **124**
Cheung Chau, Hong Kong 208, **208**
Cheval, Ferdinand 140
Chewing gum sculptures 119, **119**
Chicago, Illinois, U.S.A. 66, **66**
Chichén Itzá, Mexico 56–57, **56–57**
Chickens 54, **54**
Chile 75, **75**, 86–87, **86–87**, 96–97, **96–97**, 98, **98**
Chimney Rock, Nebraska, U.S.A. 38, **38**
China
    ancient figurine 183, **183**
    China Watermelon Museum 212, **212**
    doll-shaped building 202, **202**
    Enterprise building 199, **199**
    fireworks 209, **209**
    fossils 35, **35**
    Great Wall 188–189, **188–189**
    Lotus Building 203, **203**
    Lucky Knot Bridge 194, **194**
    Meitan Tea Museum 203, **203**
    Plank Walk hiking trail 196–197, **196–197**, 197, 200, **200**
    robot restaurant 211, **211**
    star-shaped islands 199, **199**
Chocolate 35, **35**, 251, **251**
Christmas Island 224–225, **224–225**
Cities, underwater 176, **176**
Clarke, Lewis 251, **251**
Cleopatra 159
Cleveland, Ohio, U.S.A. 29, **29**
Coconuts 233, **233**
Cocos Islands, Indian Ocean 35, **35**
Cody, Wyoming, U.S.A. 45, **45**
Coffee-grounds art 152, **152**
Colombia
    cable car 88, **88**
    Caño Cristales 77, **77**
    ceramic house 93, **93**
    clay house 101, **101**
    golden poison frogs 103, **103**
    plants 99, **99**

Colonia Tovar, Venezuela 76, **76**
"Coloso" tower, Argentina 85, **85**
Colossal squid 218
Comb-crested jacanas 237, **237**
Comb jellies 10, **10**
Conger eels 35, **35**
Congo, Democratic Republic of the 148, **148**, 162, **162**
Conklin, Frances 63
Coral islands 220, **220**, 221, **221**
Coral reefs 222–223, **222–223**
Corn Palace, Mitchell, South Dakota, U.S.A. 45, **45**
Costa Rica 44, **44**, 46, **46**, 99, **99**
Cow sculpture 39, **39**
Cox, Sam 30, **31**
Crab Nebula 286, **286**
Crabs 26–27, **26–27**, 94, **94**, 191, **191**, 224–225,
    224–225, 258, **258**
Crake, Paul 21
Crane hotel 137, **137**
Cranes (birds) 28, **28**
Craters of the Moon National Monument and
    Preserve, Idaho, U.S.A. 47, **47**
Crocodiles 16, **16**, 175
Crown Fountain, Chicago, Illinois, U.S.A. 66, **66**
Crystal River, Florida, U.S.A. 49, **49**
Cube houses 115, **115**
Cuyaba dwarf frogs 78, **78**
Cyphonia clavata 25
Czechia (Czech Republic) 120, **120**

D

Da Shuhua (fireworks) 209, **209**
Daddy longlegs 91, **91**
Darwin, Charles 95
Death Valley, California-Nevada, U.S.A. 36, **36**, 64–65,
    64–65
Deception Island, Antarctica 244, **244**, 256, **256**
Deep Dive Dubai, U.A.E. 207, **207**
Democratic Republic of the Congo 148, **148**, 162, **162**
"Desert Breath" (land art) 172, **172**
Dextre (space robot) 284, **284**
Dieffenbach, Otto 34
Diggerland theme park, England 139, **139**
"Dinner in the Sky" restaurant, Belgium 110, **110**

INDEX

Dinosaur Day 14, **14**
Dinosaurs 35, **35**, 38, **38**, 54, 61, **61**, 75, **75**
Diving and snorkeling
    Antarctica 248
    deepest 270, **270**
    Dubai pool 207, **207**
    Great Blue Hole, Belize 274
    Krupaj Spring, Serbia 112, **112**
    Micronesia 221, **221**
    oil-rig hotel 183, **183**
    underwater art 276, **276**
    underwater greenhouses 265, **265**, 271, **271**
    underwater pyramid 277, **277**
DNA 18, **18**
Dogs 22, **22**, 63, **63**, 250, **250**
Doll-shaped building 202, **202**
Dolomites, Italy 136, **136**
Dolphins 37, 104, 191, **191**, 258, **258**
Dominica 10, **10**
Doodle House, Kent, England 30, **30–31**
Dorner, Willi 114
Dorylus ants 60
Dragon Bridge, Vietnam 194, **194**
Dragonfish 35
Dragons 123, **123**, 188, 189, **189**
Dreaming 33, **33**
Drones 34, 189
Dubai, U.A.E. 207, **207**, 213, **213**
Ducks, rubber 127, **127**
"Ducks" (buildings shaped like objects) 126
Düsseldorf, Germany 34, **34**
Dwarf stars 287, **287**

E

Eagles 104, **104**
Earth 11, **11**, 14, **14**
Easter Island 232, **232**
Echo Park Time Travel Mart, Los Angeles, California, U.S.A. 41, **41**, 59, **59**
Eclipses, lunar 283, **283**
Ecuador 25, 79, **79**, 99, **99**

Eels 35, **35**
Egypt
    "Desert Breath" (land art) 172, **172**
    Heracleion 176, **176**
    King Tut 168–169, **168–169**
    Library of Alexandria 159, **159**
    Nabta Playa 173, **173**
    Nile River 145, **145**, 167, **167**
    White Desert 162, **162**
Einstein, Albert 287
Einstein rings 287, **287**
El Alto, Bolivia 100, **100**
El Ateneo Grand Splendid, Argentina 93, **93**
El Jefe geyser 75, **75**
Elands 172
Elephant shrews 151, **151**
Elephants 37, 122, **122**, 156, **156**
Elwood, Conrad Talmadge 53
Ememem (artist) 119
Emeralds, largest uncut 152, **152**
Empire State Building, New York, U.S.A. 21, **21**, 223
Endurance (ship) 261, **261**
Energy, solar 144, **144**, 154, **154**, 202, **202**
England
    Alton Towers theme park 129, 139, **139**
    Diggerland theme park 139, **139**
    Doodle House, Kent 30, **30–31**
    festivals 124, **124**
    Rollercoaster Restaurant 139, **139**
    rubber ducks 127, **127**
    shark statue in roof 141, **141**
    Tout Quarry Sculpture Park 118, **118**
Equal Playing Field 153
Erebus, Mount, Antarctica 256, **256**
Erie, Lake 29, **29**
Erie Dinosaur Park, Kansas, U.S.A. 38, **38**
Escadaria Selarón, Brazil 102, **102**
Eshima Ohashi Bridge, Japan 195, **195**
Estonia 114, **114**, 134, **134**
E.T. sponges 269, **269**
Etna, Mount, Italy 109, **109**, 135, **135**, 137, **137**
Eurasian hoopoes 113, **113**
Europe 108–143
European Space Agency 251
Everest, Mount, China-Nepal 11, **11**
Exoplanets 291
Extraterrestrials 14, **14**, 21, **21**
Extreme ironing 116, **116**
Eye of the Sahara, Mauritania 173, **173**

F

Fairview Goat Tower, South Africa 158, **158**
Fairy circles 165, **165**, 172, **172**
Falko One (street artist) 156
Faralda Crane Hotel, Netherlands 137, **137**
Ferlini, Giuseppe 177
Festivals
    2025 calendar 14–15, **14–15**
    Asia 184, **184**, 185, **185**, 208–209, **208–209**

Bastille Day 20, **20**
Europe 117, **117**, 118, **118**, 124–125, **124–125**, 136, **136**
World Penguin Day 18, **18**
Finches 75, **75**
Finland 119, **119**, 120, **120**
Fireflies 184, **184**
Fireworks 209, **209**
Fish
    Antarctic icefish 253, **253**
    creepy 35, **35**
    Great Barrier Reef, Australia 222, **222**, 223, **223**
    hagfish 278, **278**
    rays 222, **222**, 278, **278**
    sharks 10, **10**, 25, **25**, 141, **141**, 222, **267**, 279, **279**
    Trapping Zone, Maldives 267, **267**
    weirdest photo (jawfish) 29, **29**
    wolffish 76, **76**
Fishing 210, **210**
Flag colors 10, **10**
Flamingos 175
Flatwoods Monster Museum, Sutton, West Virginia, U.S.A. 53, **53**
Florence, Italy 116, **116**
Florida, U.S.A. 49, **49**, 63, **63**, 273, **273**
Flowers
    Netherlands 132–133, **132–133**
    sculptures 118, **118**
    Singapore 192–193, **192–193**
    South America 72, **72**, 87, **87**, 98, **98**
Fly Geyser, Nevada, U.S.A. 69, **69**
Fog 174, **174**
Fontanella, Dario 135
Food
    buffet for monkeys 185, **185**
    bugs as 53
    Bun Festival, Hong Kong 208, **208**
    celebrations 15, **15**
    cheese 15, **15**, 33, **33**
    cheese rolling 124, **124**
    chocolate 35, **35**, 251, **251**
    coconuts 233, **233**
    coffee-grounds art 152, **152**
    Corn Palace, Mitchell, South Dakota, U.S.A. 45, **45**
    fried air 136
    "hairy food" 240, **240**
    ice cream 15, **15**, 135, **135**
    mango sculpture 226, **226**
    new flavors and experiences 129, **129**
    pizza 40, **40**, 52, **52**, 59, **59**, 68, **68**
    in space 289, **289**
    sticky rice 188, **188**
    Waiters and Waitresses Race 20, **20**
    Watermelon Museum, China 212, **212**
    see also Restaurants
Foodom (restaurant), China 211, **211**
Forest of Knives, Madagascar 165, **165**, 170, **170**
Forests 40, **40**
Fossils 35, **35**, 60–61, **60–61**, 111, **111**
Fountains 66, **66**
France 118, **118**, 119, **119**, 122, **122**, 129, 138, **138**, 140, **140**
Fried air 136, **136**
Fried egg jellyfish 268, **268**
Frigatebirds 95, **95**
Frogs
    Bhupathy's purple frogs 190, **190**

black rain frogs 150, **150**
Cuyaba dwarf frogs 78, **78**
golden poison frogs 103, **103**
smelliest 74
Wall of Frogs 48, **48**
Fumaroles 257, **257**

G

Gabr, Ahmed 270, **270**
Gagarin, Yuri 198, **198**
Galápagos Islands 75, **75**, 94–95, **94–95**
Galápagos tortoises 95, **95**
Galaxies 286, **286**
Gamberini, Sergio 271
Gamburtsev Mountains, Antarctica 247, **247**
García Mansilla, Mario David 68, **68**
Gardens 63, **63**, 108, **108**, 130, **130**, 159, **159**, 192–193, **192–193**
Gazelles 150, **150**
Gedi ruins, Kenya 176, **176**
General Carrera Lake, Chile 96–97, **96–97**
Georgia, U.S.A. 63, **63**
Gerenuk 150, **150**
Germany
    cat-shaped kindergarten 126, **126**
    Kernie's Family Park 129, **129**, 138, **138**
    "Magdeburg Unicorn" 111, **111**
    pumpkin festival 117, **117**
    spaghetti-shaped ice cream 129, **129**, 135, **135**
    upside-down art 34, **34**
Geysers 69, **69**, 75, **75**
Ghana 158, **158**
Giant Antarctic octopuses 245, **245**, 252, **252**
Giant ants 60, **60**
Glass sponges 269, **269**
Glasswing butterflies 90, **90**
Gnomes 63, **63**
Gnomesville, Australia 240, **240**
Go-kart tours 17, **17**
Goblin sharks 10, **10**
Golden Mean (snail-shaped car) 67, **67**
Golden poison frogs 103, **103**
Google's offices 38, **38**
Gorilla costume 282, **282**
Le Grand Éléphant, France 122, **122**
Great Barrier Reef, Australia 222–223, **222–223**
Great Blue Hole, Belize 274–275, **274–275**
Great Wall of China 188–189, **188–189**
Greece, ancient 15, 131, **131**
Greek mythology 277
Green Lake, Austria 113, **113**
Greenhouses, underwater 265, **265**, 271, **271**
Greenland sharks 25, **25**
Ground pangolins 151, **151**
Guatemala 68, **68**
Guelta d'Archei, Chad 175, **175**
Guitar sculpture 227, **227**, 231, **231**

H

Hagfish 278, **278**
Hair Museum, Türkiye (Turkey) 212, **212**
Hairdos 240, **240**
Halitrephes jellyfish 268, **268**
Hannemann, Vince 44
Harpy eagles 104, **104**

Hasselhoff, David 258
Hawaii, U.S.A. 217, **217**, 221, **221**, 228, **228**, 272, **272**
Headington Shark, England 141, **141**
Heidrich, Erich 138
Heine, Johan 177
Heracleion 176, **176**
Herschel, William 286
Hierve el Agua, Mexico 42, **42**
Highlining 136, **136**
Hiking trail, most dangerous **196–197**, 197, 200, **200**
Hippopotamuses 174, **174**
Historical reenactments 138, **138**
Hitotsuyama, Chie 184, 201
Hoberman, Chuck 114
Hoberman spheres 114, **114**
Hoff crabs 258, **258**
Hoffberger, Rebecca Alban 52
Hogawood, Japan 55
Holidays *see* Festivals
Hollywood, California, U.S.A. 54–55, **54–55**
Hong Kong 208, **208**
Hoodoos 68, **68**
Hoopoes 113, **113**
Horizontal Falls, Australia 219, **219**
Horses 20, **20**
Hostal Las Olas, Bolivia 83, **83**, 93, **93**
Hot-air balloons 19, **19**
Hot lips plants 99, **99**
Hot springs 175, **175**, 256, **256**
Hotels
    crane hotel 137, **137**
    dog-shaped 63, **63**
    grain silos 234, **234**
    horse-shaped 126, **126**
    ice-bound ship 121, **121**
    igloo hotel 120, **120**
    mountainside pods 82, **82**
    oil rig 183, **183**
    ship-shaped 82, **82**, 93, **93**
    shipwreck lodge 148, **148**
    Sphinx Hotel, Australia 235, **235**
    tree house hotel 62, **62**
    with TV transmitter 120, **120**
    winged 159, **159**
House of Taga, Northern Mariana Islands 235, **235**
Houston, Texas, U.S.A. 39, **39**
Houtong, Taiwan 182, **182**
Howland Island 220, **220**
Hubáček, Karel 120
Hubble Space Telescope 286, 287
Hulík, Viktor 119
Humans, as sculpture 114, **114**, 118, **118**
Humboldt penguins 87, **87**
Hummingbirds 60, 104, **104**
Hungary 111, **111**, 124, **124**
Hydrothermal vents 258

I

Ibex 137, **137**
Ice
    Antarctica 247, 248, **248–249**, 255, 257, **257**
    ice road 134, **134**
    lighthouse covered in 29, **29**
    mummified iceman 134, **134**
    sculptures 208

ship frozen in 121, **121**
    "snow monsters" 182, **182**
Ice cream 15, **15**, 52, 129, **129**, 135, **135**
Icefish 253, **253**
Iceland 112, **112**
Idaho, U.S.A. 47, **47**, 63, **63**
Igloo hotel 120, **120**
Iguanas 94, **94**
Illinois, U.S.A. 66, **66**
Imperial measurements 11
Inca terns 104, **104**
India
    ancient board game 19, **19**
    Bhupathy's purple frogs 190, **190**
    Bollywood 55, **55**
    Pink Palace 187, **187**
    Sulabh International Museum of Toilets 213, **213**
    Taj Mahal 181, **181**, 204, **204**
    tides 183
Indian Ocean 35, **35**
Indonesia 186, **186**, 187, **187**, 234, **234**, 269, **269**
Ingenuity (Mars helicopter) 289, **289**
Insects
    ants 146
    beetles 184, **184**
    butterflies 37, **37**, 43, **43**, 90, **90**, 146, **146**
    fireflies 184, **184**
    as food 53
    fossils 60, **60**
    moths 48, **48**, 186, **186**
    restaurant shaped like 44, **44**
    South America 73, **73**, 90–91, **90–91**
    termites 91, **91**, 151
    treehoppers 25, **25**
International Highline Meeting Festival, Italy 136, **136**
International Space Station (ISS) 280–282, **280–282**, 284, **284**, 285, **285**, 288
Ironing, extreme 116, **116**
Irrawaddy dolphins 191, **191**
Islands 10, 39, 59, **59**, 199, **199**, 220–221, **220–221**
Israel, ancient 34, **34**
Italy
    chewing gum sculptures 119, **119**
    fried air 136, **136**
    highlining 136, **136**
    historic soccer 116, **116**
    ibex 137, **137**
    mummified iceman 134, **134**
    underwater greenhouses 271, **271**
    volcano 109, **109**, 135, **135**

J

Jacanas 237, **237**
James Webb Space Telescope 287
Jamsu Bridge, South Korea 195, **195**
Japan
    China conflicts 189
    Eshima Ohashi Bridge 195, **195**
    film industry 55
    go-kart tours 17, **17**
    paper animal sculptures 184, **184**, 201, **201**
    Sapporo Snow Festival 208, **208**
    see-through bathroom stalls 202, **202**
    "snow monsters" 182, **182**
    space robot 285, **285**

INDEX

Star Sand Beach 198, **198**
underwater pyramid 277, **277**
wildlife 191, **191**
World War II 221
Zauo Fishing Restaurant 210, **210**
Japanese spider crabs 191, **191**
Jardin Majorelle, Morocco 159, **159**
Jawfish 29, **29**
El Jefe geyser 75, **75**
Jellyfish 10, **10**, 268, **268**, 278
Jobs 58–59, **58–59**
Johnston Atoll 269, **269**
Joseso (car) 88, **88**
Junk, sculptures made from 38, **38**, 44, **44**, 59, **59**
Jupiter (planet) 290, **290**, 291, **291**
Jurassic Valley, Hawaii, U.S.A. 228, **228**

K

Kākāpōs 236, **236**
Kampung, Indonesia 187, **187**
Kangaroos 229, **229**, 237, **237**
Kansas, U.S.A. 38, **38**
Katydids 91, **91**
Kawah Ijen volcano, Indonesia 186, **186**
Kazakhstan 190, 203, **203**
Kelly, Paul 226
Kelly, Scott 282, **282**
Kente weaving patterns 158, **158**
Kenya 166, **166**, 175, **175**, 176, **176**
Kernie's Family Park, Germany 129, **129**, 138, **138**
Key West, Florida, U.S.A. 273, **273**
Khan Shatyr Entertainment Center, Kazakhstan 203, **203**
Kilimanjaro, Mount, Tanzania 153, **153**
Kindergarten Wolfartsweier, Germany 126, **126**
Kinetic Sculpture Race 52, **52**
Kirobo (space robot) 285, **285**
Kitefin sharks 279, **279**
Koons, Jeff 118
Korowai tribe 234
Körükçü, Galip 212
Kraken sculpture 276, **276**
Krill 248, 253, 259, **259**
Krupaj Spring, Serbia 112, **112**
Kyrgyzstan 198, **198**

L

La Amistad International Park, Costa Rica 44, **44**
La Paz, Bolivia 89, **89**
Labasin Waterfall Restaurant, Philippines 211, **211**
Lachish Ruins, Israel 34, **34**
Laguna Garzón Bridge, Uruguay 89, **89**
Laguna Verde, Bolivia 103, **103**
Lakes
    boiling 175, **175**
    green 103, **103**, 113, **113**
    under ice 246, **246**
    ice-covered lighthouse 29, **29**
    lava 162, **162**
    marble caves 96–97, **96–97**
    record-breaking 206, **206**
    spooky 50, **50–51**
    underwater park 113, **113**
Languages 75
"Larry the Lobster" sculpture 226, **226**

Lava lakes 162, **162**
Le Grand Éléphant, France 122, **122**
Leaf-mimic katydids 91, **91**
Leafhoppers 73, **73**, 91, **91**
Leafy sea dragons 279, **279**
Lego lion 111, **111**
Leijerstam, Maria 260
Lençóis Maranhenses National Park, Brazil 76, **76**
Leopard seals 248, 258, **258**
Liberia 11
Libraries 159, **159**
Lighthouse, ice-covered 29, **29**
Lightning bugs (fireflies) 184, **184**
Lightsabers 288, **288**
Lindsey, Lori 153
Lion sculptures 111, **111**
Liu Bolin 205, **205**
Liu Dejian 199
Lizards 94, **94**, 127, **127**
Llanwrtyd Wells, Wales 20, **20**
Llechwedd Slate Caverns, Wales 17, **17**
Lobb, Huw 20
"Lobster loos" restrooms, New Zealand 219, **219**
Lobster sculpture 226, **226**
Long-wattled umbrellabirds 105, **105**
Longaberger Company 63, **63**
Longo, Eduardo 78
Longo, Luca 78
Lotus Building, China 203, **203**
Louisiana, U.S.A. 50, **50–51**
Lucky Knot Bridge, China 194, **194**
Ludwigsburg Pumpkin Festival, Germany 117, **117**
Lujiatun, China 35, **35**
Lunar eclipses 283, **283**

M

Macaques 185, **185**
Macaroni penguins 254, **254**
Macaws 105, **105**
Macrobat (aircraft) 149, **149**
Madagascar 165, **165**, 170, **170**
Magnetized sand dunes 147
Magnificent frigatebirds 95, **95**
Maimela, Percy 152
Majorelle, Jacques 159
Malaysia 183, **183**
Maldives 267
Malta 139, **139**
Mamani, Freddy 100
Mammals, prehistoric 35, **35**
Man v. Horse challenge 20, **20**
Manatees 37, **37**, 49, **49**
Mango sculpture 226, **226**
Manta (sailboat) 273, **273**
Maps
    Africa 146–147
    Antarctica 246–247
    Asia 182–183
    Australia & Oceania 218–219
    Europe 110–111
    North America 38–39
    oceans 266–267
    South America 74–75
    world 10–11
Maras, Peru 80–81, **80–81**
Marathon des Sables (Sand Marathon) 22–23, **22–23**

Marble berries 173, **173**
Marble caves, Chile 96–97, **96–97**
Mariana Trench 269, 270, **270**
Marine iguanas 94, **94**
Mars (planet) 283, 289, **289**, 291, **291**
Mary River turtles 241, **241**
Maryland, U.S.A. 52, **52**
Massachusetts, U.S.A. 61, **61**
Mata mata turtles 79, **79**
Mate, Kyrsten 67
Matryoshka (nesting dolls) 202, **202**
Matschie's tree kangaroos 237, **237**
Mauritania 173, **173**
Maya 56–57, **56–57**
Mayr, Andrea 21
Measurement systems 11
Mechanical animals 122, **122**
Meitan Tea Museum, China 203, **203**
Mendoza Morales, Octavio 101
Mercury (planet) 290, **290**
Mermaids 49, **49**, 63, **63**, 276, **276**
Mermaid's wineglass alga 267, **267**
Meteorites 256, **256**
Meteors 173
Mexico
    Auditorio "El Metro" Station, Mexico City 41, **41**
    Chichén Itzá 56–57, **56–57**
    colorful houses 39, **39**
    Hierve el Agua 42, **42**
    monarch butterflies 43, **43**
    Munk's devil rays 278, **278**
    snake-shaped building 67, **67**
Meyer-Büser, Susanne 34
Microcars 88, **88**
Microlights 149, **149**
Micronekton 267
Micronesia 221, **221**
Migrations 43, **43**, 166, **166**
Mimosas (plants) 99, **99**
Mini-Trac (snow vehicle) 260
Modise, Portia 153
Moldy cheese 15, **15**
Monarch butterflies 43, **43**
Mondrian, Piet 34
Monkeys 14, **14**, 185, **185**
Montana, U.S.A. 61, **61**
Montaña Suiza roller coaster, Spain 138, **138**
Moon 283, **283**
Moons, Jupiter 290, **290**
Mopion Island 39, 59, **59**
Morocco 144, **144**, 154, **154**, 159, **159**, 174, **174**
Morse Code 14, 54
Moss Lady sculpture, Victoria, Canada 66, **66**
Moths 48, **48**, 186, **186**
Mountain goats 137, **137**
Mountains of Kong 146
Movies 54–55, **54–55**, 139, 159, 227, 228, 288, **288**
Mr. Doodle 30, **31**
Mud Festival 201, **201**, 209, **209**
Muju Firefly Festival 184, **184**
Mumtaz Mahal, Empress (India) 204
Munk's devil rays 278, **278**
Museums
    American Visionary Art Museum, Baltimore, Maryland, U.S.A. 52, **52**
    Camel Museum, Dubai, U.A.E. 213, **213**

China Watermelon Museum 212, **212**
Flatwoods Monster Museum, Sutton, West Virginia, U.S.A. 53, **53**
fossil discoveries 60
Hair Museum, Türkiye (Turkey) 212, **212**
Les Machines de l'Île, France 122, **122**
Meitan Tea Museum, China 203, **203**
Le Musée Berbère, Morocco 159, **159**
Museu do Amanhã (Museum of Tomorrow), Brazil 100, **100**
Museum of Pizza Culture, Philadelphia, Pennsylvania, U.S.A. 52, **52**, 59, **59**
Peculiarium, Portland, Oregon, U.S.A. 53, **53**
Te Papa museum, New Zealand 218
Music 29, **29**, 276, **276**
Myanmar 11
Mythology 112, 277

N

Nabta Playa, Egypt 173, **173**
Namib Desert 160–161, **160–161**, 165, **165**
Namib-Naukluft National Park, Namibia 160–161, **160–161**, 165, **165**
Namib Sand Sea coastal desert 147, **147**
Namibia 148, **148**, 160–161, **160–161**, 165, **165**, 172, **172**
Nantes, France 122, **122**
NASA 266, 267, 284, 287, 289
National Creative Ice Cream Flavors Day 15, **15**
National Moldy Cheese Day 15, **15**
National Pet Rock Day 15, **15**
National Sock Monkey Day 14, **14**
National Wiggle Your Toes Day 15, **15**
Nebraska, U.S.A. 38, **38**
Nebulae 264, **264**, 286, **286**
Neptune (planet) 290, **290**
Netherlands 115, **115**, 118, **118**, 132–133, **132–133**, 137, **137**
Neutron stars 35, **35**, 286, **286**
Nevada, U.S.A. 21, **21**, 36, **36**, 64–65, **64–65**, 69, **69**
New Andean architecture 100, **100**
New Mexico, U.S.A. 14, **14**, 62, **62**
New York, U.S.A. 21, **21**
New Zealand
    Gisborne Airport 232, **232**
    hotels 234, **234**
    kākāpōs 236, **236**
    "lobster loos" restrooms 219, **219**
    steampunk 228, **228**
    Te Papa museum 218
    world's longest place-name 11
News, weird 34–35, **34–35**
Ngorongoro, Tanzania 147
Nicaragua 10, **10**, 46, **46**
Nile River, Africa 145, **145**, 167, **167**
Nilgai (antelope) 28, **28**
Nit comb 34, **34**
Niue 220, **220**
No Homework Day 14, **14**
Noorderlicht (ship) 121, **121**
Norse mythology 112
North America 36–71
Northern Mariana Islands 235, **235**
Norway 140, **140**
Nuanquan, China 209, **209**
Nuclear power stations 129, **129**, 138, **138**
Nudibranchs 278, **278**

Numbats 15, **15**
Numbers 18–19, **18–19**, 32–33, **32–33**

O

Oaxaca, Mexico 42, **42**
"Ocean Atlas" (sculpture) 277, **277**
Oceania 216–243
Oceans and seas 264–279
Octopuses 245, **245**, 252, **252**
O'Halloran, Mykey 240
Ohio, U.S.A. 63, **63**
Oil rigs 183, **183**
Oilbirds 105, **105**
Okinawa, Japan 17
Ol Doinyo Lengai Volcano, Tanzania 163, **163**, 165, **165**
Opabinia 60, **60**
Orcas 258, **258**
Orchid bees 90, **90**
Oregon, U.S.A. 40, **40**, 53, **53**, 69, **69**
Osaka, Japan 17
Ötzi (mummified iceman) 134, **134**
Ouarzazate Solar Power Station, Morocco 144, **144**, 154, **154**

P

Pacaya volcano, Guatemala 68, **68**
Pacific Ocean 69, **69**
Pakistan 202, **202**
Palmitas, Mexico 39, **39**
Pangolins 151, **151**
Paper animal sculptures 184, **184**, 201, **201**
Papua New Guinea 233, **233**, 237, **237**
Paraguay 77, **77**, 78, **78**
Parcheesi 19, **19**
Paris, France 20, 118, **118**
Parker Solar Probe 267, **267**
Parrotfish 223, **223**
Parrots 236, **236**
Patagonia region, Argentina-Chile 75, **75**
Patagonian cypress trees 98, **98**
Peacock spiders 236, **236**
Peanut-head bugs 90, **90**
Peculiarium, Portland, Oregon, U.S.A. 53, **53**
Penguins 18, **18**, 87, **87**, 248, **248–249**, 254, **254**, 256
Pennsylvania, U.S.A. 52, **52**, 59, **59**
Perihelion Day 14, **14**
Personality quiz 58–59, **58–59**
Peru 74, 79, **79**, 80–81, **80–81**, 82, **82**, 105, **105**
Pet rocks 15, **15**
Pharaohs 168–169, **168–169**
Philadelphia, Pennsylvania, U.S.A. 52, **52**, 59, **59**
Philippines 211, **211**
Phones 33, 266
Photos, weirdest 28–30, **28–31**
Picasso moths 186, **186**
Pigs 157, **157**, 183, **183**
Pineapple maze 217, **217**, 221, **221**
Pink Palace, India 187, **187**
Pink see-through fantasias 269, **269**

Pistol shrimp 279, **279**
Pizza 40, **40**, 52, **52**, 59, **59**, 68, **68**
Place-names, world's longest 11
"Planet Nine" 290
Planets 290–291, **290–291**
Plants
    bald cypress trees 50, **50–51**
    oldest tree 98, **98**
    pineapple maze 217, **217**, 221, **221**
    seed vault 140, **140**
    smiley face forest 40, **40**
    South America 72, **72**, 98–99, **98–99**
    tree houses 234, **234**
Plastic waste, in ocean 270, 273
Plensa, Jaume 66
Poisonous animals 78, **78**, 103, **103**
Pom-pom crabs 26–27, **26–27**
Ponies 19, **19**
Poop (dung) 48, **48**, 91, **91**, 105, 175, 189, 223
Popeye Village, Malta 139, **139**
Portland, Oregon, U.S.A. 53, **53**
Portugal 141, **141**
Postman Cheval's Ideal Palace, France 140, **140**
Pretend to Be a Time Traveler Day 15, **15**
Protostars 287, **287**
Psittacosaurus 35, **35**
Pumpkin paddling 117, **117**
Puteaux, France 122, **122**
Puy du Fou theme park, France 138, **138**
Puya raimondii 98, **98**
Pyramids 56–57, **56–57**, 177, **177**, 277, **277**

Q

Quesada, Francisco 44
Quiz, personality 58–59, **58–59**

R

Races, weirdest 20–23, **20–23**
Rain Vortex, Singapore 206, **206**
Rainbow Mountain, Peru 79, **79**
Rapa Nui 232, **232**
Rays 222, **222**, 278, **278**
Red Sea 270, **270**
Reilly, Jim 288
Renewable energy 144, **144**, 154, **154**, 202, **202**
Restaurants
    Deep Dive Dubai 207
    "Dinner in the Sky," Belgium 110, **110**
    extreme restaurants, Asia 210–211, **210–211**
    floating pizzeria 40, **40**

INDEX

The Rock (restaurant), Tanzania 163, **163**
Rollercoaster Restaurant, England 139, **139**
serving fried air 136, **136**
Rhinoceroses 184
Rice, as construction material 188, **188**
Richat Structure, Mauritania 173, **173**
Río Celeste, Costa Rica 46, **46**
Rio de Janeiro, Brazil 100, **100**, 102, **102**
Roads 89, **89**, 119, **119**, 134, **134**, 148, **148**
Robots 148, **148**, 211, **211**, 284–285, **284–285**
The Rock (restaurant), Tanzania 163, **163**
Rocking horse sculpture 226, **226**
Rocks and rock formations
Africa 162–163, **162–163**
"Boulder House" 141, **141**
Bungle Bungle Range, Australia 238–239, **238–239**
hoodoos 68, **68**
National Pet Rock Day 15, **15**
sailing stones 64–65, **64–65**
Wave Rock, Australia 241, **241**
Rodríguez, José María 88
"Roller Coaster Bridge," Japan 195, **195**
Roller coasters 138, **138**
Rollercoaster Restaurant, England 139, **139**
Ross Island, Antarctica 247, **247**
Roswell, New Mexico, U.S.A. 14, **14**
Rotterdam, Netherlands 115, **115**
Rugby 18, **18**
Russia 123, **123**, 206, **206**

S

Sahara, Africa 22–23, **22–23**, 173, **173**, 175, **175**
Saharan silver ants 146
Saigas 190, **190**
Sailing stones 64–65, **64–65**
Sally Lightfoot crabs 94, **94**
Salt pools 80–81, **80–81**
Saltwater crocodiles 16, **16**
Samoa 233, **233**
Sand, pink 62, **62**
Sand cats 185, **185**
Sand dunes 76, **76**, 77, 147, 160–161, **160–161**, 165, **165**, 185, **185**
Sand Marathon (Marathon des Sables) 22–23, **22–23**
Santa Barbara, California, U.S.A. 48, **48**
Santa Fe, New Mexico, U.S.A. 62, **62**
Sapporo Snow Festival, Japan 208, **208**
Sarriugarte, Jon 67
Sarus cranes 28, **28**
Saturn (planet) 291, **291**
Savini, Maurizio 119
Schools 14, **14**, 126, **126**
Schooner Wharf Minimal Regatta, Florida, U.S.A. 273, **273**
Scooters, underwater 272, **272**
Scorpions 53
Scotland 125, **125**
Screaming hairy armadillos 77, **77**
Sculpture
"Big Things," Australia 216, **216**, 226–227, **226–227**, 231, **231**
chewing gum sculptures 119, **119**
Europe 114, **114**, 118–119, **118–119**
fire-breathing dragon 123, **123**
Gagarin, Yuri 198, **198**
Headington Shark 141, **141**

humans as 114, **114**, 118, **118**
made from junk 38, **38**, 44, **44**, 59, **59**
man at work 119, **119**
Moss Lady 66, **66**
paper animal sculptures 184, **184**, 201, **201**
Sapporo Snow Festival, Japan 208, **208**
thumb sculpture 122, **122**, 129, **129**
underwater 276, **276**, 277, **277**
Sea cows *see* Manatees
Sea cucumbers 269, **269**
Sea lions 104
Sea slugs 278, **278**
Sea sponges 269, **269**
Sea stars 252, **252**, 259, **259**
Sea turtles 223, **223**
Seabreacher (watercraft) 272, **272**
SeaCleaners 273
Seals 37, 248, **248–249**, 258, **258**
Seed vault 140, **140**
Selarón, Jorge 102
Senosiain, Javier 67
Serbia 112, **112**
Shackleton, Ernest 261
Shah Jahan, Emperor (India) 204
Shapes 114–115, **114–115**
Sharks 10, **10**, 25, **25**, 141, **141**, 222, **267**, 279, **279**
Ship, frozen in ice 121, **121**
Shipwreck Lodge, Namibia 148, **148**
Shipwrecks 55, **55**, 148, 221, **221**, 223, **223**, 261, **261**
Shrimps 248, 279, **279**
Shuster, Will, Jr. 62
Shy plants 99, **99**
Siberia, Russia 206, **206**
SiloStay, New Zealand 234, **234**
Singapore 192–193, **192–193**, 206, **206**
Sinkholes 274–275, **274–275**
Skateboarding 19, **19**
Skeleton Coast, Namibia 148, **148**
Skiing 109, **109**, 129, **129**, 135, **135**
Skydiving 19, **19**
Skylodge Adventure Suites, Peru 82, **82**
Sled dogs 250, **250**
Sleep 32, **32**
Slime 278
Slovakia 119, **119**
Slowworms (lizards) 127, **127**
Smartphones 33, 266
Smiley face forest 40, **40**
Smith, Francis Lee 45
Snail-shaped car 67, **67**
Snail-shaped villas 73, **73**, 83, **83**, 93, **93**
Snakes 67, **67**, 185
Snoop Dogg 102
Snoopy (cartoon dog) 34, **34**
Snow 182, **182**, 208, **208**, 255, 260, **260**
Snowy sheathbills 259, **259**
Soccer 116, **116**, 153, **153**
Sociable weavers 156, **156**
Sock monkeys 14, **14**
Solar power 144, **144**, 154, **154**, 202, **202**
South Africa
ancient calendar 177, **177**
art 156–157, **156–157**
Big Rush Big Swing 153, **153**
black rain frogs 150, **150**
coffee-grounds art 152, **152**

Fairview Goat Tower 158, **158**
Macrobat (aircraft) 149, **149**
soccer players 153
springhares 150, **150**
Vredefort crater 147
South America 72–107
South Dakota, U.S.A. 45, **45**
South Korea 34, **34**, 195, **195**, 201, **201**, 209, **209**
South Pole 246, 250, 251, **251**, 260, **260**
Space 280–291
astronauts 198, **198**, 251, 281, 285, 288, 289, **289**
International Space Station (ISS) 280–282, **280–282**, 284, **284**, 285, **285**, 288
planets 290–291, **290–291**
quiz 292–293, **292–293**
robots 284–285, **284–285**
space walks 282, **282**
Space shuttles 288, 289
Spain
Atocha Station tropical garden, Madrid 108, **108**, 130, **130**
bossaball 117, **117**
festivals 124, 125, **125**
theme park 138, **138**
Sphinx Hotel, Australia 235, **235**
Spider crabs 191, **191**
Spiders 236, **236**
Spiral-horned antelopes 172, **172**
Sponges 269, **269**
Sports
rugby 18, **18**
skateboarding 19, **19**
skiing 109, **109**, 129, **129**, 135, **135**
soccer 116, **116**, 153, **153**
surfing 74, **74**
surreal 116–117, **116–117**
swimming 16, **16**, 207, **207**
thrilling 16–17, **16–17**
volcano boarding 46, **46**
weirdest races 20–23, **20–23**
Springhares 150, **150**
Squeaky Beach, Australia 219
Squid 218
Staircase, colorful 102, **102**
Star Sand Beach, Japan 198, **198**
Star-shaped islands 199, **199**
Star Trek (TV show) 199, **199**
Starfish 252, **252**, 259, **259**
Stars 86, 287, **287**
Statistics 18–19, **18–19**, 32–33, **32–33**
Steampunk 228, **228**
Sticky rice 188, **188**
Stockholm, Sweden 130, **130**
Stone circles 173, **173**, 177, **177**
Submersibles 270, **270**, 272, **272**
Subway stations 130, **130**
Sudan 177, **177**
Sulabh International Museum of Toilets, India 213, **213**
Sullivan, Dennis 63
Sun 14, **14**
Supernovae 286, **286**, 287, **287**
Supertrees **192–193**, 193
Supervolcanoes 47, **47**
Surfing 74, **74**
Surrealist palace 140, **140**

Sutton, West Virginia, U.S.A. 53, **53**
Svalbard Global Seed Vault, Norway 140, **140**
Sweden 10, **10**, 130, **130**
Swimming pools 207, **207**
Swimming with crocodiles 16, **16**
Swings 153, **153**
Switzerland 111
Sword-billed hummingbirds 104, **104**

T

Taiwan 182, **182**
Taj Mahal, India 181, **181**, 204, **204**
Tanzania 147, 153, **153**, 163, **163**, 165, **165**, 166, **166**
Tarsiers 24, **24**
Teapot, giant 203, **203**
Telescopes 86, **86**, 286, 287
Temperature extremes 248, 255, 290
Termites 91, **91**, 151
Terns 104, **104**
Texas, U.S.A. 39, **39**, 44, **44**, 50, **50–51**, 59, **59**
Thailand 185, **185**, 210, **210**
Theme parks 129, **129**, 138–139, **138–139**
Thor's Well, Oregon, U.S.A. 69, **69**
Thumb sculpture 122, **122**, 129, **129**
Tides 183
Tightropes 136, **136**
Time travel 15, **15**, 41, **41**, 59, **59**
Time zones 220
Tinian, Northern Mariana Islands 235, **235**
Toco toucans 104, **104**
Toilets 33, **33**, 202, **202**, 213, **213**, 219, **219**, 234
Tokyo, Japan 17, 202, **202**
Tombs 177, **177**
Tortoises 95, **95**
Toucans 104, **104**
Touch-me-not plants 99, **99**
Tout Quarry Sculpture Park, England 118, **118**
Toys and games 14, **14**, 19, **19**
Traffic robots 148, **148**
Traffic zebras 89, **89**
Trains 111, 232, **232**
Trampolining 17, **17**
Trapping Zone, Maldives 267
Tree house hotel, British Columbia, Canada 62, **62**
Tree kangaroos 237, **237**
Treehoppers 25, **25**
Trees 40, **40**, 50, **50–51**, 98, **98**, 234, **234**
Triceratops 61, **61**
Trojan Horse 126, **126**
Tsingy de Bemaraha National Park (Forest of Knives), Madagascar 170, **170**
Tunisia 159, **159**
Türkiye (Turkey) 212, **212**
Turtles 79, **79**, 95, **95**, 223, **223**, 241, **241**
Tutankhamun, King (Egypt) 168–169, **168–169**
Twenty-five 18–19, **18–19**
Tyrannosaurus rex 61, **61**

U

U2 (band) 102
UFOs 14, **14**, 53
Uganda 146, **146**
Underwater
    cities 176, **176**
    greenhouses 265, **265**, 271, **271**
    ironing 116, **116**
    park 113, **113**
    pyramid 277, **277**
    scooters 272, **272**
    sculpture 276, **276**, 277, **277**
    sinkholes 274–275, **274–275**
Ungerer, Tomi 126
Unicorns 111, **111**
United Kingdom 19, 110, **110**, 116, **116**; *see also* England; Scotland; Wales
United States House of Representatives 18
Up Helly Aa 125, **125**
Uranus (planet) 291
Uruguay 89, **89**
U.S. Virgin Islands 40, **40**
Utah, U.S.A. 68, **68**
Utaurora comosa 60

V

Vampire finches 75, **75**
Venezuela 76, **76**, 79, **79**
Venezuelan skunk frog 74
Venus (planet) 290
Very Large Telescope (VLT) 86, **86**
Vescovo, Victor 270, **270**
Victoria Falls, Zambia-Zimbabwe 149, **149**
Video fountain 66, **66**
Vietnam 194, **194**
Vikings 112, 125
Villaggio Vista, Ghana 158, **158**
Vinicunca, Peru 79, **79**
Virgin Islands 40, **40**, 276, **276**
VLT (Very Large Telescope) 86, **86**
Vogelkop superb bird of paradise 233, **233**
Volcanoes
    Africa 162, **162**, 163
    Antarctica 244, 256, 257, **257**
    Asia 180, **180**, 186, **186**
    Europe 109, **109**, 129, **129**, 135, **135**
    fumaroles 257, **257**
    lava lakes 162, **162**
    Mars 291, **291**
    North America 46–47, **46–47**, 68, **68**
    pizza baked in 68, **68**
    skiing down 129, **129**, 135, **135**
    supervolcanoes 47, **47**
    underwater 269, **269**
    volcano boarding 46, **46**
Vostok, Lake, Antarctica 246, **246**
Voyager probes 266, **266**
Vredefort crater, South Africa 147

W

Wagon trails 38
Waiters and Waitresses Race 20, **20**
Wakata, Koichi 285
Wales 17, **17**, 20, **20**
Walking 32, **32**
Wasa Graffitilandia, Finland 119, **119**
Water harvesting 174, **174**
Water use 32, 33, **33**
Waterfalls 46, **46**, 149, **149**, 206, **206**, 211, **211**, 219, **219**
Watermelon Museum, China 212
Waterslides 83, **83**
Wave Rock, Australia 241, **241**
Wax-tailed leafhoppers 73, **73**, 91, **91**
Way, Danny 19, **19**
Weaver birds 156, **156**
West Virginia, U.S.A. 53, **53**
Wetlands 50, **50–51**
Whales 253, **253**
White, Nic 18, **18**
White Desert, Egypt 162, **162**
Wildebeest migration 163, 166, **166**
Williams, Robin 139
Winds, on Neptune 290
Wolffish 76, **76**
Wolves 189, **189**
Wood-nymph moths 48, **48**
World Living Statues Festival, Netherlands 118, **118**
World Numbat Day 15, **15**
World Penguin Day 18, **18**
World War II 221, 276, **276**
Wright Flyer 289
Wyoming, U.S.A. 45, **45**, 47, **47**, 60, **60**

Y

Year, average person's activities 32–33, **32–33**
Yellowstone supervolcano, Wyoming, U.S.A. 47, **47**
Young, John 289, **289**

Z

Zambia 149, **149**, 152, **152**, 184
Zauo Fishing Restaurant, Japan 210, **210**
Zebras 89, **89**, 166
Zimbabwe 149, **149**
Zooplankton 278
Zozobra 62, **62**
Zulu 177

PHOTO CREDITS

303

NATIONAL GEOGRAPHIC and Yellow Border Design are trademarks of the National Geographic Society, used under license.

Since 1888, the National Geographic Society has funded more than 14,000 research, conservation, education, and story-telling projects around the world. National Geographic Partners distributes a portion of the funds it receives from your purchase to National Geographic Society to support programs including the conservation of animals and their habitats. To learn more, visit natgeo.com/info.

For more information, visit nationalgeographic.com, call 1-877-873-6846, or write to the following address:

National Geographic Partners, LLC
1145 17th Street NW
Washington, DC 20036-4688 U.S.A.

More for kids from National Geographic: natgeokids.com

National Geographic Kids magazine inspires children to explore their world with fun yet educational articles on animals, science, nature, and more. Using fresh storytelling and amazing photography, *Nat Geo Kids* shows kids ages 6 to 14 the fascinating truth about the world—and why they should care. **natgeo.com/subscribe**

For rights or permissions inquiries, please contact National Geographic Books Subsidiary Rights: bookrights@natgeo.com

Trade paperback ISBN: 978-1-4263-7642-9
Reinforced library binding ISBN: 978-1-4263-7643-6

The publisher would like to thank the book packaging team at Dynamo Limited, including Claire Lister, Kate Ford, and Jeremy Marshall, as well as the book team at National Geographic Kids: Kathryn Williams, project editor; Julide Dengel, designer; Lori Epstein, photo director; Alix Inchausti, production editor; and Lauren Sciortino and David Marvin, associate designers.

Printed in South Korea
24/ISK/1

That's weird!